Poetry and Poetics after Wallace Stevens

Poetry and Poetics after Wallace Stevens

Edited by
Bart Eeckhout and Lisa Goldfarb

Bloomsbury Academic
An imprint of Bloomsbury Publishing Inc

B L O O M S B U R Y
NEW YORK • LONDON • OXFORD • NEW DELHI • SYDNEY

Bloomsbury Academic

An imprint of Bloomsbury Publishing Inc

1385 Broadway	50 Bedford Square
New York	London
NY 10018	WC1B 3DP
USA	UK

www.bloomsbury.com

BLOOMSBURY and the Diana logo are trademarks of Bloomsbury Publishing Plc

First published 2017

Library of Congress Cataloging-in-Publication Data

Names: Eeckhout, Bart, 1964- editor. | Goldfarb, Lisa, editor.
Title: Poetry and poetics after Wallace Stevens / edited by Bart Eeckhout,
Lisa Goldfarb.
Description: New York : Bloomsbury Academic, 2016. |
Includes bibliographical references and index.
Identifiers: LCCN 2016018086 (print) | LCCN 2016029393 (ebook) |
ISBN 9781501313486 (hardback) | ISBN 9781501313493 (ePub) |
ISBN 9781501313509 (ePDF)
Subjects: LCSH: Stevens, Wallace, 1879-1955–Influence. | Stevens, Wallace,
1879-1955–Criticism and interpretation. | Stevens, Wallace,
1879-1955–Appreciation. | Modernism (Literature) | Poetics–History–20th
century. | Poetics–History–21st century. | BISAC: LITERARY CRITICISM /
General. | LITERARY CRITICISM / American / General. |
LITERARY CRITICISM / Poetry.
Classification: LCC PS3537.T4753 Z7572 2016 (print) | LCC PS3537.T4753
(ebook) | DDC 811/.52–dc23
LC record available at https://lccn.loc.gov/2016018086

ISBN: HB: 978-1-5013-1348-6
 ePub: 978-1-5013-1349-3
 ePDF: 978-1-5013-1350-9

Cover image © Oriole Farb Feshbach. Courtesy of the R. Michelson Galleries.

Typeset by Integra Software Services Pvt. Ltd.
Printed and bound in the United States of America

Contents

Acknowledgments

The authors would like to thank the following copyright holders for their kind permissions to reproduce the works indicated below:

Excerpt from "The House" from *Anterooms: New Poems and Translations* by Richard Wilbur. Copyright © 2010 by Richard Wilbur. Reprinted by permission of Houghton Mifflin Harcourt Publishing Company. All rights reserved.

Excerpts from "Ideas of Disorder at Torquay" and "On the Impossibility of Translation" from *Selected Poems* by Nicholas Moore reprinted by permission of Shoestring Press.

Excerpt from "With a Cornet of Winkles" from *New Collected Poems* by David Gascoyne, edited by Roger Scott (London: Enitharmon Press, 2015). Reprinted by permission.

"Night Shift" from *Collected Poems by Sylvia Plath*, edited by Ted Hughes. Copyright ©1930, 1965, 1971, 1981 by the Estate of Sylvia Plath. Editorial material copyright © 1981 by Ted Hughes. Reprinted by permission of Faber and Faber Ltd. and HarperCollins Publishers.

Excerpt from "To Marianne Moore" December 5, 1936, Hotel Chelsea from *One Art: Letters* by Elizabeth Bishop, selected and edited by Robert Giroux. Copyright © 1994 by Alice Methfessel. Introduction and compilation copyright © 1994 by Robert Giroux. Reprinted by permission of Farrar, Straus and Giroux, LLC.

Excerpts from "Cape Breton," "The End of March," and "Questions of Travel" from *Poems* by Elizabeth Bishop. Copyright © 2011 by The Alice H. Methfessel Trust. Published by Chatto & Windus in 2004. Reproduced by permission of the Random House Group Ltd. Publisher's Note and compilation copyright © 2011 by Farrar, Straus and Giroux, LLC. Reprinted by permission of Farrar, Straus and Giroux, LLC.

Excerpt from "The House Was Quiet and the World Was Calm" from *The Collected Poems of Wallace Stevens* by Wallace Stevens, copyright © 1954 by Wallace Stevens and copyright renewed 1982 by Holly Stevens. Used by permission of Alfred A. Knopf, an imprint of the Knopf Doubleday Publishing Group, a division of Penguin Random House LLC. All rights reserved.

List of Illustrations

List of Abbreviations

The following standard abbreviations for the works of Wallace Stevens are used throughout. As a rule, references to poems and prose are to the Library of America volume edited by Frank Kermode and Joan Richardson (abbreviated as *CPP*). Page references are provided for poems in the main text only when quotations from those poems are included in the discussion.

CPP   *Wallace Stevens: Collected Poetry and Prose*. Ed. Frank Kermode and Joan Richardson. New York: Library of America, 1997.

L   *Letters of Wallace Stevens*. Ed. Holly Stevens. New York: Knopf, 1966; rpt. Berkeley: University of California Press, 1996.

SP   Holly Stevens, *Souvenirs and Prophecies: The Young Wallace Stevens*. New York: Knopf, 1977.

1

Introduction: *After* Stevens

Bart Eeckhout and Lisa Goldfarb

For Wallace Stevens, writing to José Rodríguez Feo on January 22, 1948, the case was very simple: "You are wrong, by the way, in thinking that I read a lot of poetry. I don't read a line. My state of mind about poetry makes me very susceptible and that is a danger in the sense that it would be so easy for me to pick up something unconsciously." Stevens warned the young Cuban that "Most people read [poetry] listening for echoes because the echoes are familiar to them. They wade through it the way a boy wades through water, feeling with his toes for the bottom: the echoes are the bottom." Having just denied reading other poets in order to avoid being influenced by them, Stevens laconically added he derived his habit from another poet: "This is something that I have learned to do from Yeats who was extremely persnickety about being himself. It is not so much that it is a way of being oneself as it is a way of defeating people who look only for echoes and influences" (*L* 575).

Such protestations are classic Stevens: they would have us believe that he did not read anybody else's poetry so as to be able to compose, entirely for his private delight, on a blank slate. The protestations are also classic Modernist dogma, as the enlisting of W. B. Yeats further illustrates: to be a modern poet, to be fully an artist of the twentieth century, one had to insist on "making it new." And the protestations are classic grist to Harold Bloom's mill from the 1970s—those years when Bloom was steeped in Stevens' writings and developed his theory of the "anxiety of influence" around them.

But maybe the wording in the letter to Rodríguez Feo is also, and even primarily, an illustration of Stevens' defensiveness on a specific occasion. Perhaps the sentences were rhetorically inflected so as to keep the young aficionado from firing question after question triggered by his omnivorous reading—"you are becoming so literary that you ought to understand that life fights back," Stevens tells him in the same letter (*L* 575). It may be that Stevens, on this occasion, just wanted to remind Rodríguez Feo of the need to keep a mental space open for personal experience and creativity—a space in which the young man could go for a swim of his own instead of remaining the boy wading through water. However this may be, the final sentence cited in our opening paragraph veers into hyperbole. Are we seriously to believe that Stevens wrote poetry out of animosity against those readers who love to connect poems with poems by imagining echoes and influences?

One thing Stevens' letter does is to remind us, nevertheless, that influence studies in literary criticism had better retain a tentative, speculative, occasionally even experimental character. This does not diminish their appeal. In Stevens criticism, at least, such studies have a long pedigree: time and again, the poet has been discussed as engaging in a dialogue with his main nineteenth- and twentieth-century sources of inspiration, whether these be other poets (Wordsworth, Shelley, Keats, Tennyson, Whitman, Baudelaire, Valéry, Yeats, Williams, Moore), prose writers (Emerson, Nietzsche, Santayana, William James, Focillon), or painters (Cézanne, Picasso, Duchamp, Mondrian, Klee). What has been done far less systematically so far is to undertake an investigation into Stevens' own influence on poets of later generations as well as on the development of poetics after him. To be sure, there have been a few focused inquiries—for instance, in special issues of *The Wallace Stevens Journal* devoted to the poet's influence on Elizabeth Bishop, on Adrienne Rich and James Merrill, in one case even juxtaposing him with W. H. Auden (not much influence there).[1] But the collection of sixteen chapters we are presenting here is the first to take a concerted look at the larger landscape of poetry and poetics after Stevens. It examines a great many lines that may be drawn between his verse and poetry from the second half of the twentieth century up to the present moment in 2015.

To illustrate the rich potential of this topic, we might explain very briefly how this book came about. In the wake of previous conferences on Stevens in which we were involved as organizers, in Oxford and New York, we decided to organize a small "workshop symposium" in Antwerp at the end of May 2014 with an eye to preparing another volume of critical essays.[2] We proposed the topic of Stevens' influence on later writers to a number of editorial board members of *The Wallace Stevens Journal* as well as a handful of European-based and/or up-and-coming poetry scholars with a strong knowledge of Stevens' work. To our surprise, not only was the topic received with unanimous enthusiasm, but when paper titles started to pour in, they proved to be all about different case studies.

We had worried especially about overlap between poets, and had never dreamed of the kind of diversity we are now able to put on display here. In fact, some of the usual suspects did not even make it into the discussion: Rich and Merrill, for instance, barely return in this book, and none of the chapters pursues in any substantial detail Stevens' well-attested influence on Randall Jarrell, Richard Howard, Charles Tomlinson, Mark Strand, or Jorie Graham.

What we did receive as suggested topics ranged much further afield than what we had anticipated. We were expecting to see major poets included such as Elizabeth Bishop, John Ashbery, A. R. Ammons, and Robert Hass—and indeed got a separate case study on each. We were also aware of Stevens' influence on a few writers working in traditions that are usually seen as incompatible with Stevens' Modernism, like Sylvia Plath (forever dragging along the label of "Confessional" poet) and Susan Howe (too often reduced to being a "Language" poet), though we did not yet understand how rich these two cases were. What we were wholly unprepared for, though, was the breadth of scope we were to achieve through the additional proposals we received: the case of the formalists Richard Wilbur and Howard Nemerov; two similarly canonical poets, George Oppen and Louise Glück, who are almost invariably read outside of a Stevensian framework; a series of younger poets of color, including C. S. Giscombe, Thylias Moss, Terrance Hayes, and Olive Senior; the English poets Nicholas Moore, David Gascoyne, and Peter Redgrove; the Nobel Laureate Seamus Heaney; a Franco-Belgian contemporary of Stevens', Henri Michaux; and, entirely out of left field (so to speak), the (non)response to Stevens in communist Czechoslovakia.

With such various conjunctions, it goes without saying that several contributors to this book have chosen to proceed in a questioning spirit. They also bring a lot of ambivalence to the table, allowing us to hear poetic dialogues in which later writers do not simply draw inspiration or sustenance from an old master, but frequently talk back, contesting and reshaping the Stevensian heritage to build altogether new kinds of poetics and let other voices be heard. Our contributors generally take care to resist the critical temptation Matt Miller warns against in a recent issue of *The Wallace Stevens Journal* devoted to the influence of Whitman on Stevens. As Miller complains, "influence studies are often a record of critical preconceptions, or as John Ernest brilliantly phrased it in an essay on Ashbery and William Bronk, 'narratives of influence colonize individual poets and poems, assuming critical authority over them in the name of conceptual manifest destiny'" (47). Very little of this colonizing impulse or manifest destiny is on display in the present volume, we believe.

Before providing a brief summary of individual case studies, we would still like to mention some of the more theoretical questions that have animated our project. These were offered by way of invitation to contributors, not in an attempt to narrow down perspectives or methods. One question this book hopes to address is how critical work on Stevens might continue to be integrated in broader research and scholarship on modern and contemporary poetry. In particular, what insights into later poets do we obtain from having read and studied Stevens' work, and what new insights into Stevens do we derive from reading poets coming after him? The ambiguity of the preposition in our title is intentional in this respect: although *after* may refer neutrally to chronological sequence, it also implies ways of aesthetically modeling poetry on a predecessor; indirectly, it even stages the question of what *we* are after, as critics, when we establish connections between poets, and thus stretches potentially into the future.

Besides offering a rich harvest of concrete case studies, our joint exploration also reconsiders some of the possibilities for talking about poetic "influence" in an era that no longer takes much interest in Bloom's theory of Oedipal anxiety and that has turned what was originally intended as a challenging concept, "intertextuality," into an easy shorthand for rather obvious literary allusions.[3] How can we define and refine the ways in which we establish concrete textual links between Stevens' poems and those written after him? Do we find any value in a claim such as Dana Gioia's that Stevens was "the single most debilitating influence on contemporary American poetry of the 1980s and '90s" (qtd. in Duemer 5–6)? How do we read the diverse forms of allusiveness in Dennis Barone and James Finnegan's anthology, *Visiting Wallace: Poems Inspired by the Life and Work of Wallace Stevens*? What are we perhaps *not* paying attention to—aesthetically, but also politically, historically, thematically—when we relate later poetry to someone as idiosyncratic as Stevens? And how much are we still beholden to a typically Modernist poetics when we do so? These are some of our organizing questions.

We have decided to print the following case studies in a roughly chronological sequence, beginning with figures in midcentury, on both sides of the Atlantic, and gradually moving on to the beginning of the twenty-first century. A certain amount of mental flexibility is nevertheless required of our readers, since some chapters scan a terrain of several decades, at times involving a range of poets, while others are pinpointed more specifically—in one instance even sticking to the analysis of a single poem. A monograph would be able to streamline such materials and look for an overarching narrative, but we are convinced that this relative shortcoming is abundantly compensated for by the fact that no single critic could ever cast a net as wide as our collective efforts in this volume do, whether in terms of diversity of poets and poems analyzed or variety of critical methods used. The multiplication of expertise and pluralism of perspectives that we are able to offer seem to us this book's greatest asset.

***

Now that Marjorie Perloff's question "Pound/Stevens: Whose Era?" has run its course, we begin our case studies with Bonnie Costello's proposal of an alternative question—at least, for the formalists on whom she wishes to focus her attention, Richard Wilbur and Howard Nemerov. For these two poets, the issue becomes rather "Frost or Stevens?" As Costello's subtitle, "Servants of Two Masters," moreover demonstrates, critical nuance is not always served by debates in either/or terms. Whereas Robert Frost was an obvious father figure for modern American formalists, and some of Stevens' conceptual style and abstract qualities were just as obviously too radical for such writers, both Wilbur and Nemerov repeatedly acknowledged Stevens as a precursor, too. Costello beautifully defines the nature and extent of this influence across the two poets' distinguished careers.

Our second case study refers to the same debate initiated by Perloff and takes a similarly extensive view as does Costello, but it crosses the Atlantic and engages with different kinds of poetics. Lee Jenkins investigates the resonance of Stevens' work among English poets from midcentury onwards. She explains how several of these have turned to one of Stevens' best-known poet's poems, "The Idea of Order at Key West," tilting its spatial and temporal axes in rewritings that have expanded the poem's original horizon of reception. In England, Stevens' poem has proved to be a popular resort for poets since 1942, when Nicholas Moore's "Ideas of Disorder at Torquay" drafted it into the service of English Surrealism in a time of war. Jenkins also considers David Gascoyne's "With a Cornet of Winkles," Peter Redgrove's "The Idea of Entropy at Maenporth Beach," and two neo-Surrealist seaside postcards alluding to Stevens, identifying signal differences in these various transatlantic receptions of Stevens.

Bart Eeckhout returns us to American shores and adds a conceptual dimension to discussions in the book. He introduces his analysis of the underexplored mark Stevens left on Sylvia Plath by searching for a critical vocabulary that might be adequate to this pairing of poets. In particular, Eeckhout seeks to find a language for the combined phenomenon of stylistic assimilation and creative adaptation that is not well served by theories of allusion. To illustrate his point, he unpacks one poem from what is usually regarded as the second stage of Plath's writing life, "Night Shift," detailing a wealth of Stevensian features in it. We should be careful, Eeckhout cautions us, to distinguish among varieties of connection when we look at a later poet's verse in relation to an earlier one's. Such connections may be multidimensional, are often dispersed throughout texts, and do not necessarily want to attract the reader's attention.

In Angus Cleghorn's chapter, we move on to another major poet from around midcentury, Elizabeth Bishop, to consider the latter's prosody in relation to the example set by Stevens. The chapter's title, "Moving the 'Moo' from Stevensian Blank Verse," derives from a comment Bishop made to Marianne Moore—that she disliked how Stevens could "make blank verse *moo.*" Cleghorn explores both Bishop's high regard for Stevens and how she extends his blank verse in her poetry by means of casual asides and irregular, intricate rhythms. In this account of poetic history, Bishop contemporizes Stevens' sound and language. To avoid retreading familiar ground, Cleghorn discusses verse that enacts lyrical innovations at different stages of her writing life, from "Cape Breton" to "Questions of Travel," "The End of March," and "Santarém." Thus, we learn how Bishop gradually injects prose-like rhythms into a landscape that is often still Stevensian.

We continue to crisscross the Atlantic with Axel Nesme's chapter on Henri Michaux, the first of two forays into continental Europe. In a 1950 letter to Bernard Heringman, Stevens mentions a friend who spent his whole life in Paris "avoid[ing] the Americans in order to see more of the French. Henri Michaux and Supervielle were among his friends, Michaux especially" (*L* 665). Nesme wonders how we might return to Stevens' poetic theory to shed light on the emerging work of his younger contemporary Michaux. The American poet's view that the "imagination loses vitality as it ceases to adhere to what is real" (*CPP* 645) proves to be notably relevant for Michaux's typical phantasmagorias insofar as these derive from an effort to exhibit what Freud called "psychical reality." In a work of prose poetry like *Elsewhere*, Michaux does not emulate the Surrealist association of ideas that, according to Stevens, generated an imbalance between reality and imagination. Instead, he produces "alternative universes whose very fictitiousness allows this psychical reality to emerge."

Pursuing a concrete historical example of Stevens' impact in Central Europe, Justin Quinn's chapter addresses more political and cultural questions. In 1973, a selection of Stevens' poems was published in Czech and made no impression on literary life in Czechoslovakia. Quinn explores why this was, casting light on the way poetry travels in translation, the effects of the Cold War on such travels, and what this tells us about historical notions of "American poetry." His interest lies not in anything anecdotal but in the economy of Cold War literature as part of a larger system of cultural exchange. Quinn links the universalizing tendency in American poetry criticism of the Cold War—from Roy Harvey Pearce to Charles Altieri—to US foreign policy, suggesting that, despite their pretense of universal humanism, such studies are still historically conditioned. Rather than pulling such critics back into historical relativism, however, Quinn wishes to relate their approach to "a larger global ecology in which another ideology is pitted directly against it."

In his contribution, George Lensing continues the conversation about the relation between aesthetics and politics as he addresses the work of Seamus Heaney. At first glance, Heaney and Stevens would seem to be worlds apart, yet Lensing manages to show how the Northern Irish poet's response to the American Stevens took shape over the course of his writing life. Lensing analyzes the Nobel Laureate's growing appreciation of Stevens' work as well as the subtle mark it left on Heaney's poems. In due course, Stevens came to represent "a compatible spirit congenial to [Heaney] as a political poet who prized aesthetic independence from partisan politics." In one of the interviews collected six years before his death, Heaney referred to Stevens again and allied him with great poets of old age such as Yeats.

Starting with Edward Ragg's chapter, we return to North America for the rest of our explorations. Ragg examines the overlooked affinities between the poetics of Stevens, on the one hand, and those of Oppen and Glück, on the other. He argues that "not only Glück's, but even Oppen's work is still being digested," and that both poets' relations to Stevens—though hardly obvious— prove to be compelling. On both a thematic and a stylistic level, Ragg is able to demonstrate that these poets "share repetitive, incantatory dictions combining phenomenological and ontological reflections in poems that foreground the primacy of the poem and poetry as creative forces." Thus, the currents in which poetry after Stevens has been written take at times surprising turns. As not so noble riders, Oppen and Glück have traversed poetic terrains we are only beginning to map, "not least in the sound of words: their daring gestures *as* sonority, allusion, lineation, narration, and repetition."

Al Filreis follows Ragg's discussion of poetic currents with a longer, panoramic chapter titled "The Stevens Wars." This is a slight revision of his 2009 article in *boundary 2* that we are happy to recycle here because it served as a major inspiration for our book. Situating Stevens in the landscape of American poetry after 1975, Filreis attributes the poet's widespread appeal to his poetics of everyday life. Stevens' disaffection is such, however, that it "prohibit[s] definitive legacy" and is responsible for the diffuse effect of his poetics on later writers. Filreis illustrates this through dozens of examples, ranging from the most conservative formalists (who read Stevens typically as a Romantic and post-Christian poet of meditative lyrics) to experimental voices (who find in his work a "languaged" Stevens). By concluding his contribution with the very different ways in which John Hollander and Susan Howe—coincidentally in the same year—returned poetically to Stevens' house, Filreis is able to show the radical disparity of voices the poet has been able to inspire in recent decades.

Lisa Goldfarb deepens our understanding of what Filreis deems Stevens' unfixable legacy by examining the impact of his musical poetics. She briefly reviews the contours of Stevens' musical narrative, stressing that the musical process is one the poet reenacts at all stages of his career. She then works with Barone and Finnegan's anthology, *Visiting Wallace*, to discuss how poets have tapped into diverse aspects of Stevens' musical practice—in terms of sound-play, structure, musical narrative, and his musical-poetic experimentation. This discussion includes a detailed reading of James Longenbach's "In a World without Heaven," a poem that recalls Stevens' great examples of musical-poetic variation. Goldfarb concludes with a close analysis of portions of Howe's "118 Westerly Terrace" to demonstrate the variety of ways in which Stevens' musical legacy survives.

Joan Richardson adds yet another dimension to the Stevens influence on Howe. In her reading, a version of the "imaginative power to form links across time and history" informs both Stevens' aphorism that "Poetry is a health" (*CPP* 913) and Howe's attending to what she calls "the psychic past of America." This aspect and the impact of Stevens' "studious ghost" on Howe are nowhere more explicit than in *Souls of the Labadie Tract*. Richardson understands poetry as an *over-hearing*: the lines must be experienced as *uttered*, revealing the poet as "a scribe of the sacred"—albeit with a secularized understanding that transcends anthropomorphism to include "what Stevens was more inclined to evoke as the hissing and spinning of the stars and planets, auroras and shades."

After a brief preamble in which he condenses the recent history of poetics in the West, Charles Altieri presents a crucial case study on John Ashbery, perhaps the poet most frequently anointed as Stevens' great heir. Altieri seeks to understand how Ashbery adapts Stevens' practice of analogy—what, in the wake of his book *Wallace Stevens and the Demands of Modernity*, he calls Stevens' "aspectual thinking." Altieri wonders how poets "confront the pressures created by the need to believe that their own practices are worth committing to." If we treat this question of value as basic, he argues, we find ourselves necessarily talking about the later poetry of Stevens. Ashbery in turn then picked up Stevens' aspectual thinking, partially transformed it, and made it central to his own staging of self-consciousness. To Altieri, Ashbery's writing "tests the powers of imagination not by producing a fictive world, but by calling attention to how one might produce senses of mystery, fluidity, and connectedness within the activity of writing."

Juliette Utard's chapter tackles another major poet with a complex and sure relationship to Stevens, and simultaneously adds to Altieri's reflections on Stevens' late poetry. Juxtaposing A. R. Ammons' *Glare* and Stevens' *The Rock*, Utard aims to move "beyond Bloom's notion of cultural belatedness and the construction of *post* as merely a coming after." She demonstrates how Ammons "took after [Stevens], quoting his poems, using [his] name provocatively to question the older poet's status in American academia, eventually shaping his own late style against Stevens'"—to the point where Ammons' titular metaphor suggests a *glaring* at his predecessor. Yet, despite such animosity, Ammons also relied on Stevens—besides Whitman, Yeats, and Frost—to challenge the conventions of "late writing." Thus, lateness and its validity as a critical category become the main theoretical subject of Utard's chapter, which engages in a subtle discussion of late style.

Lisa Steinman contributes the first of two chapters addressing the vexed question of Stevens and race. She notes the striking number of contemporary African American poets who actively look back at Stevens in mixed tones. To Steinman, it is the complexity of Stevens' style that triggers and accommodates these writers' ambivalent responses. Many African American poet-readers, "while dismayed by Stevens' racist language, admire how his style (seen as enacting 'lack of closure,' 'complication,' or productive watchfulness) allows [them] to position themselves … as 'unintended' readers." In a way, Stevens' poems seem to look forward self-consciously to such readers. But Steinman also manages to show how being an unanticipated reader can be "unsettlingly *productive*." Certainly in C. S. Giscombe's work, we find an invitation to read Stevens' poetry in search of what is "ambiguous, contradictory, riddled with echoes"—without these echoes always needing to be intended.

Regardless of Stevens' own disclaimers about influence, later poets have not been shy about signaling their engagements with his work, even if the writings of several poets of color have received but little commentary so far. The poets Rachel Galvin studies in her chapter, the Jamaican Canadian Olive Senior and the African

American Terrance Hayes, "engage with a tradition of resistance to the colonial logic of mimicry." Galvin argues that contemporary writers of color tend to modify the work of predecessors through "retrospective influence," as Jorge Luis Borges claimed in a deliberate anachronism, or through the related idea of a "cannibalistic poetics," as theorized by a number of Brazilian Modernists. Poems Galvin focuses on include Senior's recasting of "Thirteen Ways of Looking at a Blackbird" and "Like Decorations in a Nigger Cemetery" (where Senior deliberately misreads the word "patios" as "patois") as well as Hayes's "Snow for Wallace Stevens," which presents the older poet as a "foe" the younger poet is both for and against.

In her concluding chapter, Rachel Malkin takes us to the Pacific Coast to look into the Californian poet Robert Hass's well-known debt to Stevens. She considers the importance of the sensual world to Stevens and Hass, their mutual focus on "common experience," as well as the primacy of "acts of imagination" for both. Thinking about Stevens and Hass, in Malkin's assessment, "involves dynamics of pleasure and solace, and of doubt and guilt." Their relation also raises basic questions about what sorts of satisfaction we want from poetry as critics. Although Hass acknowledges that there is no direct link between what one of his interviewers has called "the personal world, the political world, and the world of knowledge," his writings—more than Stevens'—tend to regard the disconnect as "a source of sorrow." Malkin explores both Stevens' seductive hold on Hass and the later poet's "resistance" to the canonical Modernist, particularly in moments of political turmoil. For Hass, the problem of responding to Stevens "seems to stand in for the problem of the Modernist legacy altogether."

This is a fittingly open-ended manner to conclude our collection. In a sense, the problem for Hass applies to all case studies gathered in *Poetry and Poetics after Wallace Stevens*. We believe that this rich gathering of interventions by some of the most sensitive and subtle readers of modern poetry will stimulate, extend, and, at their best, reconfigure ongoing debates about various important aspects of the Modernist poetic legacy.

Notes

1   For these special issues, see, respectively, Brogan; Brogan and MacLeod; Eeckhout and Goldfarb.

2   We would like to take this opportunity to thank Lesley Janssen for his indispensable practical assistance in organizing our get-together in Antwerp.

3   Although most of our contributors practice forms of influence studies, there is clearly no established theoretical language in which they are able to do so. Nobody seems to have felt the urge to return to Bloom's idiosyncratic jargon about "weak" versus "strong" "misreadings" or about "revisionary ratios." In another contribution to the Whitman–Stevens issue already mentioned, Patrick Redding usefully distinguishes between three modes of diachronic textual connection in which literary critics tend to engage. He calls them analogy, influence, and theory, but warns us that these "rarely exist in strict isolation from one another. A study that begins with an analogy often blurs into one that presumes influence; studies that seek to elaborate abstract theoretical vocabularies tend to build their cases by reference to specific texts and careers" (14). Redding claims that these approaches have gone out of fashion because the historicist shift in criticism since the 1980s has tended to prioritize synchronic, extraliterary, and empiricist investigations.

Works Cited

Altieri, Charles. *Wallace Stevens and the Demands of Modernity: Toward a Phenomenology of Value*. Ithaca: Cornell University Press, 2013. Print.

Barone, Dennis and James Finnegan, eds. *Visiting Wallace: Poems Inspired by the Life and Work of Wallace Stevens*. Iowa City: University of Iowa Press, 2009. Print.

Brogan, Jacqueline Vaught, ed. "Stevens and Elizabeth Bishop." Spec. issue of *Wallace Stevens Journal* 19.2 (1995): 107–286. Print.

Brogan, Jacqueline Vaught and Glen MacLeod, eds. "Wallace Stevens, Adrienne Rich, and James Merrill." Spec. issue of *Wallace Stevens Journal* 25.1 (2001): 3–84. Print.

Duemer, Joseph. "Preface." *Wallace Stevens Journal* 17.1 (1993): 5–8. Print.

Eeckhout, Bart and Lisa Goldfarb, eds. "Wallace Stevens and W. H. Auden." Spec. issue of *Wallace Stevens Journal* 37.2 (2013): 127–230. Print.

Miller, Matt. "Whitman and Stevens: No Supreme Fiction." *Wallace Stevens Journal* 40.1 (2016): 34–49. Print.

Redding, Patrick. "Between Surface and Influence: Stevens, Whitman, and the Problem of Mediation." *Wallace Stevens Journal* 40.1 (2016): 10–33. Print.

Stevens, Wallace. *Letters of Wallace Stevens*. Ed. Holly Stevens. Berkeley: University of California Press, 1996. Print.

Stevens, Wallace. *Wallace Stevens: Collected Poetry and Prose*. Ed. Frank Kermode and Joan Richardson. New York: Library of America, 1997. Print.

2

Frost or Stevens? Servants of Two Masters

Bonnie Costello

The question "Pound/Stevens: Whose Era?" has dominated discussions of Modernist influence since Marjorie Perloff's 1982 challenge. In this chapter, I propose a different question for formalists after the Second World War: Frost or Stevens—which master?

Richard Wilbur's 1956 volume *Things of This World* is full of Stevensian moments, as are all his volumes. In one of Wilbur's most famous poems, for instance, "Love Calls Us to the Things of This World" (*Collected* 307–08), we may hear Stevens' "cry" of the sea and the "body wholly body, fluttering/Its empty sleeves" (*CPP* 105).[1] Wilbur announces "a cry of pulleys" and sees "blouses" and "smocks" on a laundry line figuring "the astounded soul/[which] Hangs for a moment bodiless and simple/As false dawn." He hangs Stevens' fluttering sleeves on his own firm if wind-plucked poetic line. Robert Frost is the other unmistakable influence on Wilbur's work, and to some extent the two masters compete for dominance in his poetry.

Frost was in many ways the father of modern American formalism. Certainly he stands behind "the other New England poet," Howard Nemerov.[2] Both Wilbur and Nemerov served in combat during the Second World War, and sometimes, with Stevens, they see the poet's struggle as part of a warlike whole, part of the "war that never ends" (*CPP* 351). But the decreative drive seldom informs their work. The poem provides "a momentary stay against confusion" (Frost, *Collected* 777) and a focus of order and beauty (dramatic or lyric) in an otherwise chaotic and often dark surround. Stevens' bold shifts of ground, his contradictions, tautologies, enigmas, digressions, qualifications, which wind through self-canceling sentences and metaphors undoing metaphors—his way, in short, of resisting the intelligence almost successfully—is not theirs. They strove for "noble accents/And lucid, inescapable rhythms" freed of the blackbird's shadow (*CPP*

75). The syntactic and metaphoric challenges of Stevens' Modernist style would find their way into the work of later poets—John Ashbery, A. R. Ammons, Jorie Graham, Susan Howe. Yet both Wilbur and Nemerov frequently acknowledge Stevens as a master and precursor. What they took from Stevens was a sense of the nobility of poetry and a set of images and phrases that established that nobility.

Unsurprisingly, dialectical and oppositional forms are prevalent in both Wilbur and Nemerov, arising in an ad hoc manner as they do in Stevens and Frost—not, that is, as part of a mythic system, as in Yeats. But beyond the similarities, the polarity between Stevens and Frost can be seen in their influence. Frost's poems pull Wilbur and Nemerov into representational scenes and stories and parables, into synecdoche, into regular rhymes, into classical chiasmus and antithesis. Stevens' poems lead them toward abstraction and transfiguring metaphor, and into meditative lyricism, tautology, contradiction, and paradox.

I would like to begin examining the dual influence of these modern masters by looking at a Wilbur poem that seems to be in conversation with both Stevens and Frost. Surely any poem of the 1950s about a snowman calls up Stevens' famous figure. "Boy at the Window" (Wilbur, *Collected* 340) may be explicitly alluding to Stevens' "The Snow Man" (*CPP* 8) with its opening lines: "Seeing the snowman standing all alone/In dusk and cold is more than he can bear." It is not just the snowman and the word "cold" in Wilbur's poem that cue us to Stevens. The tendency to project human passions onto insentient nature is explored in both works. Stevens reminds us that to have a mind of winter we are "not to think/Of any misery in the sound of the wind," and thus prompts the very thought. For Wilbur's small boy there is no resistance. He is moved to weep as he hears the wind "prepare/A night of gnashings and enormous moan." In Stevens' poem, the pathetic fallacy is tested by the mind of winter; these two push against one another through a long sentence of assertions and cancelations, ending in paradox. In Wilbur's poem, the dialectic is tidied into a two-part meditation, in two elegantly woven eight-line stanzas—one for the boy and one for the snowman. The gaze of human sympathy ("His tearful sight" covers both the gazer and the snowman) is returned by a personification, "The pale-faced figure with bitumen eyes." Thus the quartz contentment of Wilbur's snowman replaces the austerity of Stevens' challenging first idea.

Wilbur's snowman-beholder has a "god-forsaken stare"—a stare that surely mirrors "the nothing that is." But Wilbur refuses Stevens' visionary void; he melts the snowman through religious narrative, making the figure not only a "man of snow," but also implicitly a man of sorrows—"outcast Adam" redeemed by Christ, who suffers with the mortal world. But it is not only Christianity that softens the "nothing that is." Wilbur uses descriptive metaphor to enhance sentiment in the second stanza, turning rain to tears, sunlight to warmth, outer to inner weather. Wilbur's snowman is more Frostian (and less frosty) than Stevens' figure.

Indeed, the other likely source for "Boy at the Window" is Frost's famous poem "Tree at My Window" (Frost 230), which begins: "Tree at my window, window tree," establishing the reciprocity that Wilbur takes up in his poem. In Frost's imaginary exchange with the tree, the poet identifies with nature's vulnerabilities; puns and figures of speech bridge the gap. If the tree is "taken and tossed," the speaker is "taken and swept/And all but lost." Wilbur evokes a similar melancholy as he reimagines the speaker at the window as "the child at the bright pane surrounded by/Such warmth, such light, such love, and so much fear." Frost's "Tree at My Window" closes with a fourth stanza that particularly anticipates Wilbur's poem in its mirroring syntax of inside and outside: "That day she put our heads together,/Fate had her imagination about her,/Your head so much concerned with outer,/Mine with inner, weather." Like Stevens, Frost and Wilbur bind opposites together syntactically, but they emphasize correspondence more than Stevensian paradox. The domesticating window, absent in Stevens' shelterless work, protects Wilbur's boy from the rigor of the encounter. Like Frost, Wilbur confirms the priority of human sentiment even as he acknowledges its limits. He refuses the metaphysical void of "The Snow Man."

***

We see a similar domestication of Stevens through Frost in a poem by Howard Nemerov called "The Town Dump" (*Collected* 142–44) from his 1958 volume *Mirrors and Windows*. The poet on the dump has become a modern subgenre since Stevens' 1938 poem "The Man on the Dump" (*CPP* 184–86), culminating in Ammons' book-length poem *Garbage*. (Wilbur's contribution to the subgenre is "Junk.") Nemerov has likely found his prompt in Stevens, and may even allude to him. But Nemerov puts Stevens' trope into a poem modeled, it seems, on Frost's "Directive" (341–42). While Wilbur relies on Christian and classical models, Nemerov is more like Stevens in taking up the gnarly problems of modern secular philosophy that threaten the balance and hierarchy of meaning. In "The Town Dump," he exhibits hermeneutical knots of Nietzsche and Heidegger for their incongruity and poetic effects more than their conceptual force. The dump is full of phenomenological wordplay, "Where Being most Becomingly ends up/ Becoming some more." But like Wilbur, Nemerov is cautious about abstraction and about metaphor loosed from fixed allegorical structures; metaphor is less a way of making a world than of commenting on a familiar one. The lines that precede this heady play of "Being" and "Becoming" are much less abstract; they invite us to enter a mimetic scene very much in the way of Frost (and with the same "graveyard" imagery we find in "Directive"). Nemerov's dump is full of images, but they have not all been revealed as the trash of representation; they constitute a material landscape we can walk in. Illusion holds sway here over Stevensian iconicity as we are taken "A mile out in the marshes, under a sky/Which seems to be always going away." Frost's "Directive" opens with a similar "you" address. In imitation of "Directive," Nemerov takes us on a mazy tour through repetitions, parentheses, and asides that layer the primary scene with allegorical implication. "[Y]ou will find the city/Which seconds ours." The city which seconds ours has no Augustinian import at first. It is a literal, nontranscendent site, even if it is a reflection, a second city. Myth cleaves to description in self-canceling lines that highlight the experience of memory rather than directing us to a metaphysical dimension. Frost's "There is … a town that is no more a town" becomes in Nemerov "(so cemeteries, too,/Reflect a town from hillsides out of town)."

Abstraction in Nemerov, as in Wilbur, is ultimately a secondary force, which accounts for the world rather than making one. Indeed, as Nemerov starts to enumerate what is found on the dump, more echoes of Frost arise. Nemerov's "angry mackerel eyes" that "Glare at you" from "cardboard tenements,/ Windowed with cellophane" remind us of Frost's assurance not to "mind the serial ordeal/Of being watched from forty cellar holes/As if by eye pairs out of forty firkins." The bizarre incongruities of Nemerov's dump, with its lobsters and mussel shells "Far from the sea" "tenting/In paper bags," may suggest Stevens' "The Man on the Dump" with its "cat in the paper-bag" or "box/From Esthonia" and "tiger chest, for tea," but they remain more descriptive than metaphoric in Nemerov's context. What to do with this vision of the dump? Nemerov turns from aesthetic and phenomenological questions, inspired by Stevens, toward moral reflection such as one would find in Frost, or Auden, making the poem a rather casual parable. All this expensive trash, the poet reflects, "Going to show, I guess, that in any sty/Someone's heaven may open and shower down/ Riches responsive to the right dream." Nemerov plunges back into the scenic mode, this time following the "ghostly dealer"—a surrogate figure for the poet as scavenger—and here the mythic potential of the scene emerges: "heavy with fly-netting." The close of "Directive," with its playful approach to myth and archetype, certainly haunts the poem here. Frost's "broken drinking goblet … from the children's playhouse" and his "shattered dishes" turn up as Nemerov's "cut-glass goblets, lacquered cups,/And other products of his dreamy midden." This ruin of old myths is a Frostian setting.

And yet throughout, and especially at its close, the poem recalls early and late Stevens as the scene is "Penciled with light and guarded by the flies." Its dark hum and repetition of swarming flies, its shining wings and music all follow the Modernist master. The blank-verse lines rise to the kind of lyrical meditation that we would seldom find in Frost or Auden, but they are resonant for readers of Stevens. Like Stevens, he finds the sublime in the low, in "the art/Of our necessities," where he detects "new deposits" of beauty. Nemerov finds it "Among the flies, the purifying fires," and also finds "wild birds, drawn to the carrion and flies,/ … their wings/Shining with light, their flight enviably free,/Their music marvelous, though sad, and strange." While the syntax does not thicken as in Stevens, and while "I" violates the older poet's preference for the impersonal or anomalous voice, many of the words and alliterative phrases and passing details of Nemerov's "The Town Dump" recall not only "The Man on the Dump" but also some of Stevens' most famous poems, such as his early "Sunday Morning," with its assembling birds and their extended wings, and at the same time his late "The Plain Sense of Things," with its sad music and "repetitiousness of men and flies" (*CPP* 428).

Critics of Nemerov's early work called it derivative, but Frost was not his first model. As Peter Meinke remarked in his 1968 book on Nemerov, he was "writing Eliot, Yeats, and Stevens out of his system" (11).[3] Meinke picks out the opening lines of "The Master at a Mediterranean Port," an *In Memoriam* for Paul Valéry (Nemerov, *Collected* 20–21), as an example of Stevens' presence in the early poetry: "What, Amicus, constitutes mastery?/The perdurable fire of a style?" (qtd. in Meinke 11). And indeed the poem is Stevensian in other ways, too, with its rhetorical questions, its elision of "the shadow and the real," its ocean with "incessant/Organic shudders," its reflection on "the master, his image and his stance" (suggesting perhaps "To an Old Philosopher in Rome"), and with the apostrophe at the end, "O valuable glass,/Clear harbor," recalling "The Idea of Order at Key West," if also Yeats's "Among School Children."

Starting with his *Blue Swallows* (1961), critics began to identify Nemerov directly with Robert Frost, though it is worth noting that the swallow is a Stevensian, not a Frostian, bird, and blue, while rare in Frost, is one of Stevens' axial colors. Stevens remained the authority in Nemerov's thinking about what poetry is *for*, even if stylistically the younger poet turned toward Frost and other models. Nemerov's prose often plays off Stevensian tropes. *Figures of Thought*, his 1978 collection, is framed as a set of Stevensian meditations, though the title may suggest Frost's "The Figure a Poem Makes" more than Stevens' "The Figure of the Youth as Virile Poet." The opening essay in Nemerov's collection is called "Thirteen Ways of Looking at a Skylark" and the final essay "What Was Modern Poetry" closes with a section called "What Will Suffice," obviously alluding to Stevens' "Of Modern Poetry" (*CPP* 218). Beyond this collection, Nemerov wrote two substantive essays specifically honoring Stevens. "The Poetry of Wallace Stevens" appeared in *The Sewanee Review* in 1957, two years after Stevens' death. The tribute tellingly begins by identifying Stevens' work as "different from almost everything else in English" (1). His difference, the indeterminacy of his thought and anomaly of his style, makes him essential but hard to assimilate. Frost, by contrast, appears to Nemerov to belong to a logical tradition, one he can absorb and continue: "If I take at random three or four poets not usually thought of for their similarities one to the other—Donne, Pope, Tennyson, and Frost, say—and consider what poetry seems to mean to them and what poetry seems to mean to Stevens, I find a family likeness among those four and something like a generic difference in Stevens" (1). While he is not entirely clear about what that "family likeness" is that leaves Stevens an outsider, it seems implicitly to have something to do with an attitude toward the shape of content and the nature of poetic thinking. What he finds so unique to Stevens is a "subtle drama of inductions of which we lose or throw away a thousand examples daily" (3). Stevens' poetry is, for Nemerov, the "poem of the act of the mind" in that drama, an act without Frostian "momentary stay[s]" to suspend or corset the never-resting mind (*CPP* 219; Frost 777). Stevensian difficulty, he notes, unlike that of Donne or Eliot or Yeats, is not a matter of erudition; it arises "at precisely the moments of greatest simplicity" and is tied to catching "the mind in its fantastic act of deciding" (3). It is an art, we might say, of brinksmanship. Stevens is a poet of thresholds more than stays against confusion. The other poets may build neat dramatic structures, but the radical commitment to dramatic movement over the stability of concepts and conceits is unique to Stevens among major poets. Of course, another generation would soon emerge to embrace this never-resting mind. Ammons, Ashbery, Graham, and others make that "fantastic [and relentless] act of deciding" the center of their poetics.

  Nemerov's comments on Stevensian metaphor identify a tendency of mind toward abstraction that implied risks which the more logical Nemerov was unwilling to take: "metaphor also becomes arbitrary, mystical or absurd, since particulars may be said to resemble generalities as it were helplessly" (4). But if Nemerov is recognizing Stevensian difference, he does not overlook Stevensian relevance. Remarking on "Connoisseur of Chaos" and other poems, he notes, "The tone is that of philosophic conversation or meditation, but the sense is, with a touch of gentle contempt for philosophic simplicities, that philosophy is over and done with, and of no interest *except* as the poetic act of the philosopher, the poem of the act of the mind" (4). Though Wilbur and Nemerov might remain committed to the poetry of statement, they acknowledge its rhetorical nature. Statement is a shape of thought, not a simple disclosure of meaning.

Nemerov is perceptive about Stevensian abstraction even as he acknowledges its strangeness, which turns every sensation into an idea but without a controlling superstructure, as when Nemerov says about "the figurative center of Stevens' poetry":

> every object, in the poet's mind, becomes the idea of itself, and thereby produces the final illumination which in the platonic philosophy would have been produced by the view of the archetypes themselves; save that this illumination, final as it is, is meaningless, repetitious as prayer, yet "responsive as a mirror with a voice"—the epiphany not of what is real, but of the self poetizing.
>
> (8)

Such a powerful orphic conversion of things to ideas, the power to constitute the world in naming it—not ideas about things, but things *as* ideas—sets Stevens apart.

In "The Bread of Faithful Speech—Wallace Stevens and the Voices of Imagination" (1963), Nemerov again celebrates Stevens as a "man thinking" (177), but adds an emphasis on voice. There is the voice of the poet, for whom the "subjects of one's poems are the symbols of one's self or of one of one's selves" (Stevens qtd. on 179). One could easily identify this idea with Frost, whose speakers are distinctive voices and often competing aspects of the poet's sensibility (think of "Mending Wall"), and whose narratives are instances of the will exercising its agency in the world. But Nemerov argues that Stevens' voice also becomes the voice of the reader. He quotes Stevens' remark that "The poet seems to confer his identity on the reader" (qtd. in Nemerov 182). Furthermore, Nemerov finds in Stevens "the voice of an eternally other," the voice of what is not, which becomes the voice of the possible (182). We may find the first conception of voice in Frost, but not the second or third. Stevens' originality for Nemerov, his strangeness amid the family of poetry in English, has to do with this insistent engagement of the reader in the making of order and meaning, and on the voicing of the possible over and above the actual.

We encounter these qualities of the anomalous voice in Nemerov's own work. In "Mrs. Mandrill" (1960) (*Collected* 223–25), for instance, we hear a dying voice relinquishing its identity in becoming part of nature. Meinke says this is "Nemerov's equivalent of Wallace Stevens' 'Sunday Morning'" (26). Stylistically, though, the poem recalls "Mrs. Alfred Uruguay" (*CPP* 225–26); certainly some of Stevens' eccentricities, so salient in *Parts of a World*, are apparent in Nemerov's poem, which begins at a threshold moment, "On the night that Mrs. Mandrill entered Nature." Like Mrs. Alfred Uruguay, she is a naysayer as well as a searcher, whose "no and no made yes impossible" as she walks out in the moonlight, not in "the imagined land" (Stevens) but in "the unofficial land" (Nemerov). "'God?' Mrs. Mandrill said, 'I have no God,/and not afraid or ashamed to tell Him so/ either, if it should come to that.'" The narrator breaks in to comment on events surrounding her assertions: "But while she said,/her skinny feet troubled the waters, rattled/the leaves, and picked at the nervous vines." As in Stevens, saying is an action with perceptual results, in a world that affirms, alters, or contradicts what is said. Stevens' model of zany imagery suits this frame-changing moment. Nemerov describes "crickety conversations," a "moon rolled out like a marble," and "how the dark spilled up instead of down." And as in Stevens, the syntax makes distinct phenomena merge—Mrs. Mandrill's gestures reverberate out like pond circles as the vines she rattles cross the telephone wires which carry the cricket conversations that describe the marble moon. But where Stevens pushes the wildness into paradox and contradiction, Nemerov naturalizes it. "Mrs. Mandrill" ends not with "the imagined land" configured from "the martyrs' bones," but with a more organic metamorphosis. Her dying body turns into soil, and her "conversion" is a quotidian one: the stony "grasping heart" becomes vegetable matter as she relinquishes the will. Imagination describes and comments on this conversion but does not produce it; it is produced by nature and mortality.

Nemerov has admitted to having conversations with Frost (not with Stevens) in his dreams. And it is not surprising to find, toward the end of *Blue Swallows*, an explicit tribute, "For Robert Frost, in the Autumn, in Vermont" (*Collected* 405). And yet toward the end of the poem, as Nemerov imagines the *nobility* of a scene of reading, a scene removed from the mirror world of experience, yet experiential in its abstractions, his knowledge of Stevens serves him well. Though the tribute is to Frost, Stevens has insinuated himself into the remembrance at its close: "now on your turning page/The lines blaze with a constant light, displayed/As in the maple's cold and fiery shade." These lines do not really fit the poem dedicated to Frost. We hear the Stevensian "difference." Stevens is an uncanny visitor in Nemerov's Frostian work, as if the noble rider took the reins of the chariot and drove it off course.

***

Richard Wilbur loved to recount his experience hosting and introducing Wallace Stevens at Harvard in 1952. Stevens was noticeably blunt, if wholly polite, about just how little their encounter meant to him. "We said we hoped he would come and see us some time," Wilbur recalled. "I won't, but you're very kind to invite me," was Stevens' curt reply (qtd. in Brazeau 169). Nevertheless, Stevens wrote a recommendation for Wilbur to the Guggenheim Foundation, and in a brief letter to the young poet he remarked of Wilbur's work: "The greater part of the imaginative life of people is both created and enjoyed in polar circumstances. However, I suppose that without being contrary, one can say that the right spot is the middle spot between the polar and the anti-polar" (*L* 740). Presumably, Wilbur's Guggenheim application had outlined the kinds of dichotomies that would inform his lifelong poetic structure.

Like Nemerov, Wilbur turns to Stevens in his prose defenses of poetry. Stevens is especially prominent, and frequently cited, in Wilbur's beautiful essay "Poetry and Happiness." For instance, Wilbur argues, citing "Men Made Out of Words," that Stevens shows us "poetry as a self-shaping activity of the whole society": "The whole race is a poet that writes down/The eccentric propositions of its fate" (qtd. in *Responses* 91). Attractive as this idea is to him of poetry as the basis of culture, Wilbur retreats in the essay to a more modest emphasis on style. Stevens' prose imagines the river of rivers, and Wilbur concerns himself with matters of poetic craft as a "tributary form of the general imaginative activity" (92).

Wilbur certainly learned something about his craft from Stevens. He remarks in an interview with Arlo Haskell that "[Stevens'] ability to combine 'the imagination's Latin with the lingua franca et jocundissima' … was something I sought after in my own way, and with gratitude for his infectious example" (n. pag.). The mixture of elevated and demotic speech, and of religious ideas mixed with anecdotes of the quotidian, became a Wilbur trademark. But what strikes me most about Wilbur's evocations of Stevens in "Poetry and Happiness" is how much he wants to ground Stevensian abstraction, to fix it in description— how much in a sense he imagines Stevens to be like Frost, a poet of experience. Wilbur writes,

One does not think of Wallace Stevens, who so stressed the transforming power of imagination, as having much in common with Frost, and yet Stevens would agree that the best and happiest dreams of the poet are those that involve no denial of the fact. In his poem "Crude Foyer," Stevens acknowledges that poets are tempted to turn inward and conceive an interior paradise; but that is a false happiness; we can only, he says, be "content,/At last, there, when it turns out to be here."

(Responses 104–05)

The "here" in "Crude Foyer" is deeply ambiguous and may include the poem as much as the sensuous world, or to refuse the difference (*CPP* 270). Wilbur reduces Stevens' cognitive ambiguity to a moral one when he writes, "We cannot be content, we cannot enjoy poetic happiness, until the inner paradise is brought to terms with the world before us, and our vision fuses with the view from the window" (*Responses* 105). Of his own work, Wilbur writes, "What poetry does with ideas is to redeem them from abstraction and submerge them in sensibility; it embodies them in persons and things and surrounds them with a weather of feeling" (126). Does Stevens feel the need to "redeem" ideas from abstraction? The supreme fiction *"Must Be Abstract"* (*CPP* 329). Yet Stevens' use of incarnational imagery suggests a kind of redemption relevant to the Christian Wilbur. Stevensian revelation is "An abstraction blooded, as a man by thought" (*CPP* 333). But this is far more complex and paradoxical than the oppositional logic of Wilbur or the outer/inner chiasm of Frost.

We can see Wilbur pulling back from metaphor and orphic poetry in the early sonnet "Praise in Summer" (*Collected* 461), which is his own examination of the motive for metaphor. But while Stevens in "The Motive for Metaphor" turns from metaphor as evasion to metaphor as approach, Wilbur turns from metaphor to experience. What, then, is the status of Stevensian abstraction, metaphor, and linguistic flourishes in Wilbur? Are they merely parodies of Stevens? Stevens would rarely do anything so conventional as write a sonnet (whereas Frost wrote them constantly), but in Wilbur's opening lines—"Obscurely yet most surely called to praise"—we hear the elevated speech of "To the One of Fictive Music." The poem turns to the past tense, and reflection on the act of metaphoric transfiguration: "I said the trees are mines in air, I said/See how the sparrow burrows in the sky!" But this poem as it goes on becomes a conversation between the two masters. The poet questions the motive for metaphor—a Stevensian impulse itself—but turns toward Frost's preference for synecdoche: "And then I wondered why this mad *instead*/Perverts our praise to uncreation, why/Such savor's in this wrenching things awry." The inquiry ends in a Frostian rhetorical question aimed at Stevensian perversions. Why are we dissatisfied with the world of the senses, why must we "derange" the world in order to understand it? "Should it not be enough of fresh and strange/That trees grow green, and moles can course in clay,/And sparrows sweep the ceiling of our day?" That last image is of course a metaphor, and Wilbur slyly intends the contradiction, but this metaphor works to embellish, not to transfigure perception. Even when Wilbur writes of "Mind" (*Collected* 314), he binds his reflections to one extended metaphor, bats in a cave, making the poem more descriptive than conceptual in its procedures.

Critics have sometimes linked Wilbur to Stevens for his "preoccupation with reality and imagination" and seen him as a smaller-scale lyric poet in the Stevensian line (Bawer 266). And Wilbur's early penchant for abstract ideas has often been criticized for its Stevensian excesses. Bruce Michelson hears Stevens in a very early Wilbur poem, "Attention Makes Infinity," and he disapproves of the influence:

> Stevens's rhetorical flourishes seem evident here, in all this about king spinners, billowing wives, relenting air. There is an abundance of illuminated, empty "air" in early Wilbur, and to read through these first poems again is to look through a lens that seems trained a dozen degrees above the landscape, above anything one could look at hard instead. This is not simply a case of a young poet borrowing overmuch from Stevens's ethereality and trusting his own voice and imagination as yet too little; this is a refusal of any particular except the general particular, the generalized pedestrian, the laundry of "every yard."
>
> (13)

Stevensian linguistic flourishes also play across a later Wilbur poem, "All That Is" (*Collected* 112). But here Michelson attaches them to a satiric theme and a mature absorption of the master. He quotes a few lines—"It is a ghostly grille/ Through which, as often, we begin to see/The confluence of the Oka and the Aare"—and notes as follows:

> This sounds like Stevens, but a Stevens recollected in the giddiness of that hypnagogic state which is such a favorite of Wilbur's—a kind of Stevens double-talk, echoing in a mind on its way into a trance. What follows immediately is more of the same, but more broadly comic: a supreme fiction conjured out of those English words which have their being, for most of us, in crossword puzzles and there alone. If we insist on grand experiences of language to organize our days and close them out, here is what we get, and perhaps deserve …
>
> (150)

Michelson quotes more passages of whimsy, linguistic opacity, and eccentricity in the otherwise sober Wilbur. So when Wilbur adapts Stevensian rhetoric, Michelson's argument goes, he must do it tongue in cheek. Linguistic transport cannot be the real aim of this earnest poet, he assumes.

Indeed, Wilbur has been seen, and sees himself, as "a continuator of Frost" not Stevens (Interview Jason Gray 40). He has been proud of his distant relation to Frost by marriage, and in 1969 he wrote a poem, "Seed Leaves," with the epigraph "*Homage to R. F.*" (*Collected* 205–06). In its attention to minutiae of the horticultural earth, its style of wit, its use of trimeter, and of couplets and alternate rhyme, it pays homage through imitation. There is no corresponding homage to Stevens in Wilbur's canon. But in his late address to his deceased wife, Charlee, one hears Stevens again breaking through the Frostian caution. For perhaps when the mind turns to dreams and desires, to what can only be imagined rather than what can be directly felt or experienced, Stevens is the best guide. Wilbur is ninety as he writes "The House," surely the best poem in *Anterooms* (2010):

> Sometimes, on waking, she would close her eyes
> For a last look at that white house she knew
> In sleep alone, and held no title to,
> And had not entered yet, for all her sighs.
>
> What did she tell me of that house of hers?
> White gatepost; terrace; fanlight of the door;
> A widow's walk above the bouldered shore;
> Salt winds that ruffle the surrounding firs.
>
> Is she now there, wherever there may be?
> Only a foolish man would hope to find
> That haven fashioned by her dreaming mind.
> Night after night, my love, I put to sea.
>
> (1)

Here we have the abstract house, the dreaming figure, the extended syntax, the questioning commentator, the night and the sea, the sail of Ulysses—all signature Stevensian elements. It is a more formally tight, and more accessible, poem than Stevens would write. It is more confessional, not an address to an interior paramour, but to a real person known for a lifetime. Other ghosts, in addition to Stevens and Charlee, gather round the poem. We may, for instance, hear Elizabeth Bishop's "Questions of Travel" toward the end—"*home,/wherever that may be*" (75). But like the clarity of late Stevens, this late poem of Wilbur turns to metaphysics with quiet, iconic imagery. I would forgive a student on an exam if he or she said it was Stevens. It is not, by any stretch, a poem by Frost.

In postmodern poetry, Stevens' influence is hard to miss. Here is something from *The Errancy* by Jorie Graham that echoes the Stevensian wordplay of "doctrine" and "doctors": "And freedom in the room like a thin gray floating./ And doctrine./And other kinds of shine rising off the edges of things—" (42). Graham captures Stevensian simile that personifies light as mind: "as if the daylight were a doctor arriving,/each thing needing to be seen ..." (42). But much as Stevens was admired in the 1950s and 1960s, few poets during his lifetime took up the full challenge of his threshold thinking. Nemerov praised "the difficult art of a man who, so far as thought is concerned, may prove to have been the only truly *modern* poet of his time" ("Poetry" 13). Nemerov's own time seemed to require Frost's more traditional forms and structures.

Notes

1   To avoid an abundance of repetitive and intrusive page references during my readings of poems, I will systematically limit myself to providing page numbers at the first mention of a poem's title.

2   "When Robert Frost was alive," Nemerov told an interviewer, "I was known as the other New England poet which is to be barely known at all" (Interview n. pag.).

3   Stephen Metcalf in his 2003 *New York Times* review also sees Stevens' influence only in negative terms:

> Alas, like a number of university-sponsored poets, Nemerov sometimes felt compelled to write like Wallace Stevens. He tells us in "The Loon's Cry" how the "energy in things/Shone through their shapes," and about a birdsong "whose respeaking was the poet's act." In his best stab at modernist augury, "Painting a Mountain Stream," he urges the poet to "paint this rhythm, not this thing."
>
> (n. pag.)

I counter that some of Nemerov's most powerful, and indeed bold and original, passages come from his deep familiarity with the Modernist master.

Works Cited

Bawer, Bruce. "Richard Wilbur's Difficult Balance." *American Scholar* 60.2 (1991): 261–66. Print.

Bishop, Elizabeth. *Elizabeth Bishop: Poems, Prose, and Letters*. Ed. Robert Giroux and Lloyd Schwartz. New York: Library of America, 2008. Print.

Brazeau Peter. *Parts of a World: Wallace Stevens Remembered; An Oral Biography*. San Francisco: North Point, 1985. Print.

Frost, Robert. *Robert Frost: Collected Poems, Prose, and Plays*. Ed. Richard Poirier and Mark Richardson. New York: Library of America, 1995. Print.

Graham, Jorie. *The Errancy*. Hopewell: Ecco, 1997. Print.

Meinke, Peter. *Howard Nemerov*. American Writers 70. Minneapolis: University of Minnesota Press, 1968. Print.

Metcalf, Stephen. "The Other New England Poet." *New York Times*. July 13, 2003. October 18, 2015. Web.

Michelson, Bruce. *Wilbur's Poetry: Music in a Scattering of Time*. Amherst: University of Massachusetts Press, 1991. Print.

Nemerov, Howard. "The Bread of Faithful Speech—Wallace Stevens and the Voices of Imagination." *A Howard Nemerov Reader*. Columbia: University of Missouri Press, 1991. 176–82. Print.

Nemerov, Howard. *The Collected Poems of Howard Nemerov*. Chicago: University of Chicago Press, 1977. Print.

Nemerov, Howard. *Figures of Thought: Speculations on the Meaning of Poetry & Other Essays*. Boston: Godine, 1978. Print.

Nemerov, Howard. "Interview by Grace Cavalieri." *Grace Cavalieri*. October 1988. October 18, 2015. Web.

Nemerov, Howard. "The Poetry of Wallace Stevens." *Sewanee Review* 65.1 (1957): 1–14. Print.

Perloff, Marjorie. "Pound/Stevens: Whose Era?" *New Literary History* 13.3 (1982): 485–514. Print.

Stevens, Wallace. *Letters of Wallace Stevens*. Ed. Holly Stevens. Berkeley: University of California Press, 1996. Print.

Stevens, Wallace. *Wallace Stevens: Collected Poetry and Prose*. Ed. Frank Kermode and Joan Richardson. New York: Library of America, 1997. Print.

Wilbur, Richard. *Anterooms: New Poems and Translations*. Boston: Houghton, 2010. Print.

Wilbur, Richard. *Collected Poems, 1943–2004*. Orlando: Harcourt, 2004. Print.

Wilbur, Richard. "Interview by Arlo Haskell." *Littoral*. October 21, 2009. October 18, 2015. Web.

Wilbur, Richard. "Interview by Jason Gray." *Missouri Review* 27.3 (2004): 35–48. Print.

Wilbur, Richard. "Interview by Joan Hutton." *Transatlantic Review* 29 (1968): 58–67. Print.

Wilbur, Richard. *Responses: Prose Pieces, 1953–1976*. New York: Harcourt, 1976. Print.

3

The Strands of Modernism: Stevens beside the Seaside

Lee M. Jenkins

Wallace Stevens' "The Idea of Order at Key West" is a poet's poem, a self-reflexive meditation on *poiesis*, or the art of poetry itself, and on the relationship between the orders of imagination and reality, word and world, poem and place. It is unsurprising, then, that poets writing after Stevens on the other side of the Atlantic should have invoked and revoked "The Idea of Order at Key West," tilting its spatial and temporal axes in re-expressions that have, in several senses, expanded the poem's original horizon of reception. More surprising, given Stevens' belated reputation in England, is that "Key West," which appeared in the journal *Alcestis* in 1934 prior to its inclusion in the volume *Ideas of Order* (1935; 1936), has proved a popular resort for British poets since the early 1940s, when Nicholas Moore drafted Stevens' poem into the service of English Surrealism in a time of war.[1] This chapter considers Moore's "Ideas of Disorder at Torquay" with reference to a cluster of interrelated English Surrealist and neo-Surrealist poems and artworks. The chapter concludes with a discussion of Peter Redgrove's "The Idea of Entropy at Maenporth Beach," a postwar and post-Jungian restaging of "The Idea of Order at Key West" on the Cornish seaboard. The signal differences between these transatlantic receptions of Stevens, I propose, muddy the waters between the two strands of poetic Modernism, the Other Tradition and the Symbolist Tradition, traced in Marjorie Perloff's still influential position-piece of 1982, reprinted in *The Dance of the Intellect* (1985), "Pound/Stevens: Whose Era?"

Thanks to Chris McCabe and Tom Jenks for permission to reproduce two images from *Seaside Special*, the third collaboration between the poets. The full sequence can be viewed and purchased at https://cmtjthethird.wordpress.com/.

Before we turn to its English response-poems, it may be useful to revisit the reception of "The Idea of Order at Key West" itself in canonical American criticism. Helen Vendler identifies the poem with the marine verse of Stevens' first collection, *Harmonium* (1923; 1931), but hears in statements such as "The song and water were not medleyed sound" and "it was she and not the sea we heard" (*CPP* 105) a "strained" assertion of "the power of poetry over nature" (Vendler 69). That strain is audible, in particular, in the sonic proximity of "she" and "sea," phonemes representative of the orders of mind and world or of art and nature between which the poem urges us to differentiate. Both "she" and "sea" are sibilants, and Stevens defines "sibilants" as "sea-sounds" in *Harmonium*'s "Two Figures in Dense Violet Night," a Florida poem in which, in contrast to "Key West," the sea's "serenade" is identical with the seductive quality of poetic language itself (*CPP* 69). Our proneness to slip between "she" and "sea" is famously flagged in another song about a woman on a beach, the tongue twister turned popular ditty "She sells sea shells by the sea shore."[2] Stevens' "Key West" has proved harder still to parse, Harold Bloom observing that, with "its desperate equivocations and its unresolvable difficulties," "The Idea of Order at Key West" is "an impossible text to interpret" (93).

Of course, Bloom, that "impossible possible philosophers' man" (*CPP* 226), proceeds to interpret the poem nonetheless: as a figuration of the Schopenhauerian Idea. Within Bloom's wider schema, "The Idea of Order at Key West" is exemplary of the "American Romantic modification" of "the Wordsworthian crisis-poem" (93); more specifically, Stevens' poem is a revision of Emerson's "Seashore" (1856), "in which no one can sing beyond the genius of the sea" (Bloom 96). According to Bloom, "The American crisis-poem, from Emerson to A. R. Ammons, is a shore-lyric" (96), since the littoral is the liminal site of poetic crossings "between one kind of figurative thinking and another" (2). The Atlantic shore in "The Idea of Order at Key West" signifies "spirit and space," properties that, in the following poem in *Ideas of Order*, constitute a working definition of "The American Sublime" (*CCP* 107). And yet "The Idea of Order at Key West," that most equivocal of American shore-lyrics, is also an Atlantic portal through which the crisis-poem returns to its Old World origins, albeit that in its passage into English verse Stevens' poem undergoes a sea-change. In its English response-poems, "The Idea of Order at Key West" is—like Stevens' Comedian, who voyages in the other direction—"made new" (*CPP* 24).

The British domestication of "The Idea of Order at Key West," if we can call it that, begins with Nicholas Moore's "Ideas of Disorder at Torquay." Moore, the son of philosopher G. E. Moore and the nephew of artist and poet T. Sturge Moore, was an undergraduate at Cambridge when he wrote to Stevens in 1938 to solicit a contribution for his little magazine, *Seven*.[3] Stevens' "earliest champion" in England, Moore would subsequently become embroiled in the contretemps over the pirated British edition of Stevens' *Selected Poems* brought out by the Fortune Press in 1952 (Rudolf 7).[4] "Ideas of Disorder at Torquay" had appeared a decade before, in the Fortune Press volume *The Cabaret, the Dancer, the Gentleman.*

Poet, editor, and, in his later life, a prize-winning cultivator of irises, Moore was also an accomplished translator. His theory of translation gives us a purchase, if a slippery one (Moore's essay is titled "On the Impossibility of Translation"), on the relationship between "The Idea of Order at Key West" and his own "Ideas of Disorder at Torquay." Moore's essay was written as an introduction to *Spleen*, a series of thirty-one translations of Charles Baudelaire's sonnet "Je suis comme le roi" (or "Spleen (III)") in the *Spleen et Idéal* sequence of *Les Fleurs du mal*. Moore called his redactions of Baudelaire "poemenvylopes," and he posted them as serial entries in a translation competition held by the *Sunday Times* newspaper in 1968.[5] Although all thirty-one translations of Baudelaire's sonnet are in Moore's hand, these are given multiple poetic signatures: as Moore explains in "On the Impossibility of Translation," the "personages … have all grown out of or into the Baudelairian milieu of this poem and its variants. That such poets as Wallace Stevens, John Betjeman and H. D. have been sacrificed to its spleen may be misleading as I admire them all" (*Selected* 130). Christopher Ricks has argued that "translation constitutes one of the highest forms that allusion can take" (1). Moore's "Pepe-le-Moko au Montrachet-le-Jardin," one of his several versions of Baudelaire in the style of Stevens, is a double act of translation, or translation in a double sense. Dedicated to "Mrs. Alfred Uruguay," the sonnet is decked out with words and phrases—"effendi" and "The sun, in clownish yellow, but not a clown" (*Selected* 165)—that are borrowed not from Stevens' "Montrachet-le-Jardin" or "Mrs. Alfred Uruguay" but from "Esthétique du Mal," Stevens' own version of Baudelaire.[6] As Moore remarks, "putting someone else's poem into your own mind is in effect translation, or, if not that, parody or pastiche," although, he insists, "there must be some kind of critical and emotional interplay between the poet and his material" (*Selected* 131).

Like his *Spleen* sonnets, Moore's "Ideas of Disorder at Torquay" is the product of interplay between the poet and his material; in this instance, Moore's *materia poetica* is "The Idea of Order at Key West," now relocated from the Florida Keys to the "faded" English seaside resort of Torquay, in Devon (*Selected* 50). The opening lines of Moore's poem tell us that

> The trams still run in some kind of array,
> Along the seafront
>
> (49)

However, this is "an old-world order," even if Moore's seaside poem takes its terms from Stevens' New World idea of order. "The little steamers [that] puff their purple smoke/As if to say order in everything" are the staid English counterparts of the fishing boats at anchor in the more glamorous Key West. In the early 1940s—the years of the Blitz—Torquay was regarded as a safe harbor, a refuge for "old, ancient ladies,/And proud magnates from factory and bank" (49). "Order is possible" there (50), but Torquay, the bastion of "Dun dowagers" (49), is hardly a *locus amoenus* for the Muse. The idea of order at Torquay is as obsolescent as its genteel residents, the relics of an *ancien régime* that, Moore opines, will not survive the war:

> Something, the essence of a change that seems
> A breaking up of order, something grave
> Troubles the waters of contentment, moves
> The old, cold ladies to a troubled love.
>
> (50)

Where the "ladies" retreat to Torquay, "the vulgar in their hordes disdain/The imperial order" and flock instead "to Blackpool Pier,/To look for lights they used to know" (49–50). These lights are the famous Blackpool Illuminations, the Lights Festival that was founded in the year of Stevens' birth, 1879, but was suspended in 1939 for the duration of the blackout. Life during wartime means that there are no "emblazoned zones" to dazzle the vulgar hordes on the pleasure beach (*CCP* 106): in a literal sense, the lights had gone out in Europe, as Winston Churchill had said they would in his 1938 broadcast to the American people. But if the popular recourse to Blackpool is nostalgic, it also signals a sea-"change," the "breaking up" of the old order that Moore's poem anticipates (*Selected* 50).

As social commentary, "Ideas of Disorder at Torquay" comports less closely perhaps with "The Idea of Order at Key West" than with the opening poem in Stevens' *Ideas of Order*, "Farewell to Florida," which was reprinted in the July 1936 issue of *Contemporary Poetry and Prose*, the organ of the English Surrealist Group. Like the "men in crowds" of Stevens' Depression-era America,

Moore's working-class hordes at Blackpool gather in a North that in both poems is opposed to a feminized and "sepulchral South" (*CPP* 98, 97). "Ideas of Disorder at Torquay," it seems, invokes "The Idea of Order at Key West" only to countermand the "maker's rage to order" (*CPP* 106). If he is to translate Stevens' poem into an idiom appropriate to wartime England, Moore must torque the ordering trajectory of the American original. As Stevens remarks in his essay "The Noble Rider and the Sound of Words," first published in 1942, "the fate of a society is involved in the orderly disorders of the present time" (*CPP* 656), and in "Connoisseur of Chaos," from his 1942 volume *Parts of a World*, Stevens would concede that "A violent order is disorder" and that "A great disorder is an order. These/Two things are one" (*CPP* 194). For Moore, writing in the same year, the poet must be, if not a connoisseur, then a conductor of chaos, whose task is not to "order words of the sea" but to trouble the too-orderly English "waters of contentment" (*CPP* 106; Moore, *Selected* 50).[7]

"Ideas of Disorder at Torquay" reveals that Moore conducted his correspondence with Stevens in his poetry, as well as in letters, translations, and in hybrid forms like the poemenvylope. Stevens himself, who was endowed with what Alan Filreis describes as a "Postcard Imagination" (207), made poems into postcards ("A Postcard from the Volcano," in *Ideas of Order*) and postcards into poems ("The Irish Cliffs of Moher," in *The Rock*)—indeed, Stevens' verse anticipates Jacques Derrida's definition of the postcard as "neither legible nor illegible, open and radically unintelligible" (79).[8] "Ideas of Disorder at Torquay" may be classified as postcard-poetry, too, albeit that the keener affinity of Moore's poem is with a domestic type of the *carte postale*—the seaside postcard, which, with its hallmark wordplay, low humor, and lurid use of color, belongs to a demotic English tradition defended by George Orwell in an article printed in *Horizon* in 1941 (see Orwell). A year later, in Moore's "Ideas of Disorder at Torquay," we encounter Wallace Stevens beside the English seaside—where he is still to be found in twenty-first-century English neo-Surrealist artworks like Chris McCabe and Tom Jenks's *Seaside Special*, a word-and-image sequence that bears out Stevens' statement, in *The Man with the Blue Guitar*, that "The sea is a form of ridicule" (*CPP* 147).

Created in 2012, the McCabe and Jenks collaboration consists of thirty-one literary postcards that riff off the saucy seaside variety while nodding, too, to the thirty-one poemenvylopes that make up Moore's ludic sonnet-sequence, *Spleen*. Like Moore's poemenvylopes, the *Seaside Special* postcards constitute a very English take on the Surrealist perspective as defined in André Breton's *Second*

Manifesto, in which "the real and the imagined," and "the communicable and the incommunicable, high and low, cease to be perceived as contradictory" (123). J. H. Matthews has traced the trajectory of popular forms of postwar English Surrealism from *The Goon Show* (1951–60) through *Monty Python's Flying Circus* (1969–74); the line continues in the cult BBC TV comedy series *Fawlty Towers* (1975, 1979), which takes us back to Torquay, and in the *Seaside Special* postcards.

In the first of the two *Seaside Specials* in which he features, Wallace Stevens is standing in front of a bus with his name emblazoned on it; the play here is on Wallace Arnold, a now defunct British tour coach operator that carried vacationers to seaside destinations (see Figure 3.1).[9] The tourist information board to Stevens' right indicates that his bus has indeed dropped him off at a resort, an impression that, despite the drab surroundings, is confirmed by the poet's "KISS ME QUICK CUDDLE ME SLOW" hat. Like the saucy postcard and the donkey ride, the souvenir hat epitomized the English seaside experience

Figure 3.1 *Seaside Special* 1: "The Bloody Emperor of Ice Cream." Courtesy Chris McCabe and Tom Jenks.

of the 1960s and 1970s. Since the "KISS ME QUICK" catchphrase comes from Elvis Presley's 1961 hit of that title, Stevens' hat also associates him with the American "King." "It's the bloody Emperor of Ice Cream," exclaims a bystander, her remark referring, quite literally, to the gaudy ice-cream cornet that the grayscale Stevens cutout holds in his hand. The woman in the street speaks for the British public, for "the people who don't know" (to quote T. S. Eliot) who Wallace Stevens is (Eliot, "Untitled" 9). Of course, we who are in the know recognize the poet of "The Emperor of Ice-Cream," and thus a witty spin is put on the naughty *double entendre* of the comic seaside postcard.

In the second *Seaside Special*, the Emperor of Ice Cream has been crowned with his cor(o)net (see Figure 3.2). The ice cream is now on the poet's head, and guzzling it is a beach donkey, wearing Stevens' snappy Panama in place of its stock-in-trade scruffy straw hat. The ice-cream vendor, who is the British comedian Les Dawson (1931–93), cracks a lame joke: "I thought I was the donkey around here," he quips. A veteran of a 1970s BBC TV light entertainment program

Figure 3.2 *Seaside Special* 2: "The Lighter Strands of Modernism." Courtesy Chris McCabe and Tom Jenks.

called *Seaside Special*, Dawson was known for his mother-in-law gags, but it is Stevens who is the butt of his joke in the *Seaside Special* postcard. Meanwhile, a dismayed John Betjeman—British Poet Laureate in the 1970s—comments on the slapstick scene: "The lighter strands of Modernism have ripped the heart from this resort ..."

Betjeman is best remembered for "Trebetherick," his 1940 encomium to the British "Sand in the sandwiches" day out by the seaside (66).[10] The setting of McCabe and Jenks's postcard is not the Cornish village that lends its name to Betjeman's poem, but the seaside resort of Margate, in Kent. Betjeman's Second World War poem "Margate, 1940," in which the "dark" of the blackout has replaced the "fairy-lit sights," includes the lines "over the privet, commingingly clear,/I heard lesser 'Co-Optimists' down by the pier" (124–25). *The Co-Optimists* was a 1920s English variety stage revue, which was made into a movie in 1929. In the *Seaside Special* postcard, Stevens and Les Dawson are latter-day and even lesser Co-Optimists, as they perform their comic double act down by the pier.

In 1921, the year *The Co-Optimists* variety revue opened in London, Eliot was in Margate writing *The Waste Land*, a poem that hardly reflects the "lighter strands of Modernism" of which Betjeman, in the postcard, complains. Eliot may have been sniffy about Stevens, but he was an aficionado of music-hall theater. As David Chinitz argues in *T. S. Eliot and the Cultural Divide*, the music hall represented for Eliot the "possibility of reconciliation between diverging levels of culture" (103); the demise of the tradition, he therefore believed, "was closely connected with social disintegration" (102). *The Waste Land*, while it alludes to popular genres, cannot replicate the integrative function of the music hall: "On Margate Sands," Eliot confesses, "I can connect/Nothing with nothing" (*Complete* 70). By contrast, everything is connected with everything in the playful, neo-Surrealist assemblage of the *Seaside Special* postcard—Betjeman is connected with Eliot (as indeed he had been in 1915, when for a brief period Eliot was the young Betjeman's teacher at London's Highgate Junior School) and Stevens is connected with his fellow comedian, Les Dawson, and with Eliot himself. In a 1946 review, Wylie Sypher had proposed that "Stevens at moments may be Prufrock—'a most inappropriate man in a most unpropitious place'" (264); the same suggestion is tendered in the *Seaside Special* postcard, in which the lobster claw Stevens is holding connects him with Prufrock's "pair of ragged claws/Scuttling across the floors of silent seas" (Eliot, *Complete* 15).[11]

The lobster has been a prop of Surrealist art since 1936, when Salvador Dalí created his *Lobster Telephone* for the English poet Edward James. In

Stevens' judgment, "The essential fault of surrealism is that it invents without discovering. To make a clam play an accordion is to invent not to discover" (*CPP* 919).[12] To make Wallace Stevens hold a lobster claw may likewise be to invent not to discover—unless, that is, the claw in the postcard is found material, a leftover, perhaps, from the poet's meal in "Notes Toward a Supreme Fiction" of "lobster Bombay with mango/Chutney" (*CPP* 347). As Matthews argues, English Surrealism "precipitates us right into *the crisis of the object* that Breton discussed" (197). With his lobster and his ice cream, Stevens also embodies what another of the *Seaside Special* postcards—this one featuring the unlikely duo of Marianne Moore and English actor Sid James (1913–76), a stalwart of the *Carry On* comedy film franchise—terms "The poetic Americanisation of the coast," the Americanization of England's seaside between the wars that J. B. Priestley had railed against in 1934 in *An English Journey*. The phenomenon of the "Transatlantic Seaside" was registered in the United States, too—a 1926 feature in the *New York Herald Tribune*, for instance, described Blackpool Pleasure Beach as "England's Coney Island" (qtd. in Walton 115).

In the *Seaside Special* postcard, Betjeman's speech bubble—"The lighter strands of Modernism have ripped the heart from this resort"—reiterates what John Timberman Newcomb describes as the "British suspicion that Stevens was a simpering lutanist of effete fleas" (70). That suspicion, which had been aroused in 1923 with Stevens' very first British publication ("Mandolin and Liqueurs," in Harold Monro's *Chapbook*), would be allayed only partly by the publication, after decades of foot-dragging on Eliot's part, of the Faber and Faber *Selected Poems* in 1953. In the meantime, for Moore and for David Gascoyne, English poets who came of age in the interwar heyday of Surrealism, the "frivolousness" with which Stevens had been charged by Laura Riding and Robert Graves in 1927, in *A Survey of Modernist Poetry*, was a guilty pleasure (80). The role of the poet, as Stevens conceived it, lies in "giving life whatever savor it possesses" (*CPP* 661). The gaiety of Stevens' language, the "essential gaudiness" that he ascribed to his "favorite" poem, "The Emperor of Ice-Cream" (*L* 263), offered a vivid contrast to the English scene, which is described as "faded" in both Moore's "Ideas of Disorder at Torquay" and Gascoyne's early poem "Seaside Souvenirs" (Moore, *Selected* 50; Gascoyne, *New* 27).

Gascoyne's later pastiche of Stevens, "With a Cornet of Winkles," is, as Geoff Ward has suggested, a "double-edged tribute" that "remind[s] us both why Stevens has been valued, and why he has been resisted" in England (vii). What Gascoyne called his "perfectly awful attempt at a parody" is consigned to the *Light Verse* subsection of his *Collected Poems*, where a note alerts the reader to the fact that the poem was written before Stevens won the Bollingen Prize for Poetry in 1950 (*New* 226, 225n).[13] "With a Cornet of Winkles," we are to infer, pays a more equivocal tribute to Stevens than that of the Fellows in American Letters of the Library of Congress who judged the Bollingen; and indeed in Gascoyne's parody, the luscious lexicon of Stevens the "Beau linguist" (*CPP* 334), or "the Great/Gabbo," as Gascoyne calls him (*New* 225), is laced with the saltier tang of English Surrealism; as Stevens himself remarked of the difference between British and American poetry, "Taste in the two countries is quite different" (qtd. in Lensing 142). Rather than a receptacle for the milky "curds" dispensed by the Emperor of Ice Cream (*CPP* 50), Gascoyne's "Cornet" is a twist of paper filled with winkles; a traditional staple of English seaside fare, winkles are also the shellfish relatives of Dalí's lobster.[14]

A "cornet" is a musical instrument, of course, as well as a paper container and an ice-cream cone, and indeed the greater part of Gascoyne's parodic tribute to Stevens is played in the key of the "mauve melody-man" (*New* 225). As Roger Scott claims in an editorial note, Gascoyne's poem "recreates the rhythms and sounds created by players of the lute, mandolin and clavier"—Stevensian instruments all (Gascoyne, *New* 407). With his "pat-prattling lute," Gascoyne's Stevens is once again the lutanist of fleas, although Gascoyne tells us that his pastiche is more than mere "impudent snook-cocking." Stevens is the "sole plum among lute-players left/To preserve some bravura or any finesse"; he is "undeterred," Gascoyne says, by "the slums' glum goloshes-clad mummers" (Gascoyne, *New* 225–26)—presumably Marxist critics of the 1930s like Stanley Burnshaw, in whose judgment Stevens' *Harmonium* represented "the kind of verse that people concerned with the murderous world collapse can hardly swallow today except in tiny doses" (Burnshaw 139). Gascoyne, by contrast, had devoured *Harmonium* whole when he came across a copy of the first edition in Sylvia Beach's Shakespeare & Company bookshop in Paris in 1933.[15] (Later, the lean years of the war would whet the English Surrealists' appetite for Stevens; Moore's "Ideas of Disorder at Torquay" appeared in 1942, the year in which rationing was introduced in Britain.) Nonetheless, Gascoyne shares Burnshaw's reservations: "With a Cornet of Winkles" is categorized, in a parenthesis to the poem's title, as a Mallarméan "vers de circonstance" (*New* 225), the implication being that, like Mallarmé, as he is defined in Gascoyne's *A Short Survey of Surrealism* (1935), Stevens is "a disinterested experimentalist, the object of whose researches was to restore to words their pristine clarity and evocatory power" (12). "The claim to our attention of his *manner*," Gascoyne says of Mallarmé, "is undoubtedly far more important than that of his *matter*, which had not much to distinguish it from the stock-in-trade of symbolist poetry" (12).

For Gascoyne, it is in the 1937 volume *The Man with the Blue Guitar and Other Poems* that Stevens proves himself to be something more, and other, than a lutanist, or a Symbolist. In that volume, Glen MacLeod notes, Stevens "'absorbed' Surrealism as part of the growth of his own poetry" (377). Although Gascoyne would break with Surrealism at the end of the 1930s, his later work is no less attuned to Stevens' *Blue Guitar*. His recording of that collection's title poem, which was broadcast on BBC Radio in May 1955, a few months before Stevens' death, would prompt Gascoyne's subsequent experiments in the genre he dubbed the "*Radiophonic Poem*" (*New* 414).

"The Man with the Blue Guitar," Charles Altieri observes, "makes an interesting counterpart to Stevens's other major poem on music in the 1930s—'The Idea of Order at Key West'" (111). The two poems make for interesting counterparts, too, in terms of their reception in English verse. Peter Redgrove's "The Idea of Entropy at Maenporth Beach," published in his 1972 volume *Dr. Faust's Sea-Spiral Spirit and Other Poems*, takes us back to "The Idea of Order at Key West," but into very different poetic terrain from that staked out by the English Surrealists. Stevens' footprints in Redgrove's Cornish beach poem have been tracked by Erik Martiny. Without going over the same ground, I want to return to Redgrove's revision of "The Idea of Order at Key West" to make a wider point about Stevens' English legacy. Redgrove explained in an interview why he had responded to "The Idea of Order at Key West" with a poem of his own:

> The reason was that I disagreed with Stevens' philosophy there, and I think that Wallace Stevens' own poem disagrees with his philosophy, because he makes the sea so alive and says that it's only the woman's song that counts. Well, it isn't, so I'm putting this singer into a position where she is counselled by that which is usually despised, which is the mud and earth.
>
> (qtd. in Bentley 100–01)

Redgrove's poem, which embodies his "conception of the human mind existing on a largely unconscious continuum with nature," collapses the binaries that "The Idea of Order at Key West" attempts to enforce (Bentley 101).

Stevens, as Gascoyne describes him, was "that one/Still remaining Romanticist who's fully weaned of such pap" (*New* 225). Redgrove, by contrast, is a "neo-Romantic" (Bentley 101) who cleaves to the earth mother, the "black goddess."[16] The reincarnation of Baudelaire's lover, Jeanne Duval, "la ténébreuse," Redgrove's "black Venus" is reborn out of the mud on Maenporth beach, and "sprinkles substance" as "she runs into the sea" (Redgrove 117–18). Appropriately, the poem was read by Redgrove's wife, Penelope Shuttle, when, after his death in 2003, the poet's ashes were mixed with the sea at Maenporth. As Redgrove's biographer, Neil Roberts, has observed, "The Idea of Entropy at Maenporth Beach" is more than "a mere *jeu d'esprit* like his earlier 'Thirteen Ways of Looking at a Blackboard'" (*Lover* 61), but is "perhaps the pivotal work in [Redgrove's] oeuvre" (*Lucid* 162).

Redgrove's revision of Stevens in "The Idea of Entropy" takes its epigraph from Baudelaire's *Spleen et Idéal*, and so his poem, as Martiny notes, "lies at something of an intertextual crossroads" between Stevens and Baudelaire (83). The same may be said of those sonnets in Moore's *Spleen* sequence that are simultaneous translations of Baudelaire and of Stevens. Like Gascoyne, Moore belongs to a now-neglected generation of English poets who drew on Anglo-American Modernism *and* looked across the English Channel to continental models, in contradistinction to the insular Little Englandism of the Movement poets, with their suspicion of Abroad in general and of America in particular. Where Redgrove, whose own poetic had been formulated in the 1950s in resistance to the formalism of Movement verse, "attempts to draw Stevens back from his moments of modernist skepticism to a more romantic orthodoxy" (Martiny 81), Moore's Stevens is, like Baudelaire, raw material for English Surrealism.[17]

"Ideas of Disorder at Torquay" and "The Idea of Entropy at Maenporth Beach" both take their bearings from "The Idea of Order at Key West," but in doing so take English poetry after Stevens in quite different directions. For Perloff, the "aesthetic dichotomy at the heart of Modernism" between "lyric" and "collage," or between "the expressionist and the constructionist," is played out in the opposed poetics of Stevens and Ezra Pound (23). English responses to "The Idea of Order at Key West" might indicate that that dichotomy is located in Stevens' oeuvre itself. His reception in twentieth- and twenty-first-century English poetic Modernism suggests that Stevens *both* "carries on the Symbolist tradition" *and* offers "'a radical alternative to it'" (Perloff 14).

Notes

1   *Ideas of Order* appeared in a limited edition with Alcestis Press in 1935; Alfred A. Knopf brought out a trade edition in the following year.

2   Mary Anning (1799–1847), a fossil collector at Lyme Regis in Dorset, inspired both the tongue twister and Terry Sullivan's 1908 song. See Halliday.

3   Stevens obliged, and sent Moore "The Blue Buildings in the Summer Air," which appeared in issue 3 of *Seven*; Stevens' "Thunder by the Musician" is included in issue 5 and "Yellow Afternoon" in issue 8. For Moore's magazine, see Mengham.

4   On Moore and the Fortune Press, see Ford.

5   The competition was judged by George Steiner, who "drew attention to an extraordinary multiple entry, thirty-one versions of the same Baudelaire poem, obviously by the same hand and under a large number of pseudonyms, typed in brown or green ink and sent from various addresses all over the country" (Rudolf 6).

6   Pépé le Moko is the gangster antihero in a 1937 French film of that title, directed by Julien Duvivier. The film, an example of poetic realism in French cinema, is adapted from a 1931 novel by Henri La Barthe, who collaborated on the screenplay under the pseudonym "Détective Ashelbé." An American remake of the movie was released in 1938. In another of his *Spleen* sonnets, "L'eau Verte du Lethe," Moore juxtaposes epigraphs from his own (Stevensian) sequence *Recreations of a Blue Sonneteer* and Stevens' "Esthétique du Mal."

7   A selection of Moore's poetry is included in Sinclair's anthology titled *Conductors of Chaos.*

8   "The Irish Cliffs of Moher" was prompted by a postcard Stevens received from his Irish-American friend John L. Sweeney, in 1952.

9   Wallace Arnold (1912–2005) was named after its founders, Wallace Cunningham and Arnold Crowe. *Wallace Arnold Days by the Seaside* commemorative plates, which were issued into the 1990s, represent beach donkeys and other seaside images of a bygone era.

10 Betjeman, it should be noted, admired Nicholas Moore, and in his turn, as Peter Riley has pointed out, Moore would recruit Betjeman to *Spleen*'s "army of heteronyms" (415).

11 Sypher is quoting from "Sailing After Lunch," in *Ideas of Order* (*CPP* 99). Thanks to Bonnie Costello for pointing me to Howard Nemerov's Stevensian poem "The Town Dump," in which, along with fish heads, "the lobster, also, lifts/An empty claw" (142).

12 Glen MacLeod notes that Stevens' essay "The Irrational Element in Poetry" was conceived "in response to Surrealism," and that Stevens was "determined to avoid being labeled a Surrealist" (360, 362).

13 "With a Cornet of Winkles" was first printed in the section of Gascoyne's 1950 volume *A Vagrant and Other Poems* designated "Make-Weight Verse," where a footnote states that the poem was "penned" the previous year (55). I am grateful to Gascoyne's biographer, Robert Fraser, for confirming the date of the poem's composition.

14   In "Surrealism for the English" (1933), Charles Madge had argued that Surrealists in England should not merely imitate French models. Gascoyne's "First English Manifesto of Surrealism" (1935) duly draws attention to the indigenous sources of English Surrealism, albeit in a piece that was printed as "Premier Manifeste anglais du surréalisme (fragment)" in the French journal *Cahiers d'Art* in 1935. In *A Short Survey of Surrealism*, also published in 1935, Gascoyne charts Surrealism's development from Baudelaire, while emphasizing that the Surrealist mind-set "cannot be limited to any one particular time or place" (131).

15   On Gascoyne and *Harmonium*, see Fraser 242.

16   Redgrove and Shuttle explore the primal powers of the feminine in their study *The Black Goddess and the Sixth Sense*.

17   On Redgrove's resistance to the Movement, see Roberts, *Lucid* 71.

Works Cited

Altieri, Charles. *Wallace Stevens and the Demands of Modernity: Toward a Phenomenology of Value*. Ithaca: Cornell University Press, 2013. Print.

Bentley, Paul. *Scientist of the Strange: The Poetry of Peter Redgrove*. Madison: Fairleigh Dickinson University Press, 2002. Print.

Betjeman, John. *Collected Poems*. Ed. Lord Birkenhead. London: Murray, 1958. Print.

Bloom, Harold. *Wallace Stevens: The Poems of Our Climate*. Ithaca: Cornell University Press, 1977. Print.

Breton, André. *Manifestoes of Surrealism*. Trans. Richard Seaver and Helen R. Lane. Ann Arbor: University of Michigan Press, 1972. Print.

Burnshaw, Stanley. "Turmoil in the Middle Ground." 1935. Doyle 137–40.

Chinitz, David E. *T. S. Eliot and the Cultural Divide*. Chicago: University of Chicago Press, 2003. Print.

Derrida, Jacques. *The Post Card: From Socrates to Freud and Beyond*. Trans. Alan Bates. Chicago: University of Chicago Press, 1987. Print.

Doyle, Charles, ed. *Wallace Stevens: The Critical Heritage*. London: Routledge, 1985. Print.

Eliot, T. S. *The Complete Poems and Plays*. London: Faber, 1969. Print.

Eliot, T. S. "Untitled Statement." *Trinity Review* 8.3 (1954): 9. Print.

Filreis, Alan. *Wallace Stevens and the Actual World*. Princeton: Princeton University Press, 1991. Print.

Ford, Mark. "Nicholas Moore, Stevens, and the Fortune Press." *Wallace Stevens across the Atlantic*. Ed. Bart Eeckhout and Edward Ragg. Basingstoke: Palgrave, 2008. 165–85. Print.

Fraser, Robert. *Night Thoughts: The Surreal Life of the Poet David Gascoyne*. Oxford: Oxford University Press, 2012. Print.

Gascoyne, David. *New Collected Poems, 1929-1995*. Ed. Roger Scott. London: Enitharmon, 2014. Print.

Gascoyne, David. *A Short Survey of Surrealism*. 1935. London: Routledge, 2004. Print.

Gascoyne, David. *A Vagrant and Other Poems*. London: Lehmann, 1950. Print.

Halliday, Sam. "Modernism and the Seashell." *Critical Quarterly* 54.4 (2012): 74–92. Print.

Lensing, George S. "Wallace Stevens in England." *Wallace Stevens: A Celebration*. Ed. Frank Doggett and Robert Buttel. Princeton: Princeton University Press, 1980. 130–48. Print.

MacLeod, Glen G. "Stevens and Surrealism: The Genesis of 'The Man with the Blue Guitar.'" *American Literature* 59.3 (1987): 359–77. Print.

Martiny, Erik. "'From This Collision Were New Colors Born': Peter Redgrove's Reversionary Swerves from Wallace Stevens' Iconic Texts." *Wallace Stevens Journal* 31.1 (2007): 73–85. Print.

Matthews, J. H. *Toward the Poetics of Surrealism*. Syracuse: Syracuse University Press, 1976. Print.

McCabe, Chris, and Tom Jenks. *Seaside Special*. CMTJTHETHIRD July 22, 2012. November 1, 2015. Web.

Mengham, Rod. "'National Papers Please Reprint': Surrealist Magazines in Britain." *The Oxford Critical and Cultural History of Modernist Magazines. Volume I: Britain and Ireland, 1880-1955*. Ed. Peter Brooker and Andrew Thacker. Oxford: Oxford University Press, 2009. 688–703. Print.

Moore, Nicholas. *Selected Poems*. Ed. John Lucas and Matthew Welton. Nottingham: Shoestring, 2014. Print.

Moore, Nicholas. *Spleen*. 1973. London: Menard, 1990. Print.

Nemerov, Howard. *Collected Poems*. Chicago: University of Chicago Press, 1977. Print.

Newcomb, John Timberman. *Wallace Stevens and Literary Canons*. Jackson: University Press of Mississippi, 1992. Print.

Orwell, George. "The Art of Donald McGill." *The Collected Essays, Journalism and Letters of George Orwell: My Country Right or Left, 1940–43*. Vol. 2. Ed. Sonia Orwell and Ian Angus. Harmondsworth: Penguin, 1970. 194–95. Print.

Perloff, Marjorie. "Pound/Stevens: Whose Era?" *The Dance of the Intellect: Studies in the Poetry of the Pound Tradition*. Evanston: Northwestern University Press, 1985. 1–32. Print.

Redgrove, Peter. *Sons of My Skin: Selected Poems, 1954-1974*. London: Routledge, 1975. Print.

Redgrove, Peter, and Penelope Shuttle. *The Black Goddess and the Sixth Sense*. London: Paladin, 1989. Print.

Ricks, Christopher. *Allusion to the Poets*. Oxford: Oxford University Press, 2002. Print.

Riding, Laura, and Robert Graves. *A Survey of Modernist Poetry*. 1927. Manchester: Carcanet, 2002. Print.

Riley, Peter. "Nicholas Moore in the 1960s and 1970s." Sinclair 414–17.

Roberts, Neil. *The Lover, the Dreamer and the World: The Poetry of Peter Redgrove*. Sheffield: Sheffield Academic, 1994. Print.

Roberts, Neil. *A Lucid Dreamer: The Life of Peter Redgrove*. London: Jonathan Cape, 2012. Print.

Rudolf, Anthony. Preface. Moore, *Spleen* 6–7.

Sinclair, Iain, ed. *Conductors of Chaos: A Poetry Anthology*. London: Picador, 1996. Print.

Stevens, Wallace. *Letters of Wallace Stevens*. Ed. Holly Stevens. Berkeley: University of California Press, 1996. Print.

Stevens, Wallace. *Wallace Stevens: Collected Poetry and Prose*. Ed. Frank Kermode and Joan Richardson. New York: Library of America, 1997. Print.

Sypher, Wylie. "Connoisseur in Chaos: Wallace Stevens." 1946. Doyle 255–69.

Vendler, Helen. *Wallace Stevens: Words Chosen Out of Desire*. Cambridge: Harvard University Press, 1986. Print.

Walton, John K. "The Transatlantic Seaside from the 1880s to the 1930s: Blackpool and Coney Island." *Issues in Americanisation and Culture*. Ed. Neil Campbell, Jude Davies and George McKay. Edinburgh: Edinburgh University Press, 2004. 111–25. Print.

Ward, Geoff. "Foreword." *Wallace Stevens: Rage for Order*. By Lee M. Jenkins. Brighton: Sussex Academic, 1999. vii–viii. Print.

4

Hearing Stevens in Sylvia Plath

Bart Eeckhout

In March 2007, *PMLA* published an article by Gregory Machacek that offers the theoretical framework I need to be able to undertake my case study on Sylvia Plath. The article's title is, quite simply, "Allusion." Machacek sets up his topic by citing the opening of a poem by Denise Levertov: "The world is/not with us enough" (qtd. on 522). Most poetry readers will recognize what Levertov does: she is playing a riff on the first line of a well-known sonnet by William Wordsworth, "The world is too much with us." Machacek observes that to "note, evaluate, and interpret this sort of brief phraseological imitation of an earlier writer … has been an aspect of literary scholarship" for a long time, but he rightly adds that "discussion of the phenomenon is beset by limiting assumptions, conceptual murkiness, and terminological imprecision" (522). So he sets out to investigate "the nature and workings of allusion" in greater detail (523).

The methodical survey Machacek provides is useful as much for what it delivers as fails to deliver. He starts by distinguishing the "phraseological adaptations of a single identifiable precursor from the more diffuse [notion of] *intertextuality*" (523). At least in its original meaning, as proposed by Julia Kristeva in the 1960s, intertextuality refers to a general semiotic process that transcends concrete literary allusion, in which it takes no interest. Jonathan Culler admits that this turns it into "a difficult concept to use because of the vast and undefined discursive space it designates" (qtd. on 524). Machacek sees the basic impulses behind academic disciplines such as cultural studies, the new historicism, and discourse analysis as spin-offs from this post-structuralist kind of thinking about intertextuality. The orientation in such disciplines is primarily synchronic, he argues, not diachronic. As a result, practitioners take no active interest in connections between earlier and later texts. This helps to explain why none of the contributors to the present book apply methodologies from any of these disciplines.

When we wish to pursue diachronic connections between texts, Machacek notes the difficulty of finding an "adequate vocabulary." He reminds us, first of all, that the "terms *allusion* and *verbal echo* name a brief, local phenomenon" and are thus ill-suited for reflecting on the "saturation of one text by phrases from the entire literary tradition." The problem with terms such as *"source, borrowing, and echo"* is that they suggest "the allusive text is of lesser stature than the text being evoked through allusion" (524). But there are difficulties with the term "allusion" as well, since it may be used either when a poet "mentions a little-known fact or makes a roundabout reference to a well-known fact" or else for his or her "incorporation into a poem of a short phrase reminiscent of a phrase in an earlier work of literature." Although both are called allusions, the two work differently and are perceived differently (526). In the latter case, for example, "words *omitted* from the adopted phrase can come to be seen as significant, in a way for which there is no equivalent with learned reference" (527).

If "allusion" is at times unhelpfully broad, then *"echo* can be too narrow, especially if it suggests that the prior text can be evoked only through a verbatim repetition of its phraseology." After all, "the alluding author usually alters the adopted phrase" (528). In the end, Machacek feels forced to look for terminological alternatives by proposing to "speak of the echo as a *reprise* and the initial version as a *spur*," though he admits that this "slightly privileges the agency of the later author" (529–30).

For his part, Machacek defines clearly what he is after: the phenomenon of "a textual snippet" that is "distinguishable primarily by being brief, discrete, and local and evoking a single text that the culture of the alluding writer associates with an identifiable earlier author." This he sets off from four alternative diachronic connections that may likewise be explored: "parody; cento; the strategies by which a work establishes itself in a particular genre or tradition; [and] works … that answer an earlier literary work" (525). My conceptual problem on this occasion is that the phenomenon for which I will need to find a language— and which is by no means rare—is covered by none of these descriptions and definitions. If Machacek is interested in what he calls "phraseological adaptation," my concern will be rather with what I would have to define as a combination of *stylistic assimilation* and *creative adaptation*, and how best to discuss these.

My appetite for the Stevens–Plath connection as a promising case study for this book was first whetted at a conference in Oxford more than ten years ago. One of the speakers was Diane Middlebrook, the author of a number of successful biographies—on Anne Sexton and on Billy Tipton—but especially important in the current context because of *Her Husband: Hughes and Plath, a Marriage* (2003). Middlebrook was ideally placed to draw lines from Stevens to Plath because her first book (a revision of the dissertation she wrote under the direction of Harold Bloom) was half about Stevens—married, in his case, to Walt Whitman. Middlebrook started her brief exploration by digging up an interview Ted Hughes gave in the 1970s. In this interview, Hughes noted in passing that Plath's "knowledge of American poetry was pretty extensive. But she didn't have strong preferences except maybe for Wallace Stevens." Pressed further, he explained that "all along … she preserved her admiration for Wallace Stevens. He was a kind of god to her, while I could never see anything at all in him except magniloquence. Her early poetry is Wallace Stevens almost every other line" (qtd. in Middlebrook, "Stevens" 45).

To readers familiar only with received opinions about Plath and Stevens, these must seem like bizarre claims to make. Surely the psychologically tormented, self-consciously female writer of explicitly "confessional," occasionally even suicidal, verse and the cerebral mandarin who tossed off impersonal, playfully philosophical poetry are worlds apart—whether temperamentally, aesthetically, or in terms of their poetic subject matter. Furthermore, as Middlebrook concedes, "In the work Plath wrote before 1960 … it is easy to identify the poets [she] chose to imitate: they are W. H. Auden and W. B. Yeats, not Wallace Stevens." But Middlebrook then goes on to provide important counterevidence both from Plath's writings and from the archive preserved at the Lilly Library in Indiana. "The latter," she tells us, "show[s] that Plath's enthusiasm for Stevens dates back to [two] courses she took at Smith College during 1953–54." Especially Elizabeth Drew's course on modern poetry "was heavily weighted with assignments in the poetry and prose of Wallace Stevens" (46). Middlebrook selects two of the notes Plath took for the course. One of these offers a characterization of Stevens' work as "more a collection of images & incantations than … a description of a point of view, & the pleasure we get from reading it is more sensuous than intellectual." The other refers to the way Stevens liked to combine "an idea … with a color" or "a thought with an odor or perfume" (both qtd. on 46).[1]

In her own investigation, Middlebrook sets these findings to work on some of Plath's juvenilia—for example, how "Morning in the Hospital Solarium" appears to be inspired by "Sunday Morning." In this instance, she sees the influence predominantly in terms of subject matter and lexicon. More generally, she defines three ways in which we might talk of a deeper "imaginative affiliation" between Plath and the older poet. The first is with "Stevens' disposition to be pictorial" and the way "color terminology … carries metaphorical weight" (48). The second affinity "might be described as *floridity*, by which Plath reveals that she has absorbed from her fellow New Englander a fantasy about torrid geographical zones" (49). And, finally, there is the manner in which, "in some of his best-known poems, Stevens makes frequent use of a feminine point of view that carries a positive valence" (50). Middlebrook speculates that this specific aspect may have helped liberate Plath in ways that Yeats and Auden failed to do.

I want to take my time here to develop a more focused case study that enriches such a picture by pursuing a number of additional connections. Contrary to most of Middlebrook's examples, the poem I have selected is not from the juvenilia but from what is usually regarded as the second stage of Plath's writing life—the period between 1956 and 1959/1960. It is called "Night Shift" and, as far as I can tell, does not often draw attention. Before I embark upon a reading, however, let me still note that the Stevens influence on Plath has of course been raised by more than just Middlebrook: in the early 1960s, some reviewers of *The Colossus*—in which "Night Shift" appears—already insisted on the volume's indebtedness to Stevens. One of them, John Wain, even complained that a poem such as "Snakecharmer" was "too like Wallace Stevens for comfort" (Wagner-Martin, *Sylvia* 33). But very few Plath experts have given depth to the connection,[2] and we might take a moment to speculate on why this might be. After all, even Middlebrook never made it the center of her attention and broached it only on the occasion of a conference devoted to Stevens.

In her preface to *The Cambridge Companion to Sylvia Plath*, Jo Gill offers a useful survey of critical responses to the poet since her death. These responses started, famously, by Plath's being enlisted among "confessional" poets, in the label stuck to her teacher Robert Lowell by M. L. Rosenthal (Gill, Preface xii). One of the functions and effects of the label was to mark a clean break with the dogma of poetic impersonality associated with High Modernism from Eliot to Stevens; another was to establish a younger postwar generation at a time of growing generational conflict and social ferment. The inevitable corollary of this framing, propelled both by Plath's most conspicuously personal texts and the fact she ended her life at the age of thirty, was that early critical investigations tilted heavily toward the biographical. Some critics looked specifically into Plath's mythopoetic approach to her autobiography, while others developed the kind of psychoanalytical readings that were cresting during those years. Soon, moreover, Plath became an iconic figure in the second wave of feminism, so that her work came to be "read in terms of its recognition and representation of the conditions of life for women of the 1960s onwards" (Gill, Preface xiii). During the 1980s, there was a notable shift in attention to historical contexts and political inspirations (analogously to what happened in Stevens criticism). By the turn of the millennium, finally, critical responses moved on to the contested relationship with Hughes (after the appearance of his best-selling and award-winning 1998 volume of poems, *Birthday Letters*) as well as to new insights into Plath's practice enabled by the publication of expanded journal materials and the facsimile edition of the manuscript for *Ariel* (Gill, Preface xiv–xv).

From such a quick bird's-eye perspective, it becomes easy to see how none of these critical trends (with the exception of studying the journals) were much concerned with Plath's sources of poetic inspiration. For decades now, Plath appears to have been read largely in relation to either her own historical epoch or her afterlife. *The Cambridge Companion to Sylvia Plath* illustrates this well. Whereas none of the chapters are devoted to tracing the poetic traditions Plath inherited, two of them seek to identify the heritage she herself left behind: once for American poetry (Wagner-Martin), once for British poetry (Entwistle). In the first of these chapters, Linda Wagner-Martin even proclaims that "in the twenty-first century, the results of the impact of Plath's work are as pervasive as the influence of Ernest Hemingway's terse yet open prose" ("Plath" 52). It would seem, then, that the influence *of* Plath, with its frequently liberating effect on especially female poets, has received critical attention almost inversely proportional to the influence *on* Plath.

To be sure, such a formulation may be a little too pat. Wagner-Martin reminds us of exceptions, such as Jahan Ramazani's *Poetry of Mourning* (1994), where Plath's elegiac verse is situated in a longer literary tradition—even if it is one that she again, typically, recasts. In *Sylvia Plath and the Theatre of Mourning* (1999), Christina Britzolakis' emphasis is similarly on the poet's "reflexive engagement with the modernist and surrealist legacy of twentieth-century art" (qtd. in Wagner-Martin, "Plath" 59–60). And the chapter on Plath in Helen Vendler's *Coming of Age as a Poet* (2003) has sought to restore the formalist verse before *Ariel* as "a kind of phoenix of the myriad styles of modernism and incipient postmodernism that [Plath] had studied and experienced" (Wagner-Martin, "Plath" 60).

It is to one such poetic phoenix that I would now like to turn. Although poems from *The Colossus* have occasionally been regarded as "merely imitative" or as "evidence of a necessary apprenticeship" (Marjorie Perloff qtd. in Wagner-Martin, *Sylvia* 297; Gill, "*Colossus*" 92), I would prefer to steer clear of such language, which comes with a history of sexist stereotypes. Indeed, my decision to bypass the juvenilia discussed by Middlebrook and move on to the mature poetry of *The Colossus* is motivated by a wish not to treat Stevens and Plath hierarchically but as poetic equals. When we are looking into the case of an admiring young woman in her twenties full of ambition who steeps herself in the writings of an elderly statesman of poetry emerging around the same time as a giant of Modernism, we had better resist the reflex of treating the woman as a female variant of the "ephebe" Stevens instructed at the outset of "Notes Toward a Supreme Fiction" (*CPP* 329).

So let me home in, at last, on the 1957 poem "Night Shift."[3] Because of the detailed analysis of language, structure, and sound I will be undertaking, it is better to cite the text in full and even add line numbers:

> It was not a heart, beating,
> That muted boom, that clangor
> Far off, not blood in the ears
> Drumming up any fever
>
> 5 To impose on the evening.
> The noise came from outside:
> A metal detonating
> Native, evidently, to
>
> These stilled suburbs: nobody
> 10 Startled at it, though the sound
> Shook the ground with its pounding.
> It took root at my coming
>
> Till the thudding source, exposed,
> Confounded inept guesswork:
> 15 Framed in windows of Main Street's
> Silver factory, immense
>
> Hammers hoisted, wheels turning,
> Stalled, let fall their vertical
> Tonnage of metal and wood;
> 20 Stunned the marrow. Men in white
>
> Undershirts circled, tending
> Without stop those greased machines,
> Tending, without stop, the blunt
> Indefatigable fact.
>
>   (76–77)

Probably the best way to start my commentary is by acknowledging the several respects in which these stanzas do not sound or look like Stevens at all. Such differences apply to both form and content. Stevens generally preferred triplets to quatrains and, certainly after *Harmonium*, shunned the brevity of line so insistently on display in Plath's poem. He also never composed in syllabic verse. (With one exception, all the lines above have seven syllables; this is their formal challenge and explains why the poem lacks the iambic feel of Stevens' verse.) Partly as a result of this brevity and partly because of the halting, chopped-up progress of Plath's lines, with their multiple enjambments, caesuras, and irregular stresses, the rhythm is much more jagged and fractured than the ample, slow, more even pace we characteristically associate with Stevens' meditative mode. Plath's compact lines, moreover, make for a quicker succession of images and tighter clustering of sound effects than Stevens, in his spaced-out manner, tends to provide.

The differences in subject matter are, at least externally, no less obvious. Even if the opposition between indoors and outdoors is vintage Stevens, and even if the dynamic of being pulled from a domestic interior into an outside world of riddling encounters recurs in his work as well, the nature of both surroundings and encounter, as well as the affective coloring of the indoor realm left behind, are all specific to Plath. The younger poet's domestic space is one where she is in the habit of listening to her own "heart, beating" and fears the "fever" in her "blood." It is clearly not the Stevensian space of the mind in the act of finding what will suffice. What is more, Stevens does not usually leave the house to investigate mechanical sounds disrupting the pastoral idyll of suburbia. The older poet took very little interest in evoking scenes of industrial modernity, let alone that he might treat them as indirect allusions to the military-industrial complex of the Cold War. Nor was he inclined to combine the depiction of such a scene with an ambiguous eroticization of powerful male working-class bodies, suggesting both allure and threat.[4]

If the number and extent of such contrasts allow us to regard "Night Shift" as unmistakably Plath's poem and no mere pastiche *à la manière de* Wallace Stevens, then we might start our textual *rapprochement* by noting that the ulterior purpose of Plath's poem nevertheless does not seem to reside in any recording of anecdotal experience. Rather, the anecdote serves as an occasion for composing a poem whose real drive is less mimetic than metapoetic—as an expression of the aesthetic quest to convert crude reality into art. The underlying motivation for the poem seems to be close in spirit to what we find at the end of

Stevens' essay on "The Noble Rider and the Sound of Words." Plath's poem may be said to display its own kind of "violence from within that protects us from a violence without" and to demonstrate "the imagination pressing back against the pressure of reality" (*CPP* 665). This metapoetic quality invites a consideration of "Night Shift" with respect also to its "intertextual swerves" and to how it is "centred in a sense of literariness" (Axelrod, "Poetry" 74).

When we look at the poem from Machacek's perspective, in search of phraseological adaptations, we find only one real candidate: line 6—the only line with six instead of seven syllables. "The noise came from outside" is hard to read, for anyone familiar with Stevens' canonical poems, without hearing in it the "scrawny cry from outside" setting off the final lyric in his *Collected Poems*, "Not Ideas About the Thing But the Thing Itself"—the more so since that scrawny cry then morphs into two other independent verse-lines of similar length that acquire a chanting, refrain-like quality: "It would have been outside" and "The sun was coming from outside" (*CPP* 452). We may safely suppose that Plath, writing in 1957, was all too familiar with the capstone of Stevens' canonizing collection, published barely three years earlier and thus still fresh with poetic revelations.

There is a problem, though, with Plath's phraseological adaptation. As Machacek reminds us about Levertov's "The world is/not with us enough," "the alluding author usually alters the adopted phrase" (528). As a rule, the later poet does not merely repeat or replicate; he or she surprises us by casting something we recognize in a new light. Yet here this is barely the case. Stevens' poem starts with a sound he hears from outside; he calls it a cry and, in the rest of the poem, seeks to determine where it comes from and what it means. Plath's use of "The noise came from outside" is no different. She, too, hears a sound from outside, calls it a noise, and in the rest of the poem seeks to determine where it comes from and what it means. In this sense, the phraseological appropriation, by itself, has almost no aesthetic effect. For the reader who notices the reprise of "Not Ideas," the textual link can gain importance only when we move from the level of the phrase to a higher level—that of the poem's overall scene-setting. The little tableau Plath presents in her poem seems to derive a more general or diffuse inspiration from "Not Ideas," as does her formal approach to the genre of the lyric—for it is striking that Plath keeps her attention on an impersonally described scene rather than on a lyric speaker's affective first-person response to it. For this, too, she might be drawing inspiration from Stevens' poem, even if a direct link of this sort is impossible to verify, and even if she cannot quite bring herself—or simply refuses—to opt also for the third-person distancing effect of Stevens' "he"; instead, she allows the more conventional first person to slip in briefly when she talks of "my coming."

The connection between Plath's poem and Stevens' is thus more structural and organizational than phraseological. It is also considerably more dispersed, once we start to hear it. "It was not a heart, beating," in line 1 (with its typically Stevensian praeteritic antithesis in which something is highlighted by being negated), sounds like a reprise of "It was not from the vast ventriloquism/Of sleep's faded papier-mâché" in "Not Ideas" (*CPP* 452). "That muted boom" in line 2 sounds very similar to "That scrawny cry" in Stevens' poem—whether in terms of phrasal and syllabic organization or in terms of its aural imagery underwritten by sound-play (through assonance and alliteration, respectively). The way in which the noise comes from "Far off" in line 3, after the slowing down of the enjambment that evokes the depicted distance, sounds a lot like Stevens' cry that is "Still far away," also after a beautifully timed enjambment. Plath's very first stanza, in other words, already allows us to hear Stevens' "Not Ideas" in multiple ways, more or less unconsciously, before the text comes up with the recognizable line "The noise came from outside."

Yet hearing acoustic and lexical links of this sort is one thing, identifying similarities of description still another. When line 5, for instance, situates Plath's poem in the evening, with its suggestion of dusk obfuscating reality and rendering it more questionable, this proves to be analogous again to how Stevens sets up his own poem, likewise on the cusp of understanding, "At the earliest ending of winter, ... at daylight or before" (*CPP* 451). We should be careful, then, to distinguish among varieties of textual connection: sometimes the links may be acoustic or rhythmic, sometimes grammatical, sometimes lexical, figurative, or thematic.

It would of course be nice—in the sense of critically gratifying and easy to sell to a journal such as *The Explicator*—if we could conclude that "Night Shift" is a previously unnoticed rewrite of "Not Ideas About the Thing But the Thing Itself" and leave it at that. But to reduce the Stevens connection to such a cut-and-dried, one-on-one relation would be simplistic. It is too easy to say that Plath probably had one specific Stevens poem in mind and merely set out to recast the earlier poem in an oppressive landscape and disjunctive style of her own. The case before us is considerably richer and more intractable than that, which is another reason why the language of allusion, borrowing, and echo is unsatisfactory, while the language of influence is unhelpfully vague and imprecise.

As someone who professionally spends too much of his time returning to one and the same poet, I cannot help hearing a lot more Stevens in "Night Shift." There are reprises of "The Comedian as the Letter C" as well—a poem Plath apparently studied closely (Middlebrook, "Stevens" 49). The phrase in the first stanza "not blood in the ears/Drumming" has a notable affinity with "one sound strumming in his ear" from "The Comedian" (*CPP* 23). The conspicuous internal rhyme in lines 10 and 11—"though the sound/Shook the ground with its pounding"—seems to intensify the assonance in two lines from Stevens' early long poem: "So deep a sound fell down it grew to be/A long soothsaying silence down and down" (*CPP* 34). The "indefatigable fact" in Plath's final line is of the same rhetorical family as "the quintessential fact" confronted by Crispin (*CPP* 26). But even as I note such similarities, I find they are again more multiple than the single juxtaposition with the lines from "The Comedian" suggests. When Plath writes, "though the sound/Shook the ground with its pounding," she is using two of Stevens' favorite words: "sound" and "ground." "Sound" happens to be a key word in "Not Ideas" again, though its importance clearly is not limited to its occurrence there: according to the online concordance, it appears 119 times in Stevens' poetry and plays. In several of these instances, moreover, it flowers into assonance or internal rhyme—for example, in the opening couplet of "Human Arrangement": "Place-bound and time-bound in evening rain/And bound by a sound which does not change" (*CPP* 315). Likewise, "ground" occurs 39 times in Stevens, and it is used to the same musical effect, most famously in "Anecdote of the Jar," where "The jar was round upon the ground" (*CPP* 61).

Since Plath's indulgence in the luxurious eruption of such music may be inspired—or simply nourished—by these and other examples from Stevens, we might also consider the relation between the sound effect and the context in which she uses it. Her third stanza builds an opposition between a suburban environment, in which nobody seems to be aesthetically sensitive to their surroundings, and the poet-speaker, who does display such sensitivity, partly illustrated by the flowering of internal rhyme. Thanks to Middlebrook, we know that Plath liked Stevens' "Disillusionment of Ten O'Clock" as well: she actively annotated it ("Stevens" 49). And that poem works with the same opposition: all the people in the implicitly suburban houses by which the poet-speaker is surrounded are conformist and unartistic—they all wear the same "white night-gowns" without frivolous frills—with one notable exception: the drunken sailor who, as a stand-in for the artistic imagination, dreams of "Catch[ing] tigers/In red weather" (*CPP* 52–53).

And so the tentacles from "Night Shift" to Stevens multiply. As with the sound pounding the ground, it would be reductive to relate "the blunt/Indefatigable fact" in Plath's poem only to the Comedian's "quintessential fact." We should look more closely at how this cluster is constructed: the noun phrase depends for its aesthetic effect on a striking combination of contrasting and repeated phonemes, clashing lexical registers, and a mixture of abstract and sensuous terms. This is again something at which Stevens excelled, especially in his own concluding lines—think of "that alien, point-blank, green and actual Guatemala" at the close of "Arrival at the Waldorf" (*CPP* 219). And once again, we might consider how this cluster at the level of phrase-building is set to work semantically. Plath's poem shows us a sensitive poet pushing back aesthetically against a stark world of "fact," which she records in her characteristically "scrupulous" style (Vendler 51). This "reality-imagination complex" is one we recognize from Stevens (*L* 792), even if it is inflected idiomatically by Plath, who pits the artistic imagination against both the outer fact of the factory and the inner realm of the heart and the feverish blood. Despite such a difference in inflection, however, the confrontation with "the blunt/Indefatigable fact" is analogous to the way "Not Ideas" concludes, with its "new knowledge of reality" (*CPP* 452). Plath ends with "fact," Stevens with "reality," yet by the end of their respective texts both have crafted a poem to show the power of the imagination to transform a world of facts and realities into art.[5]

There are still further possibilities for establishing textual links, though they fall prey to the law of diminishing returns. In "Night Shift," Plath's love of present progressives and her handling of enjambment, punctuation, and syntactic extension are all comparable to Stevens' habits in this respect. Her reluctance to anything being "impose[d]" upon the evening recalls the warning that "to impose is not to discover" from "Notes Toward a Supreme Fiction" (*CPP* 349). "It took root" in line 12 reminds us of how easily in Stevens' verse things "took flight," "took dominion," or "took form" (*CPP* 26, 61, 223). And the anaphoric repetition of "tending/Without stop," in the final stanza, might well be inspired by the analogous repetition of "When the wind stops" in "The Death of a Soldier" (*CPP* 81). That link even helps us realize how the image of industrial and masculine energy in Plath's factory might simultaneously serve to embody the death drive, which is so pervasive in her work.

This much will be clear, then: the turning wheels in the silver factory the speaker discovers in "Night Shift," together with the title's pun on the transformative shifts performed by a young artist coining her own style, may remind us, at some deeper metapoetic level, of the way poets spin new verse out of old, even as they launch into very different orbits. A language of "phraseological adaptation" or even "allusion" is unsatisfactory to theorize such verbal shifts and spinning poetic wheels, though there are no ready-made alternatives to it. Plath's "Night Shift" is a poem that—while steeped in Stevensian sounds and images, syntactic and formal devices, even structuring elements and poetic ambitions— does not necessarily wish for readers to perceive these as ever so many intertextual links that should be activated to shape the understanding. The poem may be appreciated on its own terms by readers who do not hear Stevensian overtones in it, just as Stevens' poetry may be read without hearing any of Plath's verse announcing itself in the near distance. But our sense of both aesthetic affinity and particularity is heightened when we bring these two writers' works into the same room and treat them as scores to be performed more or less together. If this diminishes the artistic autonomy of individual poems and shows up the analytical limits of concepts like allusion and influence, then that is only what post-structuralists have told us to expect. What we may still gain by attending to the harmonies and dissonances between Stevens' and Plath's poetry is a renewed sense of the deeper value of aesthetic sharing. It is a value that informs all the links between poets in this book, and that motivates all contributors to it.

Notes

1   Later in her article, Middlebrook further reveals that the copy of Stevens' *Collected Poems* to be found among Plath's papers at Smith College is "heavily underlined" (51). In *Sylvia Plath: The Wound and the Cure of Words*, Steven Gould Axelrod additionally informs us that Plath's notes in preparation of her own teaching at Smith indicate she had a wish to include Stevens (35). Finally, a fellow student at Boston University, Kathleen Spivack, recalls Plath in early 1959 asserting with seeming self-assurance to the rest of her class that Stevens was her favorite poet (214).

2   In a 1979 essay entitled "Influence and Originality in Plath's Poems," Gary Lane builds a slight exception by spending four pages on the influence of Stevens (124–27), but I came across his essay only after finishing my chapter. Coincidentally, Lane starts off with "Night Shift" as well (124–25). His few lines of commentary add nothing to my argument.

3   I would like to thank the many contributors to this book who during the preparatory workshop in May 2014 weighed in to multiply perspectives on

the poem and open my eyes and ears to what I originally failed to notice. The imperfect manner in which I assimilated their advice remains entirely my own.

4   Quoting Plath on "the terrifying, mad, omnipotent marriage of big business and the military in America," Axelrod usefully provides context when he argues that Plath's leftist political critiques were "ideologically complex and uncertain" ("Poetry" 74). He observes, furthermore, how Plath in several poems from *The Colossus* gives "access to an uncanny … interior world" and stages "figures of immense, pervasive and frightening power" who exude a "dangerous yet sexually charged masculin[ity]" (77).

5   My reading here ties in with Vendler's discussion of "Words," a poem dated ten days before Plath's death. The adjective "indefatigable" returns there as "The indefatigable hoof-taps" (Plath 270). According to Vendler, the poem "should" end with this phrase (as the "Indefatigable fact" indeed concludes "Night Shift") and she goes on to comment, "While the fixed stars of determinism govern an individual life, the indefatigable hoofbeats of human creation simultaneously assert themselves beyond that lifetime" (62, 64). Thus, Vendler reads the insistence on indefatigability within a similar frame of artistic creation as I am proposing for "Night Shift."

Works Cited

Axelrod, Steven Gould. "The Poetry of Sylvia Plath." Gill, *Cambridge* 73–89.

Axelrod, Steven Gould. *Sylvia Plath: The Wound and the Cure of Words*. Baltimore: Johns Hopkins University Press, 1990. Print.

Entwistle, Alice. "Plath and Contemporary British Poetry." Gill, *Cambridge* 63–70.

Gill, Jo, ed. *The Cambridge Companion to Sylvia Plath*. Cambridge: Cambridge University Press, 2006. Print.

Gill, Jo. "*The Colossus* and *Crossing the Water*." Gill, *Cambridge* 90–106. Print.

Gill, Jo. "Preface." Gill, *Cambridge* xi–xvi.

Lane, Gary. "Influence and Originality in Plath's Poems." *Sylvia Plath: New Views on the Poetry*. Ed. Gary Lane. Baltimore: Johns Hopkins University Press, 1979. 116–37. Print.

Machacek, Gregory. "Allusion." *PMLA* 122.2 (2007): 522–36. Print.

Middlebrook, Diane. *Her Husband: Hughes and Plath, a Marriage*. New York: Viking, 2003. Print.

Middlebrook, Diane. "Stevens in the Marriage of Sylvia Plath and Ted Hughes." *Wallace Stevens Journal* 30.1 (2006): 45–51. Print.

Middlebrook, Diane. *Walt Whitman and Wallace Stevens*. Ithaca: Cornell University Press, 1974. Print.

Plath, Sylvia. *The Collected Poems*. Ed. Ted Hughes. 1981. New York: Harper, 1992. Print.

Spivack, Kathleen. "Some Thoughts on Sylvia Plath." *Virginia Quarterly Review* 80.2 (2004): 212–18. February 4, 2016. Web.

Stevens, Wallace. *Letters of Wallace Stevens*. Ed. Holly Stevens. Berkeley: University of California Press, 1996. Print.

Stevens, Wallace. *Wallace Stevens: Collected Poetry and Prose*. Ed. Frank Kermode and Joan Richardson. New York: Library of America, 1997. Print.

Vendler, Helen. *Last Looks, Last Books: Stevens, Plath, Lowell, Bishop, Merrill*. Princeton: Princeton University Press, 2010. Print.

Wagner-Martin, Linda. "Plath and Contemporary American Poetry." Gill, *Cambridge*, 52–62.

Wagner-Martin, Linda, ed. *Sylvia Plath: The Critical Heritage*. London: Routledge, 1988. Print.

5

Moving the "Moo" from Stevensian Blank Verse: Elizabeth Bishop's Use of Prose

Angus Cleghorn

In this chapter, I will demonstrate that Elizabeth Bishop engages Wallace Stevens' blank-verse forms with innovative prose rhythms, creating a "dazzling dialectic" in the process (*PPL* 175).[1] She often signals her variations with casual rhetorical quips. Readers hear spoken voices, so much so that Bishop's subtle changes in poetics are often missed. Casual asides and irregular, intricate poetic rhythms emerge on top of a blank-verse base, contemporizing the sound of Bishop's language. Much of Bishop's innovation appears as a dialogue in prosody with Stevens' example. Although Bishop learned most of *Harmonium* by heart when she was a student at Vassar, by the mid-1930s she told Marianne Moore she disliked how Stevens could "make blank verse *moo*" (*PPL* 740).

How Moore and Bishop admired Stevens' mind in action was the subject of George Lensing's lead essay in a 1995 special issue of *The Wallace Stevens Journal* on Stevens and Bishop. With help from essays in that volume and, more recently, Vidyan Ravinthiran's book *Elizabeth Bishop's Prosaic*, I explore how Bishop revises her Stevensian influences through verse that uses rhetorical conversation.[2] She introduces human voices that sound like speech and/or song, as well as the casual speech of prose, in an attempt to replicate "the way a poet should think" (*PPL* 740)—a notion she derived from baroque prose yet that also reveals her form of postmodern reflexivity. I will test these claims by analyzing Bishop's poetic lines, particularly from poems in the blank-verse tradition, where she plays with variations in rhythm, meter, and voice. Sometimes the lyric form itself is on the verge of being left behind, usurped by prose speech, rhythm, and detail—thereby eschewing lyric aesthetic orders.

I will not be analyzing all of the Stevens and Bishop poems that sound and look like each other, because this has been done before. Bishop's statements about her poetic maturation in the 1930s are evidence enough: "Wallace Stevens was the contemporary who most affected my writing then" (Brown 294). "At college, I knew 'Harmonium' almost by heart ... But I got tired of him and now find him romantic and thin—but very cheering, because, in spite of his critical theories (very romantic), he did have such a wonderful time with all those odd words, and found a superior way of amusing himself" (letter to Anne Stevenson, Jan. 8, 1964, qtd. in Travisano 285).

The poems I will use to flesh out her fatigue with the Stevensian manner are "Cape Breton," "Questions of Travel," "The End of March," and "Santarém." Other works that could have factored here are "At the Fishhouses," "The Moose," and "In the Village," each of those bringing different lyrical innovations. Although I am charting a course from blank verse to prose, with rhetorical voices enacting intricate changes in rhythm and meter along the way, it is worth remembering that my trajectory is selective, and its critical efficacy depends on ignoring Bishop's various other innovations, especially with forms such as the sestina, villanelle, sonnet, and ballad. Just as her verse loosens up over time, it also tightens up, though in all cases she pushes formal boundaries so that we can enjoy new dynamics in poetry. Bonnie Costello's essay "Bishop and the Poetic Tradition" (in *The Cambridge Companion to Elizabeth Bishop*) offers thorough coverage of this dimension of her work.

Lensing's title, "Wallace Stevens and Elizabeth Bishop: The Way a Poet Should See, the Way a Poet Should Think," alludes to Bishop's inheritance of "The Baroque Style in Prose," from Morris Croll's essay by that title on "a mind thinking," which she applied to her *Vassar Review* essay on Gerard Manley Hopkins (Lensing 126). Lensing's essay explains how Bishop found such a "mind thinking" performed in Stevens: "She admired [in Moore's words from *The Dial*] his 'nimbleness *con brio* with seriousness' ... and 'the effect of poised uninterrupted harmony, a simple appearing, complicated phase of symmetry of movements as in figure skating, tight-rope dancing, in the kaleidoscopically centrifugal circular motion of certain medieval dances'" (118).

Besides admiring the nimble seriousness of Stevens' poetry, Bishop also developed reservations about Stevens' blank verse, as she wrote to Moore in a letter trying to sort out *Owl's Clover*. The note of enthusiasm she strikes in her letter of December 5, 1936, is complicated by doubts:

> what strikes me as so wonderful about the whole book—because I think there are a great many rough spots in it, don't you?—and I dislike the way he occasionally seems to make blank verse *moo*—is that it is such a display of ideas at work—

making poetry, the poetry making them, etc. That, it seems to me, is the way a poet should think, and it should be a lesson to his thicker-witted opponents and critics, who read or write all their ideas in bad prose and give nothing in the way of poetry except exhortation or bits of melancholy description.

(*PPL* 740)

In further letters, Bishop expresses gratitude to Moore for clarifying Stevens' monumental critiques (see, especially, Moore's *Poetry* essay from 1937, "Conjuries That Endure"). Like *Owl's Clover*, Bishop's "The Monument" and other poems—in particular her Parisian set from the 1930s—work through statuary limitations in Depression-era poetic discourse. Lensing adds that it was the "publication of 'The Man with the Blue Guitar'" that compounded Bishop's critique of "rough spots" in *Owl's Clover* with her 1937 feeling of being "tired of his ballad-refrain words 'hi,' 'ho,' 'tick,' 'tock,' 'hoo,' 'tom-tom,' 'ai di mi,' 'ay-yi-yi'" (118).

In these comments, Bishop inadvertently announces her departure from Stevens' sonic exclamations and his comparatively staid, mechanical-bull blank verse. So Bishop evolves from two sides of Stevens' poetry: its serious moo-ing in blank verse (along the lines of "She sang beyond the genius of the sea./The water never formed to mind or voice" [*CPP* 105]) and its "Edward Lear nonsense" (those playful ejaculations critiqued as such by Hugh Kenner). Though it is fun hearing Josie and Bonnie celebrate the marriage of flesh and air by chanting, "Ohoyaho,/Ohoo" (*CPP* 65), I think Bishop realized when the poet in the steely suit merely affected Oklahoman yawps and indulged in a bit of artificial nonsense. While she certainly used a lot of Stevens' kaleidoscopic wizardry in her first volume, *North & South* (look at "Wading at Wellfleet," "A Miracle for Breakfast," "The Unbeliever," and "Seascape"), ultimately she would resolve the Stevensian contrast between heavy intonement and hooting blasts by opening up blank-verse lines with rhetorical voices of human speech and music, so that blank verse might evolve into something more contemporaneous, often with a mixture of masculine and feminine qualities that managed to expand gendered forms, as we will see in "Cape Breton," "The End of March," and "Santarém."

Lensing carefully demonstrates how some of Bishop's early poems, like "The Imaginary Iceberg" (1935) and "The Unbeliever" (1938), negotiate Stevens' dialectic of imagination and reality before she finds her own accurate style in "Florida" (1938). This poem owes some of its wondrous fascination to Stevens' Florida, yet Bishop's detailed accretions extract historical traces from the landscape through microscopic attention to its physical geography and indigenous people. Her Parisian poems of the 1930s navigate another dialectic—

of Surrealism versus monumentality—which Lensing describes as "beautiful but perilous" (125). In "Florida," Bishop rejected European styles more completely than other Modernists; on the back of Stevens' Floridian work, she nobly rode his sounds of words and what would become his necessary angel until she, like Philip Larkin a few years later, could reject the "common myth-kitty" of modern poetry in favor of fluid detail.

This is not to say that Bishop became a concrete, minimalist, or Language poet, since her favorite principles remained accuracy, spontaneity, and mystery (*PPL* 703). Her letter about Charles Darwin praises the explorer's spontaneous observations, achieved from "a self-forgetful, perfectly useless concentration" that was "almost unconscious or automatic—and then comes a sudden relaxation, a forgetful phrase, and one *feels* the strangeness of his undertaking" (qtd. in Lensing 127). Likewise, Stevens' mind in action remains part of Bishop's poetics. My first example could be dubbed, in fact, "The Idea of Order at Cape Breton." Written after having lived in Florida for nine years, the poem tells of Bishop's return to Nova Scotia in 1946 and 1947 (Ellis 45) to explore her own rock—the solid foundation that was absence, the loss of childhood and parents. These trips back led to some of Bishop's strongest poems, "At the Fishhouses" and "Cape Breton" in *A Cold Spring* (1955). While "At the Fishhouses" resembles poems by William Wordsworth and Walt Whitman, mixed with Bishop's distinctive sense of narrative, detail, and slow time, "Cape Breton" provides us with a more tantalizing poetics: we can see and hear Stevens' blank verse being renovated.

The poem's opening lines immediately display two of Bishop's signatures: her geographical precision and her use of humor to register key thematic oppositions such as nature versus technology—the baaa-ing sheep stampeding over the cliff's edge when frightened by airplanes (*PPL* 48–49). This mixture of light and heavy tones creates room in the poem; as Gillian White has argued, Bishop is a master of making space in art. Her capacity to pull two poles apart allows her to inhabit the middle ground as a real achievement of synthesis. So after the sheep descend into darkness (without extended wings) off the islands of "Ciboux and Hertford" clad with "silly-looking puffins" (*PPL* 48), entertained readers are set up in a good mood for the real action to take place. Ravinthiran explains how Bishop at the age of twenty-two thought about altering mood through poetic rhythm:

> Even as an undergraduate, when she gets to thinking about rhythm and its "irregularities," her stylistic pursuit of "effect" collides with a vocabulary of truth-claims and self-knowledge. In a letter to Donald Stanford of November 20, 1933, she insists … that she

can write in iambics if I want to—but just now I don't know my own mind quite well enough to say what I want to in them. If I try to write smoothly I find myself perverting the meaning for the sake of the smoothness ... I think that an equally great "cumulative effect" might be built up by a series of irregularities. Instead of beginning with an "uninterrupted mood" what I want to do is to get the moods themselves into the rhythm.

(*Elizabeth* 18)

It is arguably "this rejection of 'uninterrupted mood,'" "a kind of grounding skepticism about the mind's self-satisfied norms" (18), that makes Bishop's poems continually fresh with each reading. Consider the variation between the falling sheep and the serious focus on nature in these lines:

The silken water is weaving and weaving,
disappearing under the mist equally in all directions ...

(*PPL* 49)

I would suggest that while Bishop is primarily describing the landscape, she, like Penelope, is simultaneously weaving in poetics through her prosody. Readers of Stevens are accustomed to this sort of poetry about poetry. Whether we choose to see Bishop intentionally reflecting on poetics, or just demonstrating them, the lines remain astounding either way. The first line's iambic pentameter is almost standard, except that "is weaving" provides two stresses in a row, thus giving the water more power to weave (for the poem is about mist's primacy in the landscape). And the last "weaving" ends unstressed so that Bishop can stress "*dis*appearing," and so direct the mysterious game of hide-and-seek played by the water "under the mist equally in all directions"—a line with at least seven stresses emphasizing the power of water and mist to go every which way. Likewise, the next line begins with a trochee, a hard lead into an otherwise regular iambic line: "lífted and pénetráted nów and thén" (*PPL* 49). Suddenly, masculine penetration overtakes the feminine muse of fluid water, and "by one shag's dripping serpent-neck" presents a phallic form dipping into the water. This sexual dance is a dialectic that then makes space for the brilliant synthesis of the stanza's last two lines:

and sómewhere the míst incórporátes the púlse,
rápid but únúrgent, óf a mótorboat.

(*PPL* 49)

Bishop's anapest makes us wait for the expected iambic stress in "the mist," a little foreplay before the feminine misty water "incorporates the pulse." Cape Breton's seascape of mist is a natural house for the hard syllabic sounds of the pulse, which, we find out only a line later, is coming from a motorboat engine. Bishop manages to pull in the machinery from the poem's opening into the boat's sonic emanations engulfed by the harmonious mist. Machine and nature, no longer antipathetic, fuse in this landscape, which is also a marriage of masculine and feminine. The merger is formed most strongly by the brilliant assonance in combination with rhythm and meter. "Mist," which we had to briefly wait for, has a short hard vowel sound, *i*, in contrast to the longer vowel sounds of *o* and *a*. So the modest yet ever-present "mist" grows physically and sonically until it "incorporates the pulse,/rapid but unurgent, of a motorboat." Notice also the consonance of *p* and *r* in their own dance, fused together by the casual perfection of the vowels and the beat of the pulse—at once the rhythm of the poem, the boat's engine, and the personified beating landscape.

Thus, Bishop renovates blank verse with a gendered poetics, an abstraction blooded. The spontaneous mystery of the natural world embodied by the mist is maintained yet real; a sense of flux informs the whole poem, flowing into the final lines, which are at once banal, concrete, and mysteriously suggestive: "The birds keep on singing, a calf bawls, the bus starts./The thin mist follows/the white mutations of its dream;/an ancient chill is rippling the dark brooks" (*PPL* 50). The short vowels here are elongated in "the white mutations of its dream," only to be cut short by "an ancient chill is rippling the dark brooks." With a powerful last line that sounds like Stevens, Bishop leaves readers suspended in search of a sublime spirit. The line verges on the supernatural, but its mystical overtones are earned because they are rooted in the actual: this finale is the entelechy of the poem's third and fourth stanzas, where the history of Cape Breton is materialized. The chill is not just cool, watery, and pagan; its haunting is caused by the ghosts of history.

The third stanza continues the initial mechanical theme with "The wild road clambers along the brink of the coast" (*PPL* 49). Here we see the road acting in its landscape somewhat like the mist, but this encroachment threatens "the brink of the coast," which was already perceived as vulnerable with sheep falling off cliffs. What is more, in this case, the coastal landscape is itself facing obliteration because "On it stand occasional small yellow bulldozers," a typical example of Bishop's polarizing imagery, much like "a million Christmas trees stand/waiting for Christmas" in "At the Fishhouses" (*PPL* 49, 52). Here, too, the mechanical sacrifice of the landscape is set in a Christian context as the bulldozers are "without their drivers, because today is Sunday" (*PPL* 49). The Sabbath peace contrasts with nature's destruction; once again, Bishop creates a dialectical space for her punch line, which is, however, no joke: "The little white churches have been dropped into the matted hills/like lost quartz arrowheads." Because the first line about imperial and colonial settlement is excessive in length, it sets up a striking contrast with the next, short line. In just two lines of metaphor and simile, the poet tells the story of Christian triumph over indigenous people and their land. The long-inhabited place is nearly empty this Sunday, only artifacts of an ancient civilization are left over. "The road appears to have been abandoned./ Whatever the landscape had of meaning appears to have been abandoned" (*PPL* 49). "Abandoned" is a strong word in Bishop's vocabulary.

But even this "impersonal personal" historical description, as Costello describes Bishop's approach (see Costello, "Impersonal"), sets up yet another dialectic from which to move forward. Hidden beyond the emptied landscape is "the interior,/where we cannot see,/where deep lakes are reputed to be" (*PPL* 49). In these lines, Bishop briefly departs from blank verse and inserts one of her resounding end rhymes so that Wordsworthian "deep lakes" surface between "where we cannot see" and "where [we want] to be." She pulls us through "disused trails and mountains of rock/and miles of burnt forests standing in gray scratches" until the tour of Cape Breton allows us to hear "thousands of light song-sparrow songs floating upward/freely, dispassionately, through the mist, and meshing/in brown-wet, fine, torn fish-nets" (*PPL* 49). Bishop's version of "Sunday Morning" has become a paradise where the updraft of a singing flock of birds, through the mist and water, meshes with "brown-wet, fine, torn fish-nets"—both a catch from the ocean and a flock in the sky. Ravinthiran calls these lines "a rhythmical miracle," admiring how "an extraordinary prose-poetry hybrid establishes its fragile transcendence ... Exact stepping stones of sound preserve a speech-cadence finding its way" (*Elizabeth* 14–15).

The fourth stanza presents us with a bus coming along "in up-and-down rushes"—is not the whole poem doing this rhythmically?—but this bus is "packed with people, ... groceries, spare automobile parts, and pump parts" (*PPL* 50), reminding us that, in Stevens' words, "The imperfect is our paradise" (*CPP* 179). The mood suddenly changes from thoughts of a native genocide to the happy daily business that is propelled, in the language, by alliteration. Light comedy is compounded by "two preachers extra, one carrying his frock coat on a hanger" (*PPL* 50). What in Stevens' "The Idea of Order at Key West" was "a body wholly body, fluttering/Its empty sleeves" (*CPP* 105) is converted to a few preachers in excess, one in casual dress with his religious garb empty of a body on a hanger. As the riders on the bus pass "the closed roadside stand, the closed schoolhouse,/where today no flag is flying," emptiness creates more vacuous space in the almost desolate landscape: not only is the scene set on a day of rest, but it also suggests a country lacking in national identity. When the bus next stops,

> a man carrying a baby gets off,
> climbs over a stile, and goes down through a small steep meadow,
> which establishes its poverty in a snowfall of daisies,
> to his invisible house beside the water.
>
> (*PPL* 50)

In a quiet manner, the man carrying his baby seems to embody the somewhat empty space. If we recall that Stevens' "Man Carrying Thing" is about masculinity and metaphor, then "a man carrying a baby" signals a realistic if subtle and modest gender reversal. The image is complicated by another irony, "poverty in a snowfall of daisies," for we know that, in Stevens' words, "The greatest poverty is not to live/In a physical world" (*CPP* 286). So in Bishop's revision we seem to enter a bountiful physical paradise where we might want to live in the "invisible house beside the water." Bishop draws another "inscrutable house," a "proto-dream-house" cryptically set in an environment where "an ancient chill is rippling the dark brooks" (*PPL* 121, 168, 50). That final line is arguably her version of Stevens' closing at Key West "In ghostlier demarcations, keener sounds" (*CPP* 106).

Lensing aptly observes that Stevens' "elevated formality" is modified by "a corrective rephrasing, or a bathetic reversal" (128). Bishop devises a similarly corrective poetics in the larger project of getting it right as the century moves on. She questions mastery both through the pathos of artful losing and through the bathos of alternating between the sublime and the commonplace. Some of this bathos, beyond what I have illustrated in "Cape Breton," finds a Stevensian "intelligence that endures" (*CPP* 675) by revising not only the lines and rhythms of the old masters but also the rhetoric of their utterances, by means of late-twentieth-century human speech that does not drown amid indecisions and revisions.

Questions of Travel (1965) helps me further delineate the trajectory from blank verse to new rhythms, as well as Bishop's interjection of both lyrical and prosaic voices to develop a more contemporary poetics. When we read "Questions of

Travel," like almost any other poem from the eponymous volume, we hear a seemingly casual voice performing:

> There are too many waterfalls here; the crowded streams
> hurry too rapidly down to the sea,
> and the pressure of so many clouds on the mountaintops
> makes them spill over the sides in soft slow-motion,
> turning to waterfalls under our very eyes.
> —For if those streaks, those mile-long, shiny, tearstains,
> aren't waterfalls yet,
> in a quick age or so, as ages go here,
> they probably will be.
>
> (*PPL* 74)

"No writing," remarks Anne Stevenson, "could seem more natural than the loose weave of these passages, all of which would be prose if some bodiless pressure … were not making them spill over" (111). As Ravinthiran clarifies, "While the line break does not function here as a lyrically suspensive Wordsworthian or Miltonic enjambment, it needs to be admitted as a less intensive pause for consideration, a kind of sense-making rhythmic pivot" (*Elizabeth* 14). So let us try to understand how the content in this instance relates to the form.

The registration of a tourist's perspective on Brazilian abundance, treated with a paintbrush, is easy to recognize. Yet we should also think back of another voice Bishop registers—that of Dom Pedro II, the most prolific emperor of Brazil, who ruled from 1833 to 1889, as described in her *Brazil* volume for Time Life World Library: "Dom Pedro was the 'owner,' so to speak, of waterfalls three or four times greater and more magnificent than Niagara, but inaccessible, and with all his curiosity and travelling, he never laid eyes on them" (*Prose* 191). Bishop recalls Dom Pedro's departure from Brazil, with its nameless waterfalls, to go and visit the falls at Niagara (no easy excursion in 1876). He felt compelled to undertake the voyage because Niagara Falls was such an established wonder of the world. Bishop criticizes this habit of knowledge, based on following authoritative texts—as she did previously when she parodied submission to the Bible in "Over 2000 Illustrations and a Complete Concordance." In contrast, Brazil's waterfalls, "those mile-long, shiny, tearstains,/aren't waterfalls yet" because they are still without signifiers, even if "in a quick age or so, as ages go here,/they probably will be." By capturing Dom Pedro II's attitude, and including it in words spoken in her present-day voice, Bishop aligns old-school imperialism with the modern-day tourist—all without having to resort to the scholarly method of explicit allusion. However, we need only flip back a poem in *Questions of Travel* to find "Brazil, January 1, 1502," which expressly compares the original rapacious Portuguese conquistadores with the average tourist of 1952. Not much seems to have changed in 450 years.

Bishop develops various fused voices of this sort throughout *Questions of Travel*. "Manuelzinho," for instance, brilliantly merges the upper-class voice of her lover Lota de Macedo Soares and the lower-class voice of her gardener together with her own voice in a sympathetic yet parodic middle register. Unlike the Stevens of "Bantams in Pine-Woods," who exuberantly apostrophized, "Chieftain Iffucan of Azcan in caftan/Of tan with henna hackles, halt!" (*CPP* 60), we hear in the cultural rhetoric of *Questions of Travel* what appears to be plain speech and music, as in "First Death in Nova Scotia." Besides the familiar strangeness of a young child trying to figure out how the body in the open casket is to be understood in relation with the surrounding pictures of royals and a stuffed loon in the room, we witness how the young girl hears her mother's effort at consolation, yet cannot take her eyes off the white body: "Jack Frost had started to paint him/the way he always painted/the Maple Leaf (Forever)" (*PPL* 122). Further gathering information around her, Bishop's remembered younger self imagines Jack Frost whitening the corpse, as frost familiarly dusts the red maple leaves of Canada. She imagines him as the agent responsible for "the Maple Leaf (Forever)," Canada's old national anthem. Gillian White shrewdly notes the use of rhetorical voice in this poem about coming to terms with death: "The addition of 'Forever,' and the parentheses around it, complicate our ability to 'hear' particularities of a speaker's voice here" (271). The child's consciousness wrestles with various media surrounding the dead body in the room—in this example, the story of Jack Frost, the voice of the mother, red and white imagery, and then echoes of the old national anthem. Music participates with the human voice in forming perception.

But it is only when we move on to *Geography III* (1976) that we can begin to make larger claims about Bishop's poetics of prose. This volume begins with "In the Waiting Room," a poem that includes a recognition of self-conscious existence among others: after reading *National Geographic* and hearing Aunt Consuelo's "*oh! of pain*" from the dentist's office, the speaker acknowledges that "you are an *I*,/you are an *Elizabeth*,/you are one of *them*" (*PPL* 149, 150). In "12 O'Clock News," we see Bishop turn to the use of Steinian prose paragraphs. But by the time we come to the signature villanelle of "One Art," she returns us to more pure poetic terrain. Bishop never sticks to one pattern of development in her work. "The End of March" is in some ways like many landscape poems, so it fits generally with poems like "Cape Breton" and "At the Fishhouses." Here we are at the shore again.

In "'Old Correspondences': Prosodic Transformations in Elizabeth Bishop," Penelope Laurans suggests that Bishop

> parcels out her poem's appeal to the reader's emotions charily, using prose passages to contradict what she expressly states, and lyric passages to imply what she is disinclined to make plain … In "The End of March," for example, fully one third of the poem is prose arranged in verse lines … Bishop calls the shack a "proto-dream-house," a "crypto-dream-house," and thematically presents it as an unattainable ideal to be approached but never reached. Yet, while the words say one thing, the metrical impulse of the poem communicates precisely the opposite to the reader. The passage in which Bishop describes the house and her wish to reach it contains far and away the most neutral, prose-like writing of the poem … Everything in the diction and movement of the verse here—its ordinariness, its prosy, conversational sound and flow, as if Bishop were simply talking to the reader—works to diminish the excitement of the ideal she is imagining. Here is the "naturalness" Bishop likes, with a vengeance.
>
> (90–91)

Laurans traces the movement to prose poetics through the poem's proto- or crypto-dream-house "as an unattainable ideal to be approached but never reached." This has been a constant in Bishop's thematic quest for a poetic house in her characteristically homeless literature.[3] In "The End of March," Bishop revisits these houses and renovates them fancifully with "a sort of artichoke of a house" where she can—like Edwin Boomer in her prose piece "The Sea and Its Shore" or the protagonist of "In Prison"—"retire there and do *nothing*," "read boring books," "write down useless notes," drink flaming French-American grog à la Stevens in a place with stove and chimney braced with wires, as in "Sestina" (*PPL* 168; emphasis in original). "The End of March" is a greatest hits collection, but its assemblage, so physically detailed, turns out to be imaginary, as "of course the house was boarded up." Bishop's mythology of self is "perfect! But— impossible" (*PPL* 168), as J. D. McClatchy also observes (142). Her self-made place on the beach remains an unattainable fantasy. Its lyricism is checked by the prose style, but also by her dedication of the poem to John Malcolm Brinnin and Bill Read, the two friends who owned the vacation house in Duxbury, Massachusetts.

We encounter Bishop's "prose arranged in verse lines," as Laurans points out, especially in this passage:

> I wanted to get as far as my proto-dream-house,
> my crypto-dream-house, that crooked box
> set up on pilings, shingled green,
> a sort of artichoke of a house, but greener
> (boiled with bicarbonate of soda?),
> protected from spring tides by a palisade
> of—are they railroad ties?
>
> (*PPL* 168)

Returning to Laurans' analysis, Ravinthiran claims that "the real moment when prose confronts the poetic" occurs in those last three lines; the interjections there

> align with Bishop's desire to "portray, not a thought, but a mind thinking." They work as a kind of self-corrective mental speech, but spoken out loud, [the final] line jars ... If there is a drop in formality, it's from a studied poetic language to a type of wary improvisation which draws on the stylistic repertoire of prose in its play with the literary effect of speech as conventionally transcribed on the page. As Langdon Hammer remarks, Bishop's verse sometimes sounds "less like conversation than like the imitation of conversation" in her letters; her "incongruous mixing of discourses," he adds, "makes this immediacy feel arch, a reminder that the poem is not the spontaneous composition it too conspicuously pretends to be."
>
> (*Elizabeth* 30–31)

Ravinthiran further notes that this is a hybrid, "uncertain form, not quite prose and not quite poetry," and that "this isn't 'prose' as Laurans has it, a form of writing stripped of any organizing rhythmical impulse. Instead, this is 'prose-rhythm' ... with bits and pieces of regular meter 'melted or welded' into the whole—a form of rhythmical bricolage" (32).

In addition to integrating prose rhythms in blank verse, Bishop explores lyrical imaginative projections in poetry, largely through the lion-sun figure, as Harold Bloom also notes (12–13). Ravinthiran suggests that Bishop challenges Stevens' masculine lyricism by "making Stevens' 'potent' cat [his lion] clearly male, ... teasing him as the stones tease the lion sun. Then she comes out with that extraordinary last line, so long, so prosaic that it's hard even to utter, since the ear has grown used to the essentially iambic structure of the last few lines" (*Elizabeth* 40):

—a sún who'd wálked the beách the lást low tíde,
máking those bíg, majéstic páw-prínts,
who perháps had bátted a kíte out of the ský to pláy with.

(*PPL* 169)

Could that lion sun with its steady gait be Stevens the lion-poet "making those big, majestic paw-prints"? Perhaps my question is more fanciful than "The End of March" allows for, but let us nevertheless recall that major man's first idea of the sun is the foundation of "Notes Toward a Supreme Fiction" (*CPP* 329–30). Here in "The End of March," the majestic solar figure coincides with blank verse that begins to dissolve in the spondee of "paw-prints" (themselves eroded by stones and water on the beach). The beauty of the last line is that it prosaically qualifies and explains the wholly evolved mythic image of the poem. The lion sun now extends from the paw-prints to the ether as he "perhaps" swipes "a kite out of the sky," his clumsy aggression causing the kite-string to fall along the seashore like a line of breakers—the image from earlier in the poem that is picked up and completed in this poem's total projection. Costello carefully notes that this is a "unifying fiction," "not a myth of fate," as the lion sun "is a figure of imagination" (*Questions* 171). Such is what Bishop tells us, first through the proto-artichoke of a house that is really just a boarded-up shack, and then through the final blank-verse breakdown into prose aside. Costello adds, "Surely Bishop would have remembered Stevens' 'The Sun This March'" and that "the imagination, like a lion, 'can kill a man' ('Poetry Is a Destructive Force') with its power" (172). So Bishop's prose poetics makes the casual perfect, and imaginative mythical blank verse "perfect! But—impossible" (*PPL* 168).

Let us take the trajectory of Bishop's prosaic development of poetry a final step further by including "Santarém" (1978) in the discussion as well. This is a much-loved poem, I think, for its retrospective solar glow cast on Bishop's Amazonian Brazil, and its funny touches before its poignant, ironic, yet ultimately appreciative finale. But as a Stevensian I have always been a bit uncomfortable with its prosy lack of form. In 1991, Costello observed that "Santarém" shows "pleasure in the confusion and irreverence of the place, its very chaotic, faulty details, which resist all efforts at conceptual mastery" (*Questions* 173). Four years later, Mutlu Konuk Blasing had the poem conclude her feminist argument about the dissolution of masculine binary thinking in *Politics and Form in Postmodern Poetry* by referring to Bishop's "watery, dazzling dialectic" (*PPL* 175). Bishop trumps the structural anthropology of Claude Levi-Strauss that preoccupied her in Brazil (see also "12 O'Clock News"). Deconstructing any "superior vantage point" that divides and conquers, Bishop, according to Blasing (108), dissolves dialectics through the blue–brown suspension of adjacent rivers and "blue eyes in brown faces," as James Merrill said of the poem (see the video documentary *Voices and Visions: Elizabeth Bishop*). We are left with dialect instead of dialectics, Blasing concludes: "Dialect maintains 'crazy' differences without opposition or the resolution of oppositions; it links to the 'mongrel' combinations—the legacy of a history of 'crazy shipping'— [and] possibly 'remembering it all wrong' … within this paradisal space" (109).

"Then—my ship's whistle blew. I couldn't stay": Bishop again uses sound to transport readers into the so-called "real world." She does so, even more impressively, with the casual reaction to the gift of the "empty wasps' nest" that the poet received: "Mr. Swan,/Dutch, the retiring head of Philips Electric,/really a very nice old man,/who wanted to see the Amazon before he died,/asked, 'What's that ugly thing?'" (*PPL* 176–77). Mr. Swan's voice of capitalist superiority does everything here to crudely undercut the poet's lyrical gift. When he speaks, we recognize the awkwardness of travel in today's world—or simply of living in a global diaspora, where we encounter such cultural differences all the time. The casual closure of "Santarém" builds a kind of home for us as global citizens hearing funny voices that make us smirk and carry on. Bishop's late poem is far from the modern angst of T. S. Eliot's Prufrock ("Till human voices wake us, and we drown"). Stevens' American yawps were joyfully cathartic, but with Bishop's prosy conversation that registers the "up-and-down rushes" of her mind thinking (*PPL* 50), we are left to consider our world again in a language that is at once familiar and strange. Lyrical gifts remain on display—if in jeopardy—and as they flicker in the flux, we cherish them even more.

In *The Art of Twentieth-Century American Poetry*, Charles Altieri broadens Bishop's innovative impact in the following terms:

> Rather than ask Lowell's question—"Who am I as the world besets me in various ways?"—she uses the role of tourist to focus instead on the question "Where am I standing?" Her poems then become explorations of location—of angle and relative distance. That mode of questioning allows others—other people and the entire world of nature—a significant and mobile existence. The self does not measure situations by the binary oppositions between resistance to the will or complicity with it; rather, everything becomes a matter of degree and position. The other has as much reality as the self, but in a different place changing at different rates. So Bishop may be the first white American major poet fully aware of what we all were to learn about the de-centering of the West and the limitations of the oppositions on which its imaginary world was founded.

(193)

As a "sister of the Minotaur" embodying "the intelligence that endures" (*CPP* 675), Bishop picks up where Crispin leaves off. Lensing has been the first to point this out and Ravinthiran follows through: "Crispin, the protagonist of the early poem 'The Comedian as [the] Letter C' (1923), is said to grip 'more closely the essential prose' of a disenchanted world, while looking forward to the moment when 'prose should wear a poem's guise at last'—he claims a 'prose/ More exquisite than any tumbling verse'" (*Elizabeth* 35). Crispin's foresight strangely anticipates the integrations of prose into poetry advanced by Elizabeth Bishop.

Notes

1   All citations from the Library of America edition of Bishop's *Poems, Prose, and Letters* are referenced as *PPL*.

2   For a detailed critical evaluation and analysis of Stevens' blank verse, see Ravinthiran, "Blank."

3   Recall the "invisible house" that the man with the baby approaches in "Cape Breton" (*PPL* 50), the "inscrutable house" the child draws in her grandma's kitchen in "Sestina" (*PPL* 121), and, in her early prose stories, Edwin Boomer's shack on the beach where as a janitor he brings back torn newspapers to read by drunken firelight, as well as the protagonist of "In Prison," who designs the interior of her cell so she can read with free imagination and write notes in "an almost illegible scrawl" to be discovered by those coming after her (*PPL* 588).

Works Cited

Altieri, Charles. *The Art of Twentieth-Century American Poetry: Modernism and After.* Oxford: Blackwell, 2006. Print.

Bishop, Elizabeth. *Elizabeth Bishop: Poems, Prose, and Letters.* Ed. Robert Giroux and Lloyd Schwartz. New York: Library of America, 2008. Print.

Bishop, Elizabeth. *Prose.* Ed. Lloyd Schwartz. New York: Farrar, 2011. Print.

Blasing, Mutlu Konuk. *Politics and Form in Postmodern Poetry: O'Hara, Bishop, Ashbery, and Merrill.* Cambridge: Cambridge University Press, 1995. Print.

Bloom, Harold. "Introduction." *Elizabeth Bishop: Comprehensive Research and Study Guide.* Ed. Bloom. Broomall: Chelsea House, 2002. 11–13. Print.

Brown, Ashley. "An Interview with Elizabeth Bishop." Schwartz and Estess 289–302.

Costello, Bonnie. "Bishop and the Poetic Tradition." *The Cambridge Companion to Elizabeth Bishop*. Ed. Angus Cleghorn and Jonathan Ellis. New York: Cambridge University Press, 2014. 79–94. Print.

Costello, Bonnie. *Elizabeth Bishop: Questions of Mastery*. Cambridge: Harvard University Press, 1991. Print.

Costello, Bonnie. "The Impersonal and the Interrogative in the Poetry of Elizabeth Bishop." Schwartz and Estess 109–32.

Croll, Morris W. "The Baroque Style in Prose." *Style, Rhetoric, and Rhythm: Essays by Morris W. Croll*. Ed. J. Max Patrick and Robert O. Evans. Princeton: Princeton University Press, 1966. 207–32. Print.

Ellis, Jonathan. *Art and Memory in the Work of Elizabeth Bishop*. Aldershot: Ashgate, 2006. Print.

Laurans, Penelope. "'Old Correspondences': Prosodic Transformations in Elizabeth Bishop." Schwartz and Estess 75–95.

Lensing, George S. "Wallace Stevens and Elizabeth Bishop: The Way a Poet Should See, the Way a Poet Should Think." *Wallace Stevens Journal* 19.2 (1995): 115–32. Print.

McClatchy, J. D. *White Paper: On Contemporary Poetry*. New York: Columbia University Press, 1989. Print.

Moore, Marianne. "Conjuries That Endure." *The Complete Prose of Marianne Moore*. Ed. Patricia C. Willis. New York: Penguin, 1987. 347–49. Print.

Ravinthiran, Vidyan. "The Blank Verse Moo of Wallace Stevens." *Thinking Verse* 3 (2013): 108–30. Print.

Ravinthiran, Vidyan. *Elizabeth Bishop's Prosaic*. Lewisburg: Bucknell University Press, 2015. Print.

Schwartz, Lloyd, and Sybil P. Estess, eds. *Elizabeth Bishop and Her Art*. Ann Arbor: University of Michigan Press, 1983. Print.

Stevens, Wallace. *Wallace Stevens: Collected Poetry and Prose*. Ed. Frank Kermode and Joan Richardson. New York: Library of America, 1997. Print.

Stevenson, Anne. *Five Looks at Elizabeth Bishop*. Newcastle: Bloodaxe, 2006. Print.

Travisano, Thomas. "Bishop's Influence on Stevens?" *Wallace Stevens Journal* 19.2 (1995): 279–86. Print.

Voices and Visions: Elizabeth Bishop. New York: New York Center for Visual History, 1988. Video. Viewable at Annenberg Learner.

White, Gillian. "*Words in Air* and 'Space' in Art: Bishop's Midcentury Critique of the United States." *Elizabeth Bishop in the Twenty-First Century: Reading the New Editions*. Ed. Angus Cleghorn, Bethany Hicok, and Thomas Travisano. Charlottesville: University of Virginia Press, 2012. 255–73. Print.

6

Henri Michaux's *Elsewhere* through the Lens of Stevens' Poetic Theory

Axel Nesme

In a letter to Bernard Heringman dated February 10, 1950, Stevens mentions a friend who spent his whole life in Paris "avoid[ing] the Americans in order to see more of the French. Henri Michaux and Supervielle were among his friends, Michaux especially," Stevens writes (*L* 665). Michaux's name comes up again in a letter of November 5, 1950, to Thomas MacGreevy, in which Stevens mentions a critical work that reproaches the French poet Léon-Paul Fargue for having remained "superficial" and never having gone "to the extremes of Rimbaud or Michaux" (*L* 696). This letter suggests that to Stevens, Michaux was a poet capable of following "the imagination in its own right" instead of letting reality prevail as it did in Fargue's poetry, which "substituted Paris for the imagination" (*L* 696). Taking my cue from these lines, I want to explore Michaux's own poetic fictions in that "elsewhere" of the imagination he depicts in *Ailleurs* (Elsewhere) (1948) and *La Vie dans les plis* (Life in the Folds) (1949), as seen through the prism of Stevens' poetic theory.[1]

I will argue that this "elsewhere" often overlaps with what Freud in *The Interpretation of Dreams* called that other "scene" where the barrier of repression is lifted and the superego's collusion with transgressive desire is exposed (574). As a result, even though the lands Michaux's traveler roams have no equivalent on the map, they too result from the Stevensian effort of "the imagination to adhere to reality" (*CPP* 650)—if by "reality" we understand those commonly unacknowledged forces at work within the unconscious psyche.

Stevens' view that the "imagination loses vitality as it ceases to adhere to what is real" (*CPP* 645) may thus prove compatible with Michaux's phantasmagoria as stemming from a sustained effort to exhibit what Freud called "psychical reality," namely, that mix of "subjective representations which are a product of symbolic and imaginary articulations" (Evans 161). In order to achieve this, however, Michaux does not emulate the Surrealist association of ideas that, according to Stevens, generated an imbalance between reality and imagination to the detriment of the former (*CPP* 651). Instead, he produces highly lucid though otherworldly alternative universes whose very fictitiousness allows this psychical reality to emerge. This is what André Gide meant when he portrayed Michaux as pursuing "strange, odd, or downright bizarre sensations or ideas" by "letting poetic breath carry him away he does not even know where, with total abandon, in a manner reminiscent of Nietzsche's saying that only in our dreams are we perfectly sincere" (15–16).[2]

In *Wallace Stevens and Poetic Theory*, B. J. Leggett shows that the Stevensian dictum "It Must Be Abstract" is "a sign of the necessary condition of the symbolizing process of any fiction or myth" (39) whereby the ephebe's world "is of necessity an invented world" (40). Thus, Stevens

> is not making a distinction between levels of language (i.e., abstract versus concrete) or levels of thought (concepts or ideas versus particular details) but stating the premise of an epistemology by which even the most sensuous detail remains radically a product of abstraction. He is … using the notion of abstraction as the basis for a dissolution of the imagination-reality conflict …
>
> (40)

It is in this sense that we may understand Gide's depiction of Michaux, who, "although as characteristic a product of our time as any, nonetheless succeeded in remaining utterly untimely" (9–10). In this chapter, I will attempt to determine to what extent "It Must Change" and "It Must Give Pleasure," the other two precepts around which "Notes Toward a Supreme Fiction" is ordained, are equally relevant to Michaux's poetry.

In Leggett's reading, "It Must Be Abstract" may be interpreted as referring to the need for the supreme fiction to be both *ab*stracted from reality as we know it and *ex*tracted from that reality. This process of abstraction is recognizable in Michaux's imaginary world, many of whose individual features are borrowed from ours—most noticeably perhaps the ethnographer's persona that Michaux adopts in his accounts of his travels to Great Garaban and the Land of Magic. These accounts often read like articles from the *National Geographic*, although not without mocking the unabashed ethnocentrism often exhibited by such articles, as may be judged from two examples chosen at random in early-twentieth-century issues of the magazine.

In an article entitled "Untoured Burma" by Charles H. Bartlett, a photograph of Chin girls is followed by a caption that is a concentrate of colonial prejudice:

> These girls belong to a tribe that have hardly come into contact with civilization. Unlike the Burmese, who are Buddhists, they are worshipers of nature spirits, and, although some missionaries have settled among them, but *little progress has been made.*
>
> (849; emphasis added)

Another illustration from the same 1913 *National Geographic* draws our attention to details that are presented as objectively odd, though obviously the oddity lies mainly in the observer's perspective:

> The peasants marry very early in Rumania, and the ceremonies accompanying a country wedding still preserve the tradition of marriage by capture. In some districts a flower is painted on the walls of the cottage which is the home of a girl of marriageable age. Note how *curiously* the babies are bundled.
>
> (Moore 1065; emphasis added)

Michaux's descriptions of the peculiarities of the tribes he visits in Great Garaban suggest a similar intimacy with readers who share in his worldview and amused interest in the other cultures, with the small nuance that those cultures do not exist, so that the form of the ethnographic report is abstracted from its unreal contents. The ethnographer's stylistic mannerisms thus become purely vocal effects unrelated to any referent. As a result, their paternalistic tone is exposed no less powerfully perhaps than the voice of civilization was parodied by Joseph Conrad in his story "An Outpost of Progress." For instance, at the beginning of the chapter on the utterly fictitious Emanglons' "*Manners and Customs,*" Michaux explains that when an Emanglon suffers from respiratory disease, he is kindly choked to death by his fellow villagers, and that it is considered a great privilege for a "beautiful young virgin" to perform the merciful operation (*Selected* 145). Written in 1936, between the two world wars and their cortege of atrocities, this passage praising the sense of "duty" of those who help the sick cross "the bridge between life and death" seems nevertheless uncannily close to reality (*Selected* 145).

Although with different means, Michaux achieves a similar effect to Freud in his *Reflections on War and Death*:

> In reality there is no such thing as "eradicating" evil. Psychological, or strictly speaking, psychoanalytic investigation proves, on the contrary, that the deepest character of man consists of impulses of an elemental kind which are similar

in all human beings, the aim of which is the gratification of certain primitive needs. These impulses are in themselves neither good or evil ... These primitive impulses go through a long process of development before they can become active in the adult. They become inhibited and diverted to other aims and fields ... The formation of reactions against certain impulses give[s] the deceptive appearance of a change of content, as if egotism had become altruism and cruelty had changed into sympathy.

(11)

Michaux's mock-ethnography offers his readers an insight into another form of social organization where the demands of the superego have not disappeared but simply taken a different route. While requirements of propriety, and even the notion of charity, still hold sway, primitive impulses just happen to have been "diverted" in a less stringent manner than is the case in "civilized" societies. As a result, in Great Garaban mercy killing becomes desirable though somewhat improper to mention as such, as witnesses the Emanglons' reluctance to admit that one of their own was choked to death, preferring instead the vague statement that he has stopped breathing (*Selected* 144). Michaux's notion of his fellow human beings' potential savagery is no less sobering than Freud's, and no less effectively portrayed by means of a series of dystopian evocations combining macabre humor and a detached tone that confront us with an impossible choice between moral outrage and sheer relish of the poet's experiments in elaborating his *esthétique du mal*.[3] Thus, when Michaux explains that a "truly feminine nature" is required to perform a task for which amazons and coquettes are equally ill-suited (*Selected* 145), he is also exposing the arbitrariness of gender roles, and disqualifying the essentialist presuppositions underlying his contemporaries' ideas of femininity as well as the veil of sentimentality in which those are cloaked.

It is perhaps no accident if Gide, who introduced Michaux to the French public in 1941, interestingly described the disquieting characteristics of the writer's style in terms of the specific balance between reality and imagination that is also Stevens' main concern in "The Noble Rider and the Sound of Words" (composed in the same year). Michaux, writes Gide,

narrates mores, customs, pleasures, diseases, foods that are only remotely akin to ours, and a sort of mysterious poetry, but also an indefinable malaise, is born of all this. The malaise comes from the relationship that is involuntarily established in our mind between the imaginary and the real. And this malaise sometimes goes beyond the buffoonish and turns into anxiety. After all, we say to ourselves, all that which does not exist could exist, and all that we know to exist might very well not be much more real. What happens on this earth of ours is not fundamentally much more reasonable than what Michaux depicts for our benefit.

(41)

According to Gide, the phenomenon we experience while reading Michaux is thus one where, in Stevens' language, the "violence from within" Michaux's writings achieves a precarious balance with the "violence without" (*CPP* 665) in a mutual unsettling of reality and the imagination that translates into "an interdependence of the imagination and reality as equals" (*CPP* 659).

This is why, although *Voyage to Great Garaban* begins with a fight to the death that is one of many local forms of entertainment and that, the speaker tells us blandly, happened to involve a contest between two brothers when he attended it, we would nonetheless be mistaken to infer that chaos reigns from the mere fact that within the first three pages of the book the ban on fratricide, one of the founding interdictions of human society since Cain and Abel, has been lifted. Much to the contrary, the myriad strange customs observed in Great Garaban lend themselves to a variety of numeric and taxonomic distinctions. "Traditionally," Michaux explains, the aforementioned performance "is given the number 24" (*Ailleurs* 12). Performance number 3, which is an equally bloody avatar of the previous one, takes place in a swamp, which to the contestants poses the additional challenge of having to struggle with the mud. Therefore, when the speaker tells us that "Sleep has in fact always been Problem Number One for the Emanglons" (*Selected* 149), we are to take this literally as the first item on a much longer list where every aspect of Emanglon life is categorized and catalogued. Indeed, much as murder shows are held for the public's recreation in an orderly fashion, the supreme form of pleasure that is sleep, like death, calls for a complicated, well-established ritual that involves the Emanglons being "Rolled around on a drum" or "sewn into a mattress" while they are being tapped with "paddles" until they realize they are "beaten in advance" and might as well surrender to sleep. The central signifier Michaux uses in this context is the verb "delight" (*jouissent* in French), which points to the "infinity of methods" in which pleasure is given and received, notably by means of the sadomasochistic scenario involved in this Kafkaesque torture to which the Emanglons are, it seems, happy to consent (*Selected* 149).

"Reading Michaux makes one uncomfortable," Richard Ellmann notes at the beginning of his introduction to Michaux's *Selected Writings* (vii). Indeed, many episodes narrated in *Voyage to Great Garaban* create in the reader the uneasy feeling that he or she is both spectator and accomplice in the elaborate theater of cruelty that Michaux stages by depicting situations where the quasi-universal legal principle of proportionality is overturned to the benefit of absurdly and comically gruesome avatars of disproportionality—for instance, when he explains that the Emanglons cannot abide loud sneezes, which, in their tribe, can last hours on end—a problem easily solved, as it turns out, if "a relative, a sister, a friend of the family" lends a helpful hand by crushing the sneezer's "skull with a hammer blow" (*Ailleurs* 43).

This collusion of social codes with the raw violence they are meant to contain, I would suggest, may be read as a symptom of the tension between the law and enjoyment that, although in much sublimated fashion, already underlies the three commandments around which "Notes Toward a Supreme Fiction" is neatly structured into three sections, each comprising ten tercets. If poetic enjoyment or "expressible bliss," as Stevens calls it (*CPP* 349), is a matter of order, if the Barthesian pleasure of the text requires the poet's abiding by a set of prescriptions, then an aesthetic avatar of the Freudian superego oversees the operations of the imagination. And while its scope may be limited to the realm of the supreme fiction, it is nonetheless capable of what Stevens calls "the difficultest rigor" (*CPP* 344)—a rigor equal to that of the agency that regulates the odd distribution of crime and punishment, pleasure and pain, in Michaux's "Emanglia."

The fact that Stevens' aesthetic creed is voiced in the deontic form of the moral imperative signals the connection between poetic enjoyment and the law that commands the pursuit of the sovereign good. That law, as Slavoj Žižek points out, "is only the mask of radical, absolute Evil" (161) if we follow Lacan's revision of the Freudian conception of the superego and his suggestion that the demands of this prohibitive-normative agency are the flip side of the imperative to enjoy beyond the pleasure principle. In that beyond, *eros* and *thanatos* are joined, as they are wherever Michaux depicts avatars of what Alenka Zupančič calls "a kind of bodying forth of the cruel, unbridled and menacing superego— the 'real or reverse side' of the moral law (in us), of the superego as the place of *jouissance*" (156). We encounter this *jouissance* not only throughout *Elsewhere* but also in *Lointain intérieur* (The Far-Off Inside) and *La Vie dans les plis*, where extremes of lawlessness are often inseparable from manifestations of a punitive or regulatory order that Michaux allegorizes as "necklaces of eyes in her neck which roll feverishly every which way, or the emissaries of the Judge who look from everywhere at you under stony lids with the implacable eyes of grandeur joined to meanness or remorse" (*Selected* 203).

While Michaux consciously cultivates the uncomfortable sense that the blurring of the boundary between the law and its other may elicit in the reader, he also frequently affords his reader moments of comic and poetic relief—as he does, for instance, in the extract I quoted earlier by describing an uproariously counterintuitive manner of fighting against insomnia, but also, more interestingly, by refocusing our enjoyment on the workings of the signifier. Thus, when we are told that the candidate for sleep is "beaten in advance," the phrase is doubly meaningful, since it puns on the familiar expression "struggling for sleep" and on the immediate context, where the Emanglon is indeed beaten over the head.

Puns, according to Freud in *Wit and Its Relation to the Unconscious*, are characterized by their "double-dealing" (756): they satisfy both the demands of the ego and those of the id. The specific enjoyment they trigger comes from a partial lifting of the barrier of repression. Michaux's creatures, in the image of the passage's central trope, straddle two realms. When they wake up, their facial expression makes them look "almost outside the bounds of humanity": they have a "dark look … such as you find in sick and rheumatic old dogs with a master to whom, in spite of his wickedness, they have become attached" (*Selected* 149). In other words, Emanglons look like beaten dogs when beaten dogs most resemble human beings: the pseudo-human and the inhuman thus contaminate each other beyond recognition, so that the border between the two realms becomes as porous as that between the ego and the id, culture and barbarity, and literal and figurative sense.

Although the most noticeable feature of Michaux's *Voyage to Great Garaban* is its visionary quality, and although very few generic markers differentiate these texts from ordinary prose, we are thus seldom allowed to forget that a poet is running the show. We may at first be amused by the description of the Emanglons' favorite beast of burden, "la ranée" (*Ailleurs* 48), which, we are told, is a bit like a donkey, but has the inconvenient habit of constantly falling asleep—something of a contradiction when it comes down to a work horse or donkey. Yet we perceive that Michaux's elaborate and pathos-laden description of the unfortunate animal, too lazy to fight off the smallest predators, builds only on a semiotic nucleus that has little to do with the poet's interest in chimerical creatures.

Only the logic of the signifier is at work in this passage built on the French phrase "bête de somme" (*Ailleurs* 48), which puns on the homophones *somme*, feminine, meaning "burden," and *somme*, masculine, meaning "quick nap." Beasts of burden, therefore, can only be prone to napping. The reader is thus deluded into giving the *imaginary* preeminence whereas it is on the *symbolic* stage that most of the action takes place. Set phrases and standard metaphors turn out to provide the foundation of some of the oddest situations depicted not only in *Voyage to Great Garaban* but also in its companion piece, *In the Land of Magic*.

The premise of this volume, published in 1941, is contained in its title: it is a literary travelogue in which the speaker, adopting the same analytical voice as in *Voyage to Great Garaban*, describes the living habits of dwellers in a land where the laws of physics are suspended. Here again, however, the erasure of the limit between reality and imagination is only the more visible aspect of processes that affect the poetic medium itself. Thus, Michaux writes that whenever a young boy happens to be grabbed by a lion, he "identifies" with the animal and finds such "delight in being devoured that a teenager who had been pulled out of a lion's mouth immediately began to cry" (*Ailleurs* 155). Michaux's primary focus in this case is not on the amusing reversal whereby someone cries about having been rescued from certain death. His interest lies, rather, in the poetic treatment through which a trope commonly found in textbooks of rhetoric can be turned into poetic material. "This man is a lion" is a familiar phrase used to exemplify the workings of metaphor *in praesentia*. Here again the metaphor provides the semiotic matrix of the passage as a whole, which revolves around Michaux's attempt to create an alternative poetic universe where being "rescued out of the lion's mouth" means no more than what it says, where tropes no longer function as poetic currency, and change may still be generated even when the motive for metaphor, by magical necessity, no longer exists. The reader thus realizes that he or she has fallen for Michaux's own favorite conjuring trick throughout the volume. To the same extent that we are intrigued, if not fascinated, by the infinite possibilities offered by a world where the rules of causality no longer apply, we are also blinded to the subtler transformations that occur on the surface of the poem's signifying fabric. Indeed, what supernatural operations take place in the Land of Magic are primarily experiments in literalization.

"The imagination loses vitality as it ceases to adhere to what is real," Stevens writes (*CPP* 645). How, then, do we reconcile such a statement with Stevens' praise of Michaux as a poet capable of following "the imagination in its own right" (*L* 696), when Michaux's poetic "elsewhere," though undeniably vital, is so blatantly unanchored in ordinary experience? I would argue that Stevens himself answered the question when he wrote that "the moment of exaltation that the poet experiences when he writes a poem that completely accomplishes his purpose, is a moment of victory over the incredible, a moment of purity that does not become any the less pure because, as what was incredible is eliminated, something newly credible takes its place" (*CPP* 676). Michaux achieves such a victory over the incredible when he strips the two aforementioned phrases of the metaphorical dead weight that made them no longer credible in their literal sense, and thus restores their poetic potential in a magical setting where "identifying with the lion" is once again a credible operation. To this extent, Michaux shares with Stevens the view that "the poet must … move constantly in the direction of the credible. He must create his unreal out of what is real" (*CPP* 679).

By the same token, Michaux reminds us that what reality and unreality we deal with primarily is not referential, but of a linguistic nature. Thus, in "Ici, Poddema" (Live from Poddema), the third and last section of *Ailleurs*, Michaux poses as the master of an imaginary language, one of whose main oddities is the existence within its phonemics of two mutually canceling signifiers. The first one, "*Nag*," "triumphantly steps into discourse," Michaux tells us. "*Nag* is like a king, it is pure force, it is the wing that flies, briefly glimpsed over one's head, and it is also meditation" (*Ailleurs* 222). Though endowed with the energy of illocutionary statements and, conceivably, with the force of the poetic word in the manner of the letter *h* that in Hebrew carries the breath of life and of God's creative power, this lexeme, however, serves only a stopgap function in the imaginary idiom of the Poddemai. Indeed, Michaux, posing as an expert in exotic languages, immediately adds that "*Nag* fills *Hag*," the latter word being defined as the "syllable of uncertainty," which, once added to a statement, makes its validity questionable. The existence of such a syllable, in and of itself, would not pose any logical difficulty if we were not told that it appears in "virtually all sentences" (*Ailleurs* 222). Thus, not only does it annul the seemingly boundless force of "*Nag*," it also suggests that among the Poddemai, any *referential* use of language is considered practically impossible, and that only skeptical utterances hold sway—utterances that, in other words, are as good as saying nothing at all.

"[U]nreal things have a reality of their own, in poetry as elsewhere," Stevens writes in "The Noble Rider and the Sound of Words" (*CPP* 644). He then adds that what happened to Plato's charioteer and horses is not that the images were any more or less extravagant in Plato's time than they seem to us now: it is simply that they have lost their currency. Michaux's endeavor is to create "gorgeous nonsense" for modern times, to invent conditions that make it possible for us to "yield ourselves to the unreal" (*CPP* 644) as Plato's antiquated imagery no longer allows. If, according to Stevens, when reading Plato's *Phaedrus*, "We do not feel free" (*CPP* 645), then Michaux's own effort is one of liberation and redefinition of the real as that which we experience as beings-in-language.

In his treatment of puns as well as dead tropes, Michaux's work is thus consistent with Stevens' notion of "the naked poem" as "the imagination manifesting itself in its domination of words" (*CPP* 639). This is even more strikingly the case when it comes down to verbal invention. Whereas Stevens only occasionally resorts to coinages, preferring remote etymologies, rare words, and polyglossic hybridization, as in "We enjoy the ithy oonts and long-haired/ Plomets, as the Herr Gott/Enjoys his comets" (*CPP* 305), Michaux's own way of heeding the precept that "It Must Change" involves naturalizing words of his own making, so that our experience of his "elsewhere" is also, if not primarily, one of linguistic estrangement.

To ascertain this, one need go no further than the table of contents of *Voyage to Great Garaban*, which lists the imaginary tribes the traveler has visited. These may be quoted in French, since all the names in question, though quite genuine-sounding, are equally meaningless: "les Omanvus" (*Ailleurs* 67), "les écoravettes" (68), "les rocodis et les nijidus" (69), "les arnadis" (70), "les garinavets" (71), "les bordètes" (73), "les mirnes" (74), "les mazanites et les hulabures" (76), and "les ossopets" (77). In Michaux's coinages, the imperatives "It Must Be Abstract," "It Must Change," and "It Must Give Pleasure" are combined: these transformations inflicted on the French language result from a process of abstraction of its main phonemic characteristics allowing for re-combinations that, though utterly fictitious, still bear the seal of authenticity. Finally, the pleasure we derive from these verbal artifacts is a direct function of this process of abstraction and transformation, which does not preclude the surprise of occasional, and often humorous, encounters with recognizable verbal fragments, as in the word "ossopet," where the French word for "flatulence" is clearly heard, or "garinavet," whose last syllables are the French equivalent of the word "turnip."

The most emblematic of these coinages, however, does not merely communicate language's infinite ability to renew itself. At the very end of his account of the Emanglons' often cruel and consistently weird customs, Michaux's speaker offers with great aplomb a conclusion whose veracity few readers will be in a position to ascertain, or contest: "The Emanglons, in a nutshell, are Yoffes" (*Ailleurs* 52). Such a statement, connecting two made-up words, means nothing, but it nonetheless makes *sense*, at least if we take this term as Gilles Deleuze understood it when he wrote that "we can never say what is the sense of what we say. From this point of view, sense is … that which in its empirical operation cannot be said … There is only one kind of word which expresses both itself and its sense—precisely the nonsense word" (*Difference* 155). Michaux, in his own poetic fiction, thus heeds the double imperative that "It Must Be Abstract" and "It Must Change": as he undertakes to transform ordinary language by means of verbal invention, he also abstracts from meaning the pure element of sense, the realm we have unwittingly been exploring with him throughout his *Voyage to Great Garaban*.

***

Michaux's poetry is often described as too metamorphic to lend itself to a unifying vision. This lack of a recognizable *principium individuationis* in his work as a whole is reflected in the poet's choice to locate the lyrical subject "Between Center and Absence," as a section of *Lointain intérieur* is entitled (7). Even more explicitly, Michaux once declared that "There is no one self. There are no ten selves. There is no self. SELF is only a position of equilibrium. (One among a thousand others continually possible and always ready)" (qtd. in Ellmann xvi). Whatever self we thus identify in *Elsewhere* is always supremely fictitious in its a-topicality and inconsistency.

Helen Vendler once analyzed Stevens' preference for third-person utterance as a means for the poet to allow his speaker to maintain analytical distance from himself. Vendler shows how this de-multiplying of lyrical subjectivity helps Stevens "work toward an objective view of his emotions and convictions" (134). "Each of these personae," Vendler writes, "embodies some aspect of Stevens himself or the world as he perceives and conceives it" (137). One might well argue, though, that behind this monolithic subject relating to its masks as Aristotelian substance relates to its attributes, there is little more than the mere fiction of a unified poetic self, and that the proliferation of personae witnessed throughout Stevens' oeuvre may be read as opening up what Deleuze calls "impersonal and pre-individual … nomadic singularities which are no longer imprisoned … inside the sedentary boundaries of the finite subject" (*Logic* 107).

Michaux, similarly, maintains subjectivity in a limbo, in an embryonic state reminiscent of Deleuze's notion of the larva-like condition that presides over the genesis of true ideas (*Difference* 219). In "La Ralentie" (The Slower One; *Plume* 41–52), a poem that features in *Lointain intérieur*, Michaux takes on a feminine persona who seems only a pulse away from physical and psychological exhaustion, passively trapped in a half-life where the possibility of human agency has been practically erased. The poem entitled "Naissance" (Birth) further drives a wedge into the ordinary definition of the biographical subject as having one birth and one death by inventing a Protean character named "Pon," who, within less than three pages, experiences a variety of new births: "Pon was born of an egg, then he was born of a codfish and while being born made it explode, then he was born of a shoe … then he was born of a woman and greatly surprised" (*Selected* 69–71). The creature named "Pon" emanating from such a multiplicity of mutually exclusive, monstrous, or bizarre origins that its being born of a woman qualifies as a surprise, we come to realize that what we perceive as the basis of subjective unity is little more than a flimsy, monosyllabic name, a fragile unitary fiction barely concealing the fact that *ab ovo*, from the egg onward—as is literally the case here—the individual's alleged indivisibility is threatened with atomization by the manifold causes that have brought it into existence.

Michaux's work in which this de-subjectivizing movement culminates is *La Vie dans les plis*, where many poems are variations on the motif of "vanishing, bordering horror without subject, bordering 'nothing left'" (*Vie* 57).[4] Such vanishing may be brought about by situations that change so rapidly that the melancholy speaker they involve can barely keep up with them, as is the case in "Situations étranges" (Strange Situations), a prose poem where dreamlike sequences appear in quick juxtaposition, connected only by the refrain-like recurrence of the phrase "Mais il y a changement" (But there is change), sometimes imperceptibly varied into "Mais il y eut changement" (But there was change), so that even within that which signifies change, more change occurs.

The Modernist dogma of impersonality may arguably reverberate from Stevens' "The Snow Man," with its gnomic "One must have a mind of winter" (*CPP* 8), to "The Plain Sense of Things," where "the absence of the imagination had/Itself to be imagined" (*CPP* 428), as if the imagining were no longer traceable to the agency of a speaking subject. Michaux, however, does not merely comply with the equivalent Mallarméan request for the poet's "elocutionary disappearance." What we witness instead, in *La Vie dans les plis*, is a gradual simplification of subjectivity, a folding upon itself of the subject that is also a prelude to a later unfolding. In "Entre ciel et terre" (Between Heaven and Earth), Michaux thus writes, "Far from being an individual weighted with bones, muscles, flesh, organs, memory, intentions, I would gladly imagine myself—so weak and indeterminate is my sense of life—as a microscopic amoeba, hanging by a thread" (*Vie* 98). In a poem like "Dans l'attente" (Waiting), the thread the poet hangs by may be a single letter, like the letter "f" in the litany of temporary beings with which the speaker identifies: "Un être fou,/un être phare,/un être mille fois biffé" (*Vie* 78). To this being who is "mad," then "beacon-like," then "crossed out a thousand times," only the alliterative sound /f/ provides a minimal degree of—phonemic—continuity.

The phrase "hanging by a thread," however, becomes even more unavoidable in the section of *La Vie dans les plis* misleadingly entitled "Portraits des Meidosems"—misleadingly, that is, to the extent that Michaux's Meidosems, as we soon find out, are representations of the unrepresentable. Being defined by their "extreme elasticity," they may indifferently resemble "a hanging piece of wire, a sponge that absorbs liquid and is already almost full, another one that is empty and dry, condensation on a window pane, a phosphorescent track" (*Vie* 120). Meidosems, in other words, have remarkably few intrinsic, essential features. They mostly exist in the eye of the beholder, if at all, since Michaux's paradoxical portraits seem designed to thwart our efforts to visualize them. Even gender distinctions, which somehow still apply to them, seem to have been distributed at random, as in the case of the "young female Meidosem [who] is all flags ... that mean nothing" (*Vie* 135). We learn that the "legs that make them run to the far end of the world are not hairy, not supported by bones, and not attached to a solid circular pelvis" (*Vie* 169). We have a very precise notion of what their legs do not resemble, but the one positive analogy Michaux consents to draw—"They are like erasers, like boredom on the run" (*Vie* 169)—tells us only that they defy our efforts of analogy and will not yield to "the intricate evasions of as" (*CPP* 415).

Meidosems are thus mere emblems of what is known in French as *dépaysement*, roughly meaning a radical "change of scene": they signify the reader's exile from the coordinates that allow him or her to make sense of his or her surroundings. In Michaux's poetic fiction, they embody a principle of constant mutability: "From mist to flesh, there are infinite transitions in Meidosem land" (*Vie* 156). Yet this does not preclude our occasionally recognizing individual human features, which, instead of cohering into a whole, remain free-floating within the space of these vignette-like portraits, like scattered fragments of larva-like, incipient subjectivity. A Meidosem fearing immediate danger is unable to act, for he is torn between the antithetical demands of his "right dominator" and of his "left terrorizer" (*Vie* 136). Whether those are organs, functions, or mere dispositions, they reflect the split subjectivity of the post-Freudian psyche, although we are sooner or later reminded that such metaphorical characterizations somewhat contradict the Meidosems' essential plasticity.

Elsewhere Michaux portrays these imaginary beings as transfixed by a "great diagonal spear stuck from top to bottom in the weakening Meidosem in order to prop him up ... From his forehead to his knee, it is a tall, marrowless crutch, an imperious T-bar of military rigidity," the poet writes, before asking, "You ferocious stake, do you want to kill or do you provide support?" (*Vie* 144). The last two clauses of the original French text are heavily alliterative: "Traverse impérieuse, à la dureté militaire. Tuteur féroce, tu veux tuer ou tu soutiens?" The all-too-obvious recurrence of the /t/ sound and of the corresponding letter that is twice capitalized in these lines thus makes both visible and audible the artificial, prosthetic nature of the deadly imperative on which, in spite of their ectoplasmic constitution (*Vie* 147), Meidosems are crucified—the same imperative we saw at work in Michaux's poetic fantasies of well-regulated barbarity in *Voyage to Great Garaban*. And, much as in this earlier work, behind the seeming dichotomy between the Meidosems' ability to "molt into waterfalls, crevices, fire ... all things that shimmer" and the rigid spear that supports them (*Vie* 166), we understand that complementarity rather than opposition prevails.

In order to conclude this reading of Michaux after Stevens, I will venture to suggest that, although prone to speculate on infinity, Michaux's Meidosems, too, "live in an old chaos of the sun" (*CPP* 56) since their reach for transcendence is limited by the small size of their ladders, suggestive of their longing for the absolute and of their terrestrial nature as creatures of the earth-bound imagination: "Everywhere ... there are ladders, ladders ... And everywhere there are the heads of Meidosems who climbed up those ladders ... The Meidosems below who walk between the ladders work, take care of their families ... They are said to be impervious to the call of the ladder" (*Vie* 177).

Although they dwell on terraces, roofs, and promontories, Michaux stresses the futility of their all-too-human reaching for "vain heights" (*Vie* 181). In a way, then, they remind us of how, "in the isolation of the sky,/At evening,/casual flocks of pigeons make/Ambiguous undulations as they sink,/Downward to darkness, on extended wings" (*CPP* 56). Much as Stevens' pigeons are "casual" in these familiar lines from "Sunday Morning," Michaux's Meidosems surrender to whirlwinds of joy that lift them off the ground only to experience their own casualness: "Meidosems are constantly falling from the sky ... Only close relatives notice it. Some have their eyes lifted toward the sky for the sole purpose of seeing them fall" (*Vie* 183). As Stevens' pigeons "make/Ambiguous undulations as they sink,/Downward to darkness, on extended wings," Michaux's Meidosems "fall for the sake of falling" and "prefer to fall obediently, in the light drift of the breeze" (*Vie* 152). Yet they, too, make ambiguous undulations. While acknowledging their inevitable downward motion, Michaux ends "Portrait des Meidosems" with his own version of Stevens' "extended wings," acknowledging gravity while also asserting those human-inhuman creatures' ability to become one with the instrument of flight without relinquishing what Stevens calls "the heavenly fellowship/Of men that perish and of summer morn" (*CPP* 56): "Headless, birdless wings ... fly toward sunlit sky, which is not yet resplendent, yet working hard toward resplendence ... /Silence. Liftoff./What Meidosems so intensely longed for, they have finally achieved. Here they come" (*Vie* 184).

Notes

1 Where possible, I have used Richard Ellmann's translations of Michaux's *Selected Writings*. For quotes not included in Ellmann's selection, I refer to the original French titles and provide my own translations.

2 All translations from Gide's *Découvrons Henri Michaux* are mine.

3 Gide, in his 1941 essay on Michaux, insists that the element of Swiftian satire is lacking in Michaux's imaginary travels (39), a view briefly echoed by Maurice Blanchot in his essay of the same year, "L'Ange du bizarre" (21). Those critical judgments themselves may well have borne the imprint of the colonial context in which they were written.

4 All translations from *La Vie dans les plis* are mine.

Works Cited

Bartlett, Charles H. "Untoured Burma." *National Geographic Magazine* 24.7 (1913): 835–53. *HathiTrust Digital Library*. September 5, 2015. Web.

Blanchot, Maurice. "L'Ange du bizarre." 1941. *Henri Michaux ou le refus de l'enfermement.* Tours: Farrago, 1999. 11–25. Print.

Deleuze, Gilles. *Difference and Repetition.* Trans. Paul Patton. New York: Columbia University Press, 1994. Print.

Deleuze, Gilles. *The Logic of Sense.* Trans. Mark Lester with Charles Stivale. Ed. Constantin V. Boundas. New York: Columbia University Press, 1990. Print.

Ellmann, Richard. "Introduction." Michaux, *Selected* vii–xxi.

Evans, Dylan. *An Introductory Dictionary of Lacanian Psychoanalysis.* London: Routledge, 1996. Print.

Freud, Sigmund. *The Interpretation of Dreams*. Trans. James Strachey. New York: Avon, 1965. Print.

Freud, Sigmund. *Reflections on War and Death*. Trans. A. A. Brill. N. p.: Floating Press, 2014. Print.

Freud, Sigmund. "Wit and Its Relation to the Unconscious." Trans A. A. Brill. *The Basic Writings of Sigmund Freud*. Ed. A. A. Brill. New York: Random House, 1938. 633–803. Print.

Gide, André. *Découvrons Henri Michaux*. Paris: Gallimard, 1941. Print.

Leggett, B. J. *Wallace Stevens and Poetic Theory*. Chapel Hill: University of North Carolina Press, 1987. Print.

Michaux, Henri. *Ailleurs*. 1948. Paris: Gallimard, 1967. Print.

Michaux, Henri. *Plume*. 1938. Paris: Gallimard, 1963. Print.

Michaux, Henri. *Selected Writings*. Trans. Richard Ellmann. New York: New Directions, 1968. Print.

Michaux, Henri. *La Vie dans les plis*. 1949. Paris: Gallimard, 1972. Print.

Moore, Frederick. "Rumania and Her Ambitions." *National Geographic Magazine* 24.10 (1913): 1057–86. *HathiTrust Digital Library*. September 5, 2015. Web.

Stevens, Wallace. *Letters of Wallace Stevens*. Ed. Holly Stevens. Berkeley: University of California Press, 1996. Print.

Stevens, Wallace. *Wallace Stevens: Collected Poetry and Prose*. Ed. Frank Kermode and Joan Richardson. New York: Library of America, 1997. Print.

Vendler, Helen. "Stevens and the Lyric Speaker." *The Cambridge Companion to Wallace Stevens*. Ed. John N. Serio. New York: Cambridge University Press, 2007. 133–48. Print.

Žižek, Slavoj. *Looking Awry: An Introduction to Jacques Lacan through Popular Culture*. Cambridge: MIT Press, 1991. Print.

Zupančič, Alenka. *Ethics of the Real: Kant, Lacan*. London: Verso, 2000. Print.

7

Stevens across the Iron Curtain

Justin Quinn

Humanist approaches to literature have gone through many phases in the United States, and great claims have been made by native critics for the different ways in which the novels and poems of the country advertise fundamental human dignity and freedom. Many such claims have remained markedly consistent in the second half of the twentieth century, and the poetry of Wallace Stevens has often played a key role in these arguments. Yet how does his poetry fare when it crosses the borders—national and linguistic—of the United States and travels abroad? To what extent do the claims of these critics stand up? This chapter attempts to answer this question by following Stevens as he voyages from America into another linguistic, cultural, and political climate.

***

In 1973, a selection of Wallace Stevens' poems was published in Czech, but made no impression on literary life, or culture, in Czechoslovakia. For several reasons this is hard to understand. The translator, Jan Zábrana, was one of the best in the land. During the preceding twenty years, he had translated a wide range of work, both formal and free verse, mainly from Russian and English, into Czech. He had coedited one of the most influential anthologies of American poetry, in 1967. His translations of the Beats had dramatically transformed Czech literature in the 1960s, and he was widely recognized as a bellwether. As his afterwords show, he was an agile and intelligent critic of US poetry—his assessment of the anthology wars between Donald Allen and Hall–Pack–Simpson of the 1960s remains pertinent to this day. The Stevens translations were published by Odeon, one of the best houses for literature, which had consistently pushed the boundaries of censorship since the beginning of the Cold War. The knowledge and critical intelligence of its editors (among them Zábrana's wife) exceeded those of most humanities professors in the country; and indeed, many of its prominent figures took up positions in universities after the revolution of 1989. And, finally, Zábrana was a poet himself—in fact, as critical consensus is now coming to recognize, one of the finest in the twentieth century.

One possible reason for the negligible interest in his Stevens translations may have been that everyone was in a bad mood in the 1970s in Czechoslovakia. Before Warsaw Pact tanks invaded in August 1968, the country had opened itself to Anglophone culture to an unprecedented extent, and this had helped precipitate many changes—social, political, and poetic. Now, people felt as though they had been catapulted back to the bad old days of the early 1950s, as the state cracked down on any expression of dissent. Part of this was the curtailment of cultural institutions—sometimes they were shut down, sometimes they were purged—as well as a thorough revision of the publishing policies of houses like Odeon.

Translation never occurs in a vacuum. The author's reputation in the source language canon is always moving. In the case of Stevens, his reputation in the United States was high throughout the 1960s and 1970s (which Zábrana knew about). The target language culture is also in movement, so that it is important *when* a particular poet is translated (thus, perhaps the problem of the 1970s in Czechoslovakia). Translators stand between the two fast-flowing rivers, looking for the right moment, attempting to guess when they should divert some of one river into the other. These are difficult decisions, and in order to succeed the translator must have a complex understanding of both the source and target cultures, as well as some luck. These are some of the considerations involved before translators decide *how* to translate the texts themselves.

I mentioned above the Beats' influence on Czech culture from the 1960s on, to which Zábrana was integral. Poets such as Lawrence Ferlinghetti and Allen Ginsberg were acceptable to Czechoslovak authorities, at least at the outset, because of their wide-ranging critiques of Eisenhower's United States. Communist censors waved them through passport control, presuming that the enemy of my enemy is my friend. However, the Beats subsequently released expressive forces in translation that influenced Czech poetry, its oral performance, and popular music, as well as consolidating a movement toward greater explicitness in literature more generally—from the outright denunciatory texts of the underground to the more subtle ironies of Miroslav Holub. By the end of the 1960s, communist censors had become wary of revolutionary American poets. Stevens was perhaps viewed as a safer bet.

The Stevens selection was entitled *Muž s modrou kytarou* (The Man with the Blue Guitar), and the afterword was written by Zdeněk Vančura, considered by hardline communists to be a safe pair of hands in this period—his name insured that there would be no trouble. This points to another reason for the possible failure of the translation: if the communists allowed it to be published in such dark days, and if it was endorsed by one of the apparatchiks, then *de facto* it could not be of interest. If Zábrana had published it in samizdat, or even tamizdat (i.e., smuggled in from abroad), with their difficult and precarious distribution, then arguably it might have done better.

Vančura's first paragraph in his afterword is instructive:

> It is better to listen to the poet than explain him. A range of critics has tried to interpret Stevens' poems and come to different conclusions each time. The poet did not make life easy for them. He is clear as air and as untransparent as deep water. But always pure and true as a natural element. He at once dazzles and obscures. It is hard to sum him up more distinctly for the time being, as he hides behind numerous semblances, from which it is not easy to frame the true one.
>
> (103; translation mine)

Here Vančura identifies some of the features that have endeared Stevens to generations of readers, but it is also important to register the cultural context of such remarks as the poetry arrives across the Iron Curtain from the United States. At the very outset, he emphasizes the focal ambiguity of Stevens' poetry. Its clarity is described as a natural element (thus, it cannot have an ideological angle). A reader who would try to present Stevens as an American ideologue will be engaging in pointless labor: how do we really know, Vančura equably asks us, who the real Stevens is?

Since the political-historicist readings of Stevens by James Longenbach and Alan Filreis over two decades ago, we know that certain passages in the poetry would make for interesting reading behind the Iron Curtain. In "Owl's Clover," "Idiom of the Hero," "Esthétique du Mal," "Description Without Place," "Botanist on Alp (No. 1)," "Mountains Covered with Cats," "A Dish of Peaches in Russia," and several essays in *The Necessary Angel* (1951), Stevens' ideas about socialism and communism played an important and evolving role in his work. Imaginatively engaged with it earlier, he would later, at the onset of the Cold War, refer to communism as "this grubby faith" (*CPP* 730).

Czechs, among many other nations of the Eastern Bloc, would have agreed with the lines "Marx has ruined Nature,/For the moment" (*CPP* 109). Surrounded by gigantic failed industrial projects, large swathes of the landscape destroyed by open-cast mining, the routine pollution of air, earth, and water, living in buildings that rust, warp, and crack before they are even completed, readers would have enjoyed the pithy accuracy of Stevens' pronouncement. But "Botanist on Alp (No. 1)," along with all the other work that engaged overtly with twentieth-century political ideology, was not translated. Zábrana mainly chose short lyrics, with two exceptions: "The Man with the Blue Guitar" and "Like Decorations in a Nigger Cemetery," which were translated in their entirety. Both these poems of the mid-1930s have important things to say about the relations between poetry and politics, and would have been of intense interest to Czech culture, which had endured the diktats of Zhdanovist literary theory from 1948 to the late 1950s, then a subsequent loosening of that, to be followed by a more cynical and opportunist translation policy in the 1970s. Stevens' idiom, especially in "The Man with the Blue Guitar," is so abstract that it took Filreis' close reading to embed it, once again, in the political debates of the 1930s, after many decades of idealizing criticism. Certain lines and stanzas of "Like Decorations" can be seen as engaging in some of the same currents of thought, but they do so at a distance, and employ such various disguises and ironic ventriloquism, that it is difficult to pin down the drift of the thought, just as Vančura pointed out.

Granted, Stevens often writes at rarefied levels of philosophical abstraction. One of the damning comments on him was that his images were "less like a poet's imagery than those eternal hypothetical tigers and rhinoceroses of the philosophers. They are chosen because they are, if nothing else, clear; there is no sense of their having chosen themselves" (Alvarez 128). On the other hand, abstraction can be a powerful tool for intervening in mundane matters, and we have learned to read Stevens' abstractions as "blooded, as a man by thought" (*CPP* 333)—that is, to acknowledge the ways in which his philosophical tigers and rhinos often take on the more familiar forms of the actual world around us. However, to get to this point, we needed the historicist readings of Longenbach and Filreis, as antidote to the large body of criticism that figured Stevens as celebrant of the human imagination, meditating magisterially on fictions, weather, and suspiciously empty landscapes. In its broad outlines, such an approach fitted neatly with US Cold War cultural ideology, which Filreis, again, has thrillingly detailed in his more recent book, *Counter-Revolution of the Word: The Conservative Attack on Modern Poetry, 1945–1960* (2008).

More particularly, several critics have examined Stevens in a Cold War context. Paul Bauer helped us to understand Stevens' politics as they developed from the Second World War into the Cold War, marking his distance from McCarthyism and communism alike. Mark Schoening finds a Cold War thematic in "Description Without Place," viewing this as part of Stevens' desire to locate poetry *outside* the binary of East and West; such an apolitical aesthetic would become stealthily politicized later in the Cold War, but that need not concern our ideas of Stevens. Schoening places this stance in a broad European intellectual history. Filreis, in "Stevens/Pound in the Cold War," uses Stevens' legacy as an index of changing paradigms in American poetry criticism in the decades following the poet's death. He argues that during the 1950s, it had not yet become polarized in a choice of Pound or Stevens (or in further morphs, each of which shifts the debate in slightly different directions: Donald Allen or Hall–Pack–Simpson; Marjorie Perloff or Helen Vendler; Language poetry or New Formalism). "In the fifties," he writes, "Stevens floated freely among the spheres of influence" (186). He hopes the pitting of Stevens against Pound has changed again by 2002, when he can conceivably imagine Bob Perelman choosing Stevens as his Modernist precursor for a program held at the Kelly Writers House in 2000, where nine poets were invited to read themselves through Modernism (though Perelman remained true to type and chose Louis Zukofsky instead) (189–90).

Here I wish to consider two studies that are, in my view, symptomatic of the way Stevens' reputation evolved in the Cold War critical context. They are bookends of a kind, one from the beginning of the war, one from the end. The first is Roy Harvey Pearce's *The Continuity of American Poetry* (1961), which began as a series of lectures at the Salzburg Seminar in American Studies in February 1954. It is worth stressing that neither the seminar nor Pearce's book was Cold War boosterism. While Pearce acknowledges, though does not specify, the forces in US society that are inimical to poetry, his general intention is to present a success story, where poetry—American poetry—achieved a continuity and a kind of autonomy. This was in stark contrast to the uses to which poetry was being put about 120 kilometers (75 miles) away from Salzburg, across the Iron Curtain. Pearce says that "The real subject of this narrative, I repeat, has been the dignity of man in the United States—how achieved, and at what cost" (421). He identifies this as a humanist agenda. American poets have successfully fought off "threats" to "the dignity of man," and thus their work is of exemplary interest to the world (4). Though he does not directly link such threats to the Cold War, except in a general vague way, it is not hard to connect the dots when, at the end of the book, he states, "Recently we have been much troubled by the question of this responsibility and all it implies for the bearing of American literature on American life" (420). Stephen Matterson has remarked that the book "belong[s] to a cold-war ethos of stabilizing a separate American identity at home and promoting it abroad" (112). Pearce wishes to explain that since US poetry learned to survive and prosper, finding an autonomous space for itself, so too can poetries in other cultures, no matter what the political pressures. This is poetry as democratic export.

In his argument, Stevens is the capstone of the American poetic tradition. He comes at the end of the book, and no other poet—not Whitman, not Dickinson—receives an entire chapter to themselves, reflecting what Pearce believed to be Stevens' "culminating place in the continuity of American poetry" (378). So, what did he praise in Stevens?

> The poem [Stevens] sought—and, especially toward the end of his life, with superbly lucid awareness of what he was seeking—was one of a creative process purified in such a way that all men could share in it. It was to be a poem in which all men could come to behold, stripped of its antecedents and consequences, that which made them human.
>
> (378)

We may be tempted to read this in the purely nationalist terms that Pearce's title implies; however, he makes clear that the humanism promoted by Stevens and his other poets is available globally, and not just nationally:

> Stevens' goal is one toward which some Americans have long aspired—a collective egocentrism, a universal humanism, an American way of life negating itself, and thereby creating something larger, precisely by being itself.
>
> (393)

This view of "an American way of life" that can be shared beyond the borders of America is obviously germane to US democratic ideology as figured in the nation's foreign policy through many different periods. Such global humanism is, in Pearce's view, prior to, and provides the ground for, both religious belief and political conviction. In other words, it precedes ideology, and is in its nature, unideological.[1] Pearce's framework is generally typical of the 1950s and early 1960s—and some critics still hold to the humanist idea of literature. But it created a problem for American poets and critics, as it implied that any overtly political poetry was missing the point: to be an American poet, to be a poet of the great world, one had to address themes *prior* to politics, of more general import.

It is striking, then, to skip to the end of the Cold War and encounter another large and complex survey (though not solely of American poetry) that takes a similar position. Rather, it is the story of the evolution of Romantic poetry, through French Symbolism, which ends with a consideration of American Modernist poetry. Once again, however, Stevens is offered as the culmination of this story. Although not nationalist in its overt framework, Charles Altieri's *Painterly Abstraction in Modernist American Poetry* (1989) presents Stevens as a poet who releases radical powers, resources, energies, investments, nobilities, and models of agency in his poetry, free of ideological content. By engaging ourselves with the interpretive difficulties of reading Stevens' poems, we come to an awareness that "there are not worlds and interpretations, but worlds as interpreted in a variety of ways, each perhaps best articulated, not by descriptions, but by making manifest the energies involved" (347). This reveals to us "portents of our own powers" as readers, to quote Altieri quoting Stevens (340). These are a kind of poetic content "without the traps of ideology" (322). Acknowledging this achievement in Stevens, Altieri can thus posit "powers that we all share, powers that we can even imagine building a community around" (356–57).

Altieri is a vastly different reader from Pearce, but both share a humanist approach to the reading of literature, shadowed by a democratic ideology that had specific Cold War applications in the cultural financing of both the State Department and the CIA. In his later work, Altieri slots this hermeneutics into a story of a generous American exceptionalism ("Spectacular" 58–59). To access these powers, you do not have to be an American citizen or even the holder of a Green Card: they are available to any reader who engages with the poems on a profound level. Such readers are atomized and unencumbered by other cultures or languages—Altieri presumes that the ideal reader of Stevens will be able to shuck these off, as they would a hard-to-pronounce surname at Ellis Island. Much as the true Muslim must learn Arabic to gain access to the Koran, so too must Stevens' ideal reader speak a language of the atomized individual of Anglo-American philosophy, the subject, or consciousness, that seems to exist prior to imbrication in language, culture, nation, and family. For Altieri, in a key passage, presumes the existence of the individual prior to all ideologies; if he did not, his claims for Stevens would collapse (*Painterly* 327). And yet in doing so, he assumes that which he would prove. We are reminded here of Pearce's view of poetry readers as stripped of antecedents and consequences so that they can get to their essential humanity, something which dovetails not coincidentally with the claims that US democratic ideology makes for the individual.

I am skeptical of such idealism, because it confuses the way in which Anglo-American philosophy universalizes its view of human beings as packets of consciousness, or subjectivity, or essences, that exist *prior* to socialization, as well as their entrenchment in various languages. It does not concede that many of the nuances, complexities, and deeper structures of consciousness are created precisely through socialization and language acquisition. As several generations of philosophers and critics have pointed out, this is a limited, Anglocentric view of the matter, in which the atomized individual can, like Jay Gatsby, spring from the Platonic idea of itself. But there is a further cause for wariness.

So far, with a fairly broad brush, I have linked the universalizing tendency in American Cold War poetry criticism—from Pearce to Altieri—to US foreign policy, suggesting that despite their pretense of universalism, of validity beyond history, they are much more limited and historically conditioned. However, my point is not to pull Altieri and Pearce back down into historical relativism, where they would truly hate to be. Rather, I am interested in the way their approach to culture and ideology—which framed so much American culture of the mid-twentieth century—is part of a larger global ecology in which another ideology is pitted directly against it. The counterargument to this American humanism was sounded early in the twentieth century by Vladimir Ilyich Lenin when he declared that the "freedom of the bourgeois writer, artist or actress is simply masked (or hypocritically masked) dependence on the money-bag, on corruption, on prostitution" (n. pag.). This states it fairly strongly (and many contemporary bourgeois poets might complain that not much of the money bag is thrown in their direction). Lenin's statement set the cultural direction for much of the Soviet sphere of influence up to the 1960s, revalidated at the very beginning of the Cold War by Andrei Zhdanov. If humanist literary criticism in the United States during the Cold War up to 1960 designated politically engaged poetry as not really poetry at all, then communist literary criticism reciprocated inversely, designating any text that did not express socialist ideals as non-culture, non-literature, non-poetry. Historians and sociologists call this phenomenon of Cold War culture a mirroring mechanism.

Then, in the second phase of the Cold War, beginning around 1960, translators, writers, critics, and editors found ways for work to travel across the Iron Curtain, despite the ideological strictures on both sides. In poetry, we have Czesław Miłosz, Joseph Brodsky, Miroslav Holub, Zbigniew Herbert, and many others who are brought to the West in various forms and celebrated as humanist, apolitical poets (even when this is patently not an accurate characterization of them all). Similarly, Central and Eastern European communist regimes search through Anglophone literature for writers who will suit them ideologically. Thus, in Czechoslovakia, the country I know best, poets such as Edwin Rolfe, Thomas Mcgrath, Dalton Trumbo, and many other 1950s radical poets are translated— then later the Beats. This shuts down in 1968, with the end of the Prague Spring, which brings us to 1973, when Stevens appears in Czech.

At this point, it is interesting to inspect the humanist claims of both Pearce and Altieri and to see how they fare beyond US borders. Their American exceptionalism does not engage itself in the business of translation and cultural transfer of poetry—they simply presume that those individual powers, resources, and energies, released by poetry and its interpretation, *must* be understandable and available across such divisions. Pearce, lecturing at the Salzburg Seminar, might indeed have felt that he was able to communicate this global American humanism to Europeans from both sides of the Iron Curtain. However, he perhaps was not aware of how select his audience was, especially if they came from a communist regime. He also perhaps was not aware of how far these people had traveled linguistically to be able to appreciate what he said. And, thus, perhaps he assumed a kind of global cultural community existed, one that could appreciate the exceptionalist story of American poetry. Whatever the reason, critics such as Pearce and Altieri frequently underestimate the linguistic, cultural, and national contexts of the understanding of poetry and the ways that it travels across borders and languages. (Altieri in another essay declares that "The US democratic subject cannot be reduced to a set of rights emerging within history" ["Spectacular" 59].) They believe that the abstract humanism of Stevens can travel unimpeded and unimpaired across such divisions.

It is a Cold War wager; and the communist critics on the other side, such as Zdeněk Vančura, call their bluff and say, "Be our guest. Try out your abstractions on our readers." At the end of his afterword, Vančura even allows Stevens a kind of universal truth: "Although Wallace Stevens is very unique and individual as a poet, he is moving towards the universal" (106; translation mine). As the poetry goes through Checkpoint Charlie, as it is transformed from English into a Slavic language and literary tradition, its abstractions are sapped of their force. A universal truth can challenge politics and societies anywhere; but in its degenerate form, it merely becomes a trivial statement about the world. This is the bland universal of Vančura's sentence above. If Stevens dreamed of an abstraction blooded as a man by thought, then his were drained of blood when they left the English language in this Cold War journey.

Moreover, Altieri has written of Stevens' poem "Large Red Man Reading" as a model for the release of pre-ideological powers in the individual

(*Painterly* 354–56). Such an idea of readers, ensconced in their homes, realizing great powers within themselves, and given no hint about how to implement these powers in public forums, was a neat fit for the cultural policy of communist Czechoslovakia during the 1970s. Its citizens were allowed their small freedoms in private conversations, after-hours pursuits, and small cottages in the countryside, but if they raised their voices so that they could be heard across the village, or in the town hall, the authorities would rise to repressive action. What seems like a radical release of powers to the US humanist critic turns out, once again, to have a different effect in another political environment.

I disagree with Massimo Bacigalupo when he says, "Studies of influence can be tedious, unless they throw some light on the original writer" (227). Writing about Italian and French translations of Stevens, he tells us that through examinations of his linguistic and cultural crossings we can learn something new about Stevens. My interest, however, lies in what Stevens' reputation can tell us about the particular economy of Cold War literature, as part of a larger system of cultural exchange. Cold War literary studies, in the American context, tend merely to append Cold War thematics to a national canon, from Thomas Schaub to Alan Filreis. However, it was a transnational economy, with translation playing an integral role on both sides. How else are we to understand the anomalous fame of Soviet and Central European dissident writers in the United States and United Kingdom? How else can we understand the fame of a minor talent such as Miroslav Holub in English? Conversely, the readership of this book might be surprised to hear that two of the most famous American novelists in communist Czechoslovakia were Warren Miller and Anton Myrer. These are not merely glitches in the system, but are symptomatic of wider and deeper patterns of cultural exchange that we ignore at our peril as literary critics of the era.

Returning to the US context, we might ask what warrants Pearce's and Altieri's respective claims that Stevens, and by implication a major current in American poetry, offers powers to readers beyond the language and borders of the United States. Surely this claim can be made only by people *outside* America and *outside* English? It can be tested only after it has made the journey into another language and culture. A further difficulty is the reluctance of such critics to acknowledge the ideological uses to which this kind of humanist criticism was put during the Cold War, excluding the political as theme from mainstream US poetry well into the 1960s, and also mounting a strong rearguard action afterwards. In the last ten years, we have seen a resurgent humanist criticism, marked most dramatically in the theoretical turn of Edward Said's *Humanism and Democratic Criticism* (2004). Said argues that while humanism's reputation was indubitably tarnished by the Cold War, it is not ultimately defined by that involvement and remains available as an important resource. When a preliminary version of this chapter was presented at a Stevens symposium in Antwerp in 2014, Charles Altieri remarked that humanism was not invented in the United States after the Second World War, but came from other places. Such powerful ideas are always on the move, changing the cultural and political terrain, and being changed in their turn.

I would like to conclude with two alternative bookends, the first from the 1970s and the second from the beginning of the Cold War, as they will allow us to extrapolate from the positions of Said and Altieri in the preceding paragraph. Stevens' first translator, Jan Zábrana, did not hesitate to read Stevens' abstractions in raw political terms, finding in poetry a way to understand the conditions of his own life. He died in 1984 and his diaries were published after the fall of the Iron Curtain. The following passage is an excellent example of how an abstraction can be taken down from its rarefied air and given explanatory force in a particular historical moment, that of communist Czechoslovakia:

> I will die in a falsified history ... One generation after another rots away in it— at seventeen, they tattoo their biceps; at forty, they wallpaper their bidets ... For the cleverer ones, there awaits the fetish of faculty positions. Or they are metamorphosed into regime Cerebuses in offices and administrations, bell-jar parrot cages dolled up as academic institutes, with their ass-licking subordination and cementing over of brains in exports, imports, machine-tools, chemical industries. That line by Wallace Stevens, "It is equal to living in a tragic land/To live in a tragic time," is about that. Few people will understand what it means. It is one of the most inspired and universal lines that I have ever read. This lying, cheating, murderous regime—this regime that sets out to gradually stupefy the people—it keeps on going. This regime, passing off its prostheses and cheap imitations, obscuring reality in human speech, this regime keeps going ... I will die in a falsified history.
>
> (403–04; translation mine, ellipses in original)

In Zábrana's ear, Stevens speaks politically. Even so, the American poet does not lose his abstract glint. A truth is upheld here, one that is largely consonant with the interpretations of Pearce and Altieri. If Stevens' lines do not give Zábrana a model of agency, or power, or nobility, that would allow him to transform his political circumstances and that of his fellow Czechs, they do yet serve to remind him of his dignity as a human being, and the ways in which it is compromised by his daily life in a repressive state. If this is poetic humanism at work, then we should perhaps take its measure not from Pearce or Altieri, but from Zábrana, who in strategic choices of poets to translate also presented Czech readers with the strong poets of the American left, such as Kenneth Patchen, Thomas McGrath, Edwin Rolfe, Lawrence Ferlinghetti, and, most importantly, Allen Ginsberg—poets, it should be noted, who were routinely excluded from the canons of US poetry compiled by humanist critics. However, in his life and in his work his revolt was ultimately quietist—he kept his head down and worked hard.

The second bookend is from 1947, when F. O. Matthiessen was teaching at the Charles University in Prague for a semester. He recorded his impressions in his memoir of the time, *From the Heart of Europe* (1948), which also covers his travels through a Central Europe that had yet to recover from the Second World War. A committed leftist, he hoped that Czechoslovakia would be able to exist as a socialist country without having to choose between the emergent superpowers. Late in the year, only a few months before all such hopes were extinguished in the communist putsch of February 1948, when the country was definitively embraced by the Soviets, Matthiessen found himself teaching Stevens to his Czech students:

> They may have been a little bewildered (as the poet would have wanted them to be) by the opening lines of "Bantams in Pine Woods" … But after "The Emperor of Ice Cream" they surely began to realize what Wallace Stevens meant by "the essential gaudiness of poetry." And in selections from "The Man with the Blue Guitar," their own knowledge of Picasso could illuminate the conception of how the artist achieves fresh reality only by breaking through the conventionally expected appearances … As I read "Sad Strains of a Gay Waltz," I felt, even more fully than when I had first read it in the middle of the depression, that here in the contrast between a played-out tune and a new skeptical music which might spring from the very heart of our disbelief, lay one of the most resourceful "ideas of order" for our broken time.

(179)

Matthiessen's pedagogical insistence on "the essential gaudiness of poetry" is made to a group of people many of whom would have lost family members in the war and who were still living in difficult material and political conditions. Given Matthiessen's own political convictions and the attentive, if overly optimistic, impressions that his memoir provides, we understand that this gaudiness is anything but insouciant. Here, it has its joy as necessary obverse of the violence, disease, and repression that had coursed and would course through Europe in this time. If this kind of joy is at the root of a new, resurgent humanism, if it is an aesthetic ideology that is engaged in conversation with other cultures and languages, as it was in the early winter of 1947, and not merely the fellow traveler of an imperial foreign policy, then it has a fair chance of success.

It remains only to add that a more extensive selection of Stevens' poems was published in Czech in 2008, translated by Daniel Soukup.

Notes

1   Cf. "The poetry which Stevens wanted was to be grounded in a humanism so powerful that even God would be under its sway" (Pearce 381). And: "Stevens' faith was that the ultimate poem contained within itself the ground of political belief because it contained within itself the ground of belief in man. The ultimate poem would be chaotic too, and reality and imagination would be aspects of the chaos. Man's burden—in politics as in others of his ways—is that he must learn to live proximately in the light of what he can know ultimately" (417).

Works Cited

Altieri, Charles. *Painterly Abstraction in Modernist American Poetry*. Cambridge: Cambridge University Press, 1989. Print.

Altieri, Charles. "Spectacular Anti-spectacle: Ecstasy and Nationality in Whitman and His Heirs." *American Literary History* 11.1 (1999): 34–62. Print.

Alvarez, A. *The Shaping Spirit: Studies in Modern English and American Poets*. London: Arrow, 1963. Print.

Bacigalupo, Massimo. "Reading Stevens in Italian." *Wallace Stevens across the Atlantic*. Ed. Bart Eeckhout and Edward Ragg. Basingstoke: Palgrave, 2008. 216–29. Print.

Bauer, Paul. "The Politics of Reticence: Wallace Stevens in the Cold War Era." *Twentieth-Century Literature* 39.1 (1993): 1–31. Print.

Filreis, Alan. "Stevens/Pound in the Cold War." *Wallace Stevens Journal* 26.2 (2002): 181–93. Print.

Lenin, Vladimir Ilyich. "Party Organisation and Party Literature." 1905. Marxists Internet Archive. December 2, 2013. Web.

Matterson, Stephen. "'The Whole Habit of the Mind': Stevens, Americanness, and the Use of Elsewhere." *Wallace Stevens Journal* 25.2 (Fall 2001): 111–21. Print.

Matthiessen, F. O. *From the Heart of Europe*. New York: Oxford University Press, 1948. Print.

Pearce, Roy Harvey. *The Continuity of American Poetry*. Princeton: Princeton University Press, 1961. Print.

Schoening, Mark. "Sacrifice and Sociability in the Modern Imagination: Wallace Stevens and the Cold War." *Contemporary Literature* 41.1 (2000): 138–61. Print.

Stevens, Wallace. *Wallace Stevens: Collected Poetry and Prose*. Ed. Frank Kermode and Joan Richardson. New York: Library of America, 1997. Print.

Vančura, Zdeněk. "Afterword." *Muž s modrou kytarou* (The Man with the Blue Guitar). By Wallace Stevens. Trans. Jan Zábrana. Prague: Odeon, 1973. 103–06. Print.

Zábrana, Jan. *Celý život* (A Whole Life). 2nd ed. Prague: Torst, 2001. Print.

8

Stevens and Seamus Heaney

George S. Lensing

In the mid-1960s, just a few years after his death in 1955, Wallace Stevens was largely unknown in Ireland and the United Kingdom and would remain so for years to come. In Belfast, Northern Ireland, however, two young student-poets—Seamus Heaney and Seamus Deane—who had been schoolmates for six years at St. Columb's College (middle and high school) in Londonderry, found themselves reunited as students at Queen's University in Belfast. Deane had somehow "discovered" Stevens and was sufficiently impressed by the American poet to laud his work to Heaney. Moreover, Deane's sonnet "To Wallace Stevens" was included in his first published collection, *While Jewels Rot* (1966). (Heaney's own chapbook *Eleven Poems* had appeared in the same series in the previous year.) The poem's overwrought language aims at capturing something of the style of Stevens. It begins: "Of the svelte diction, Master; of the colours/Of things the most prismatic poet/Who ever tautened meaning in the rainbow/Of his verse" (n. pag.). Years later, Heaney would recall those opening words, and in writing his own poem "The Ministry of Fear," addressed to Deane, cites the "svelte diction[s]" from the lines just cited. In the 1960s, however, Heaney saw Stevens as Deane's poet, not his own. Deane's "opulent flourish of language," in partial imitation of Stevens, enabled him, in Heaney's eyes, to "[wear] the mantle" of poet; of himself, however, Heaney recalled, "I on the other hand was far from confident" (O'Driscoll 185). He would also remain "far from confident" about Stevens—unlike, for example, the poetry of Robert Frost, who was an early and important influence.

The young Heaney was also hearing about Stevens from two other contemporaries who were in Belfast during the 1960s, Michael Longley and Derek Mahon, both of whom were making their own way as poets. In Heaney's poem "The Bookcase," from *Electric Light* (2001), he remembers fondly his personally owned volumes located on the bookcase in those years, adding these two lines: "Voices too of Frost and Wallace Stevens/Off a Caedmon double album, off different shelves" (60). That Caedmon album has taken on a kind of notoriety. Edna Longley, the critic and wife of Michael, has noted that "Northern Irish poetry of the 1960s, I would argue, initiated … a [new aesthetic] cluster in the tradition of the English lyric, and these American poets … influenced its formation"; she goes on to list Stevens, along with Frost, Hart Crane, Robert Lowell, Richard Wilbur, and Theodore Roethke (260). She also mentions the recording: "a Caedmon record of American poets reading their work was endlessly played by Mahon and Longley at Trinity College, Dublin in the early 1960s. Top of the pops was Wallace Stevens reading 'The Idea of Order at Key West'" (263). Heaney would later admit in an interview with John Brown that the bookcase and Caedmon album were not his own: "The album they [Mahon and Longley] played is probably the very one I listened to in the Longleys' flat in Malone Avenue [in Belfast]. And that's actually the Longleys' bookcase I'm describing" (Brown 80). Even so, Heaney was reluctant to register the same enthusiasm for Stevens that was exhibited by his peers.

In various interviews, Heaney has attempted to explain his slowness to appreciate Stevens. Although Deane, Longley, and Mahon were all poets of Northern Ireland, his own rural Northern Irish roots made him suspicious of Stevens' elegant syntax and acoustical melodies that were so admired by Deane:

> No place in the world [he is speaking of Northern Ireland] prides itself more on its vigilance and realism, no place considers itself more qualified to censure any flourish of rhetoric or extravagance of aspiration. So, partly as a result of having internalized these attitudes through growing up with them, I went for years half-avoiding and half-resisting the opulence and extensiveness of poets as different as Wallace Stevens and Rainer Maria Rilke …
>
> ("Crediting" 418)

But there is something more than Northern Irish reticence at work here. In writing the poems that would make up his first volume in 1966, *Death of a Naturalist*, Heaney was deliberately embracing a less refined, less elegant style to complement the poems he was beginning to write centered in the rural setting in County Derry, where he had grown up. When Heaney, Longley, and other young Northern Irish poets in Belfast began meeting in the apartment of Philip Hobsbaum, beginning in 1963 (later becoming known as the "Belfast Group"),

Heaney found his own work favored by the older Hobsbaum, who had founded, hosted, and tutored the meetings: "Hobsbaum didn't go for their work [Longley and Mahon] because he thought it was too elegant. He was a strong believer in the bleeding hunk of experience. So there was an edginess therefore, and I was favored and they weren't" (Randall 15). Citing the influence of Lowell and Ted Hughes, Heaney restated the contrast in another interview:

> When we were young poets together in Belfast, Michael Longley and his wife Edna were always forwarding the Larkin-Wilbur line. And I would line up on the Lowell-Hughes side of things. It was partly because the sound I made in my lines was closer to the Anglo-Saxon roughage of Hughes and the head-on, less melodious note of Lowell. [Longley and Mahon] were sponsors of immaculate melody.
>
> (Heaney and Cole 125)

It is easy to see how Stevens during those years would fade as an exemplar for the young Heaney—even as, in succeeding years, he would himself go on to become a highly accomplished lyricist and connoisseur of his own "immaculate melody."

By the time Heaney was in his late forties, it was clear that he had continued to read Stevens, unable to dismiss him entirely, but nonetheless failing to find a unifying "gestalt" in his work—though he was now beginning to regret his remove from the poet:

> Wallace Stevens I am helplessly in awe of but my response is as helpless as it is awed. When I open the door into that great cloudscape of language, I am transported joyfully. And I have got to a stage of reading Stevens where—to mix the metaphor—I can feel the bone under the cloud. I love his oil-on-water, brilliant phantasmagoria. And there is deep mind-current under the water, and a kind of water-muscle mind at work, but I find it difficult to hold that in my own reader's mind. I find it difficult to see a Stevensian gestalt in the way that I can see Frost as a whole. I can see Frost defined against a sky or landscape. Somehow with Stevens, I cannot see the poetry defined. It is coterminous with the horizon. That says a lot for him but it also means he is difficult to think about.
>
> (Brandes 15–16)

At this stage in 1988, Heaney concedes that he "love[s] his oil-on-water, brilliant phantasmagoria" in spite of his failure to "see a Stevensian gestalt," even as he was beginning to point to the richness of the American poet's echoing sound-chambers and musical virtuosity.

A few years later, he became noticeably more sympathetic to Stevens' aestheticism, especially in his last poems. In one essay, he compares Stevens to Marlowe and Milton for demonstrating just this quality:

> The power of the final chorus of *Doctor Faustus*, or the opening lines of *Paradise Lost* or the whole somnambulant drift of a late Wallace Stevens poem such as "The River of Rivers in Connecticut" has not to do simply with its author's craft. The affective power in these places comes from a kind of veteran knowledge which has gathered to a phonetic and rhythmic head, and forced an utterance.
>
> ("Dylan" 134–35)

Earlier he had made similar comments about Stevens' "The Irish Cliffs of Moher." What he admired in the poem was not the attempt to construct a "conjectural meaning" so much as the poem's "body of sound":

> The stateliness, the pomp of its progress, the solemn march established in three-time at the beginning—"in this world, in this house,/At the spirit's base," "My father's father, his father's father, his—," "before thought, before speech,/At the head of the past"—all this contributes to a deep horn music, the rounded-out, lengthened-back note ... Yet for all its shadowy effectiveness, the poem is not a mere "somnambulation" [a word he had applied to "The River of Rivers in Connecticut" in the previous quote, though here he employs it only to deny it]. [The poem] is rather a definite matter of sensation, arising from the cliffiness not of the cliffs themselves but of the word-cliffs in the poem, the vowel-caverns of "house," "father," "shadows," "Moher."
>
> ("Place" 40)

***

What repeatedly drew Heaney to Stevens has less to do with the style of the American poet, which in time he came to value, than with Stevens' aesthetic self-justifications in the face of attacks for his social and political "irrelevance." The American poet, writing largely in the first half of the twentieth century, lived through the First World War, the Great Depression, the Second World War, the Korean War, and the emergence of communism as a world force leading to the Cold War. Although his poems address all these pressing events, they do not embrace ideologies or consign propagandistic endorsements or condemnations. Indeed, his very "oil-on-water, brilliant phantasmagoria," in addition to his musicality, seemed to militate against a gritty realism that one might more readily associate with political poetry. During the 1930s, and following the publication of Stevens' first volume, *Harmonium*, in 1923, the critic and poet Stanley Burnshaw wrote a review that is perhaps the most cited of all the reviews of the poet's work then and later. The poems of Stevens' first volume, he said, make up "the kind of verse that people concerned with the murderous world collapse can hardly swallow today except in tiny doses" (42). Though the title was later changed, Stevens published the original version of the second part of his long poem "Owl's Clover" separately under the title "Mr. Burnshaw and the Statue."

Initially, Heaney's reaction to Stevens indulged some of the same imputations. In a lecture given at the University of Surrey in 1978, he set Stevens in opposition to William Butler Yeats, making clear his own preference: "Unlike Wallace Stevens, for example, that other great apologist of the imagination, Yeats bore the implications of his romanticism into action: he propagandized, speechified, fund-raised, administered and politicked in the world of telegrams and anger ... I admire the way that Yeats took on the world on his own terms" (*Preoccupations* 100–01). Such comparison, made here in broad and sweeping strokes, would undergo reconsideration and revision.

It was not only Stevens' defense of his own poetic aims that increasingly appealed to Heaney but also, and equally importantly, the uneasiness with which he put forward those defenses, knowing that a poem could not directly prevent or stop a war, correct social injustices, or overthrow tyrants. On the other hand, he would argue, the poem can become a mode of survival for those who are otherwise subjected to such social cataclysms and atrocities. What hovers behind Stevens' defenses, however, is a lingering regret that art cannot do more to prevent or undo these very realities in the face of widespread human suffering.

Heaney endured similar accusations in the wake of his own poems written in the worst years of the Troubles in Northern Ireland. Between the years 1969 and 1998, when the Good Friday Accords were signed, bombings and other acts of terrorism between the Protestants of Northern Ireland (loyalists to the prevailing English government) and Catholics, whose numbers were fewer in the six counties of Northern Ireland (leading to their favoring Irish independence from England and unification with the rest of Ireland), were constant. Born into a family in Northern Ireland that was devoutly Catholic, though not militantly political (*Stepping* 28), Heaney found himself caught between the demands of the Catholic nationalists for a more overtly pro-independence viewpoint in his work and the attacks of certain Protestants who saw his work and his popularity as a threat.

When Heaney's second-cousin became the victim of a killing following a fake roadblock while driving home from a soccer match, the poet commemorated his death with one of his most moving elegies, "The Strand at Lough Beg." In the tradition of the pastoral elegy, and shaped by lines from Dante's "Purgatorio," Heaney resets the actual scene of the attack in a pasture in Heaney's hometown where the cousin had actually herded cattle. As the cousin is shot, now falling beside Heaney and the surrounding cattle, the poem movingly responds, "I dab you clean with moss/Fine as the drizzle out of a low cloud" and "plait/Green scapulars to wear over your shroud" (*Opened* 146). The poem first appeared in 1979, but five years later, in a longer poem called "Station Island," Heaney summons the ghost of the same cousin who now addresses him in what are, of course, words of self-reproach. The cousin-as-ghost addresses the poet in these words:

> You confused evasion and artistic tact.
> The Protestant who shot me through the head
> I accuse directly, but indirectly, you
> who now atone perhaps upon this bed
> for the way you whitewashed ugliness and drew
> the lovely blinds of the *Purgatorio*
> and saccharined my death with morning dew.
>
> (*Opened* 239)

That mode of self-accusation recurs in numerous Heaney poems. In 1972, he moved with his family out of Northern Ireland to a cottage in the republic near Dublin. The compulsion to defend that decision and to justify his own political poems on their own terms, rather than terms that were externally imposed, remained with him until the last years before his death. It also led to constant attempts to define and redefine the nature of political poetry itself. And here is where he found the example of Stevens increasingly salient.

Stevens' own attempts to justify the role of political poetry in a time of war, for example, came to the fore in a poem like "Gigantomachia." Here, in the context of the Second World War, he demands that the poet "expel … seductions" and "confront with plainest eye" those realities that "war magnified" (*CPP* 258). Nonetheless, such efforts on his part at drawing his poetry into contemporary history, of which there are many, left him at moments feeling inadequate and insufficient. In a letter written in the year after the war, Stevens noted that "The misery of Europe … seems not to have been so real to us then [during the war] as it is now" (*L* 525). He then gives voice to his own self-accusation, not unlike Heaney's. Commenting on some recently published poetry, including his own, and finding it "academic and unreal," he adds, "One is inclined, therefore, to sympathize with one's more unsympathetic critics" (*L* 525). The words of Heaney's ghostly cousin addressed to him constitute just such an "unsympathetic critic."

As Heaney became more familiar with Stevens' work and his estimation of the American poet's supple richness of language rose, he also began to identify with Stevens' political consciousness and with his own awareness of the limitations of such language. In one of his best-known essays, "The Redress of Poetry," Heaney begins by noting that "apologists" for poetry, "from Sir Philip Sidney to Wallace Stevens, all sooner or later are tempted to show how poetry's existence as a form of art relates to our existence as citizens of society—how it is 'of present use'" (1). He implicitly identifies his own views of the role of politics in poetry with those of Stevens. In the essay "The Noble Rider and the Sound of Words," Heaney notes, Stevens had defended the social content of the imagination by calling it "a violence from within that protects us from a violence without. It is the imagination pressing back against the pressure of reality. It seems, in the last analysis, to have something to do with our self-preservation; and that, no doubt, is why the expression of it, the sound of its words, helps us to live our lives" (*CPP* 665). But to some would-be heckler, Heaney imagines in his essay, such protective interior violence would never be sufficient: "The heckler … is going to have little sympathy with Wallace Stevens" ("Redress" 2). Heaney, however, mouths his defense of both Stevens and, implicitly, his own poetry. The poem can introduce "a counter-reality in the scales—a reality which may be only imagined but which nevertheless has weight because it is imagined within the gravitational pull of the actual and can therefore hold its own and balance out against the historical situation" (3–4). Four years later, in "Frontiers of Writing," Heaney recalled his earlier singling out of Stevens in defense of poetry's "redress" against the pressure of reality, but now adding confidently, even triumphantly, that "the theme is in fact an aspect or consequence of my autobiography" (190).

Even in his Nobel Lecture, "Crediting Poetry," he nods once again toward Stevens: "I went for years half-avoiding and half-resisting the opulence and extensiveness of poets as different as Wallace Stevens and Rainer Maria Rilke." Such "costive attitudes" (toward Stevens and Rilke), he continues, were influenced by his "having to conduct oneself as a poet in a situation of ongoing political violence and public expectation" (418). If Stevens had once come up short by such defense of the imagination, it was no longer the case. Heaney had found in Stevens a useful model for how the poet could defy "public expectation" and remain faithful to his own aesthetic goals and standards. In the face of taunts from his own "heckler," who, in the poem "The Flight Path," had demanded that he "'write/Something for us,'" Heaney replies, "'If I do write something,/ Whatever it is, I'll be writing for myself'" (*Opened* 385).

***

Heaney's first reference in a poem to Stevens occurs in "Fosterage," from *North* (1975), a poem that is dedicated to Michael McLaverty, the principal of St. Thomas Intermediate School in Belfast, where Heaney taught for a year in 1962–63 after obtaining his teaching certification. McLaverty was himself a novelist and short story writer of some repute. The poem begins with three words set in quotations: "'Description is revelation!'"—words taken from a longer poem by Stevens called "Description Without Place." The poet, however, is not named in the poem in spite of the quotation marks and exclamation mark. Rather, it goes on to remember affectionately the advice given to him by McLaverty: "Listen. Go your own way," almost the same words of the ghost of James Joyce, for example, in the last part of "Station Island." McLaverty makes reference to two proposed exemplars for the young aspiring poet: Katherine Mansfield and "Poor Hopkins." He quotes Mansfield in the poem as saying, "*I will tell/How the laundry basket squeaked.*" McLaverty calls this a "note of exile" and then adds, "But to hell with overstating it" (*Opened* 134). If precision of ear and eye without overstatement constitutes the gist of McLaverty's advice, the three words from Stevens as the poem's beginning—"Description is revelation"—introduce a complicating irony.

Stevens' poem identifies description as always an act of the imagination, an approximation—or "seeming"—of reality, not a mirror thereof. As the poem, "Description Without Place," states at the beginning of part VI, such description is "an artificial thing that exists,/In its own seeming" (*CPP* 301). To describe the squeaking of the basket, in other words, may create a facsimile of sound that is *not* false, but for Stevens it remains "an artificial thing" and must not be "too closely the double of our lives." He insists that such "seeming" of the world is "Intenser" than any imitation of "actual life," such as the sound of the basket. Stevens, I suggest, hovers in interesting ways behind McLaverty as a second and somewhat competing mentor in "Fosterage."

In Heaney's final volume, *Human Chain* (2010), appears a poem entitled "'The Door Was Open and the House Was Dark.'" By its very title it recalls Stevens' "The House Was Quiet and the World Was Calm."[1] Heaney's poem is an elegiac tribute to his friend David Hammond, who had died in 2008. He had met Hammond during his Belfast years following his graduation from Queen's University. Hammond, Heaney, and the poet Michael Longley spent a month in 1968 traveling on a reading tour sponsored by the Arts Council of Northern Ireland. Their performances consisted of reciting poetry and singing songs; Hammond was the musician. Their friendship would continue for forty years: Hammond and Longley are the dedicatees of Heaney's third volume, *Wintering Out*, and one of Heaney's best-known poems, "The Singer's House" from *Field Work*, celebrates Hammond without naming him, though Hammond is named in another poem from the same volume, "September Song." Hammond would go on to become a director of Field Day Theater Company and a documentary film maker. One of his films is about Heaney himself, for which Heaney wrote the script. He would later say of his friend, "This Hammond name kept coming up … so I was glad to meet him. I once described David as a natural force masquerading as a human being. Halfway between a lord of misrule and a tuning fork" (O'Driscoll 53–54).

Stevens' title, "The House Was Quiet and the World Was Calm," seems a tacit invitation to the reader to enter the house and room and thereby share the silence and calmness in which the words being read by the occupant offer "access of perfection to the page" (*CPP* 312). The poem begins as follows:

> The house was quiet and the world was calm.
> The reader became the book; and summer night
>
> Was like the conscious being of the book.
> The house was quiet and the world was calm.
>
> The words were spoken as if there was no book,
> Except that the reader leaned above the page,
>
> Wanted to lean, wanted much most to be
> The scholar to whom his book is true, …
> (CPP 311–12)

Heaney's title first appears to be a similar beckoning: "The door was open," as if the speaker was and the readers are being invited inside. But with the second part of the title, "the house was dark," the invitation is immediately qualified, if not thwarted, and here in the very title is a swerve away from Stevens. (Note that in both poems, the first line repeats the title.) Heaney's poem begins thus:

> The door was open and the house was dark
> Wherefore I called his name, although I knew
> The answer this time would be silence

That kept me standing listening while it grew
Backwards and down and out into the street
Where as I'd entered (I remember now)

The streetlamps too were out.
I felt, for the first time there and then, a stranger,
Intruder almost, wanting to take flight ...
                                        (*Human* 81)

The poem echoes in several places Alfred Tennyson's elegy to Arthur Hallam, "In Memoriam A. H. H."[2] In section VII of that poem, Tennyson's speaker also stands alone before a darkened and empty house whose occupant (Hallam) has been removed by death:

Dark house, by which once more I stand
    Here in the long unlovely street,
    Doors, where my heart was used to beat
So quickly, waiting for a hand,

A hand that can be clasped no more ...
                        (870–71)

The poems of both Stevens and Heaney present figures in self-conscious isolation. Heaney as speaker, sensing "withdrawal" and "Emptiness" in the darkness (*Human* 81), is hauntingly alone in the absence of his deceased friend; Stevens' speaker points to a "reader" who is enveloped in the silence of his house. The words "The house was quiet" appear in the title and in lines 1, 4, and 10. Hammond's house is also identified with quietness, as the first stanza indicates: "I called his name, although I knew/The answer this time would be silence." Calm is one with darkness in both poems. (One notes that the title and first line in "'The Door Was Open and the House Was Dark'" are an unmistakable echo of the title of Heaney's second volume, called *Door into the Dark*.) The darkness is described again in line 7: "The streetlamps too were out."

The word "calm" is prominently employed in Stevens' poem—in the title with five additional recurrences. The peacefulness of the scene is reinforced by the poem's suggestion that the implied noise and lack of calmness are, on this occasion, canceled. Calmness is also implied in Heaney's poem (though the word itself is not used) in the description of his speaker as "Yet well aware that here there was no danger" (*Human* 81), no cause for alarm to displace the calmness. In section XI of Tennyson's "In Memoriam A. H. H.," the word "calm" appears in all five quatrains, beginning: "Calm is the morn without a sound,/Calm as to suit a calmer grief,/And only through the faded leaf/The chestnut pattering to the ground" (874).

In both poems, the season of "summer" is identified, mentioned three times in Stevens' poem, and it is the final word of Heaney's poem.

In short, both poems subtly create an aura of isolation—in Heaney's poem an isolation that is "not unwelcoming" (*Human* 81), in Stevens' poem one that is ostensibly consoling. The elegiac absence and emptiness that underlie Heaney's poem are replaced in Stevens' poem with the words that the reader in the poem is absorbing as he leans forward toward the book and "wanted much most to be/The scholar to whom his book is true," thereby creating what the poem calls something "like a perfection of thought" (*CPP* 312). For Stevens' reader, there is no disturbance except for the sense that the quietness and calmness may not be the usual state of affairs. His poem does not go so far as to claim an exemption for a stated "danger," one from which Heaney's speaker is now protected. I might add in passing that the word "danger" in Heaney's poem is difficult not to associate with the politics of Northern Ireland, now notably cooled at the time of Hammond's death in 2008.

For all their differences, the two poems, to whatever degree Heaney is consciously echoing Stevens, share a harmonious unity—solitude, calmness, darkness, quietude, and summer.

It must be said that very rarely does one hear the cadences and diction of Stevens in reading Heaney. Their differences as poets are, of course, greater than their similarities. Occasionally, one hears a distant echo, as in poem xliv of "Squarings," where a line, "For the nothing there—which was only what had been there" (*Opened* 362), recalls Stevens' "The Snow Man": "Nothing that is not there and the nothing that is" (*CPP* 8). Or the "spirit music" of Heaney's "The Given Note" caught from sea and air (*Opened* 36) has a faint echo with Stevens' "The Irish Cliffs of Moher," with its own "spirit's base" located in the ancient cliffs and revealing "the race of fathers: earth/And sea and air" (*CPP* 427). But these are hardly allusions or direct borrowings on Heaney's part.

Heaney did absorb Stevens, however, even if it was slow in coming—as such absorption has also been for other Irish and English readers. But it is clear that he was reading the American poet as early as the 1960s (and listening to him on a recording) even as he struggled to locate what he called the "gestalt" behind the body of work. That effort, however, has yielded salubrious results for Heaney, as Stevens came to represent a compatible spirit congenial to him as a political poet who prized aesthetic independence from partisan politics—both poets attacked for just such independence. In the book-length collection of interviews published six years before his death, Heaney drew upon the name of Stevens again. Now, instead of dismissing Stevens in comparison with Yeats, Stevens is allied with "certain great poets" of old age (even as Heaney himself was approaching the age of seventy): "But in certain great poets—Yeats, Shakespeare, Stevens, Miłosz—you sense an ongoing opening of consciousness as they age, a deepening and clarifying and even a simplifying of receptivity to what might be awaiting on the farther shore … No poet can avoid hoping for that kind of old age" (O'Driscoll 466).

Notes

1   In response to a query from the author (July 25, 2013), Heaney replied that he was aware of Stevens' title but was not consciously in dialogue with the poem in the writing of "'The Door Was Open and the House Was Dark.'"

2   I am grateful to Charles Altieri for suggesting a possible connection between Heaney's "'The Door Was Open and the House Was Dark'" and Tennyson's "In Memoriam A. H. H."

Works Cited

Brandes, Randy. "Seamus Heaney: An Interview." *Salmagundi* 80 (1988): 4–21. Print.

Brown, John. "Seamus Heaney." *In the Chair: Interviews with Poets from the North of Ireland*. Cliffs of Moher: Salmon, 2002. 75–85. Print.

Burnshaw, Stanley. "Turmoil in the Middle Ground." *New Masses* 17 (1935): 41–42. Print.

Deane, Seamus. *While Jewels Rot*. Belfast: Festival Publications, Queen's University Belfast, 1966. Print.

Heaney, Seamus. "Crediting Poetry." *Opened Ground* 413–30.

Heaney, Seamus. "Dylan the Durable? On Dylan Thomas." *The Redress of Poetry* 124–45.

Heaney, Seamus. *Electric Light*. New York: Farrar, 2001. Print.

Heaney, Seamus. "Frontiers of Writing." *The Redress of Poetry* 186–203.

Heaney, Seamus. *Human Chain*. New York: Farrar, 2010. Print.

Heaney, Seamus. *Opened Ground: Selected Poems, 1966–1996*. New York: Farrar, 1998. Print.

Heaney, Seamus. "Place, Pastness, Poems: A Triptych." *Salmagundi* 68/69 (1985–1986): 30–47. Print.

Heaney, Seamus. *Preoccupations: Selected Prose, 1968–1978.* New York: Noonday, 1980. Print.

Heaney, Seamus. *The Redress of Poetry.* New York: Noonday, 1995. Print.

Heaney, Seamus. "The Redress of Poetry." *The Redress of Poetry* 1–16.

Heaney, Seamus, and Henri Cole. "The Art of Poetry No. 75." *Paris Review* 144 (1997): 88–138. Print.

Longley, Edna. *Poetry and Posterity.* Highgreen: Bloodaxe, 2000. Print.

O'Driscoll, Dennis. *Stepping Stones: Interviews with Seamus Heaney.* New York: Farrar, 2008. Print.

Randall, James. "An Interview with Seamus Heaney." *Ploughshares* 5.3 (1979): 7–22. Print.

Stevens, Wallace. *Letters of Wallace Stevens.* Ed. Holly Stevens. Berkeley: University of California Press, 1996. Print.

Stevens, Wallace. *Wallace Stevens: Collected Poetry and Prose.* Ed. Frank Kermode and Joan Richardson. New York: Library of America, 1997. Print.

Tennyson, Alfred. *The Poems of Tennyson.* Ed. Christopher Ricks. London: Longman, 1969. Print.

9

The Not So Noble Rider: Stevens, Oppen, Glück

Edward Ragg

This chapter examines the essentially unexplored convergences between the poetics of Wallace Stevens and George Oppen, two poets whose devotees are seldom well versed in both figures, but whose writings, especially when comparing later Oppen with later Stevens, may be revealingly read together. The chapter also considers Louise Glück's responses to Stevens, in her poetry and in her influential 1994 collection of essays, *Proofs and Theories*, both of which represent Stevens ambivalently as well as, perhaps, revealing a debt to Stevensian abstraction. Abstraction is, at least, variously embraced and resisted in Glück's work, such that reading her *after* Stevens, both in terms of poetic inheritance and divergence, proves to be compelling.

Glück is a poet, volume-upon-volume, of trenchant new beginnings. Her departures partly illustrate her handling of Oppen's influence, detectable as early as *Descending Figure* (1980). But Stevens also appears in Glück's early poetry and, equally ambivalently, in her 1996 collection *Meadowlands*. For Glück struggles with, and aims to transcend, a grudging Stevensian legacy. The theme of abstraction appears most strongly in *Vita Nova* (1999) and *The Seven Ages* (2001). Not that Stevens has a monopoly on abstraction. However, how Glück writes of abstraction notably draws on a Keatsian and Stevensian inheritance of the concept and its implications.

Assessing the dynamics of Glück's career to date is now easier thanks to the appearance of her *Poems 1962–2012*. Oppen is also better served by the 2002 *New Collected Poems* than any prior edition. My point is that not only Glück's but even Oppen's work is still being digested (see Shoemaker 1 and *passim*); and, as this chapter argues, these poets' relations to Stevens, though on first glance hardly obvious, are gradually emerging. Indeed, it is by bringing Stevens, Oppen, and Glück into discussion together that this chapter aims to transcend the more formulaic grouping of writers that can characterize Modernist and Postmodernist studies. Traditionally, admirers of Oppen tend also to have absorbed Ezra Pound, William Carlos Williams, Charles Olson, Louis Zukofsky, Charles Reznikoff, and the Language Poets. Admirers of Stevens tend to have absorbed Marianne Moore, Delmore Schwartz, William Bronk, John Ashbery (and other New York School poets), Robert Lowell, Richard Howard, and James Merrill. But a far more diverse range of poets has tussled with Stevens, Oppen and Glück being no exceptions.

Superficially, therefore, Stevens and Oppen have so little in common that they rarely attract comparative discussion. George Oppen was, in a sense, the George Orwell of twentieth-century poetry. Born in 1908 in New Rochelle, New York, to a wealthy Jewish family—the Oppenheimers were gem dealers and Oppen's father later ran a chain of San Francisco movie theaters—the poet eschewed his bourgeois life and turned to poetry. The epiphany that prompted this decision arose from enrolling in a poetry course (where he met his future wife, Mary) and from hearing Carl Sandburg read in 1927—both formative experiences at the then Oregon Agricultural College, now Oregon State (Englebert and West 13).

Oppen's precocious development resulted in *Discrete Series* (1934), published by the Objectivist Press he cofounded, with a preface by Ezra Pound saluting him as "a serious craftsman" (*NCP* 4).[1] But the book appeared once Oppen had already decided to stop writing, instead committing himself to alleviating the social ills of the Depression. In 1935, he and Mary joined the American Communist Party; by 1936, he was the party's Brooklyn campaign manager. Deliberately losing his military exemption as a machinist in the Second World War, Oppen took the fight to fascism literally, serving in France with the Anti-Tank Company of the 411th Infantry Regiment of the 103rd Infantry Division. Following action in the Battle of the Bulge and subsequent wounding in Alsace, he was awarded a Purple Heart in 1945 (*NCP* xxiv–vi). Oppen's dramatic return to poetry, resulting in *The Materials* (1962)—appearing twenty-eight years after his first book—occurred only after exile in Mexico during the McCarthyite era, apparently following an inspirational dream discussed in therapy (*NCP* xxvii). Oppen the Objectivist, political agitator, soldier, exile, and subsequent author of politically resonant Cold War poems seems to have little in common with the stay-at-home abstractionist Stevens, a poet who never got over having to pay income tax (see *L* 843).

Clearly, one can elide Oppen with Reznikoff and Zukofsky, fellow cofounders of the Objectivist Press, as well as with Williams, who appears in Oppen's "Five Poems about Poetry" from *This in Which* (1965). But Oppen's return to poetry was also influenced by readings in phenomenology and ontology, spurred by Jacques Maritain and Martin Heidegger (Nicholls 30 ff.). Oppen's new poetry addressed "being" and the role of poetry in a violently changing world, thereby chiming with Stevens' own poems on these themes. As Peter Nicholls has explored, Oppen read Maritain's *Creative Intuition in Art and Poetry* (1953) in Mexico. Stevens also owned that volume, discussing it briefly with Barbara Church in early 1953: "Maritain is an extraordinary person, who fascinates me" (*L* 772). Maritain was on the committee for the transplanted Entretiens de Pontigny series of lectures at Mount Holyoke to which Stevens had contributed a decade earlier. Undoubtedly, Stevens was also known to Oppen early on, at least in print, as the Objectivist Press published Williams' *Collected Poems, 1921–31*, including Stevens' idiosyncratic preface to that volume (*CPP* 768–71).

Admittedly, Stevens' occasionally flamboyant poetic style grated on Oppen. Nicholls cites a 1963 letter in which Oppen refers dismissively to "Stevens and his little elegances" (37). However, as Nicholls further reveals, Oppen would later write, in assessing Carl Rakosi's own return to poetry in *Amulet* (1967), of "a rich, imaginative and supple rhetoric" similar to Stevens'; intriguingly, Oppen qualified this assessment by asserting Rakosi had "Not the final depth of Stevens" (qtd. in Nicholls 37).[2] Although Nicholls understandably asserts of Oppen that "Stevens's work seems, in fact, not to have occupied him much at all" (37), I would suggest Oppen was not only sufficiently familiar with Stevens to make that comparative assessment of Rakosi but was also, by the early 1960s, writing poems that coincide with Stevens' later work both thematically *and* stylistically.

Nicholls also observes how Oppen—who began his poetic career in the grip of Modernism, resuming only in its aftermaths—looked back on the American poetry of his times (including Stevens, albeit tangentially):

> one may think of one current of American poetry as deriving primarily from Williams and Pound, and a second stream as deriving from Eliot thru Auden and including—a bit remotely, Stevens, then Bronk is in the current of Eliot and Stevens.
>
> (qtd. in Nicholls 36)

Note how Oppen places Stevens "remotely," himself writing in a loose syntax emphasizing *currents* and *streams* of poetry rather than groups, camps, or categories. This perhaps illustrates Oppen's later Postmodernist leanings—although, as Nicholls argues and as Oppen's interviews reveal, this was a poet, despite or maybe because of his involvement with Objectivism, often resistant to literary camps (a trait shared with Stevens; see Shoemaker xiv–xv). Stevens also represented to Oppen a kind of exemplar, at least in how the older poet found means to support himself while writing poetry. Speaking on this subject in a 1975 interview, Oppen observed, "It is a question of class, finally. And the people we knew made every kind of solution. Williams, Stevens. Reznikoff, who planned very carefully. And also was probably a bit short on sleep" (Englebert and West 11).

But the larger point of my discussion is not to what extent Oppen read Stevens or how Oppen conceived of Stevens as a poet, but whether aspects of Oppen's poetry coincide with Stevens' and whether or not the two poets can be usefully read together. Consider the following sentence: "We cannot assert the poet's relation to reality, nor exhort him to face reality, nor do any of these desirable things, nor be sure that we are not insisting merely that he discuss only those things we are accustomed to talk about, unless we somehow manage to restore a meaning to the word." A seasoned reader of Stevens might suggest this is a Stevens letter or even an extract from *The Necessary Angel.* It is, in fact, a passage from Oppen's 1963 essay "The Mind's Own Place" (*SP* 30). Admittedly, one could argue that Oppen's position contrasts with the Stevens who writes of "reality" in his essays and lectures sometimes unquestioningly. Oppen's essay is certainly wary of "an abstract noun" (*SP* 31) that may replace the cumbersome word "reality," perhaps an indirect broadside to Stevens the abstract poetic theorizer of this very term. But Oppen's poetry of the 1960s and after clearly addresses some of the themes that captivated Stevens before him.[3]

Moreover, I want to suggest not only on a thematic but on a *stylistic* level that these poets share repetitive, incantatory dictions combining phenomenological and ontological reflections in poems that foreground the primacy of the poem and poetry as creative forces. Undeniably, Oppen is a much more visual poet than Stevens. Witness his attention to the page—Glück calls him a "master of white space" (*PT* 29)—and his radical lineation, the full force of which can be lost in reading aloud; indeed, Oppen in later life preferred not to read publicly and observed, "I feel very strongly—not as a theory or an exhortation to anybody else, but for myself—that the poem is supposed to be on the page" (Englebert and West 11). Oppen's syntax is also more demanding even than Stevens'. But Oppen's writing results in an intensely musical poetry—these visual poems scoring that music— with its *own* modes of "abstraction." Though Oppen might have resisted the term, Glück revealingly contrasts Williams and Oppen on this very theme: "Oppen has not got Williams' scampering vitality, but he seems Williams' celestial counterpart. A difference, it seems to me, is that Oppen's mind more craves abstraction" (*PT* 30).

The differences between Oppen and Stevens also help define the space Oppen creates for his later work *after* Stevens—how he compares and contrasts with Stevens (who died seven years before Oppen returned to poetry in book form) in addressing experience, Heideggerian Being, and what Maritain describes as the process in which "Things and the Self are grasped together" (30). The relationship between "Things and the Self" is a constant preoccupation of both poets. Oppen rewrites Maritain in the quotation opening *The Materials* ("*We awake in the same moment to ourselves and to things*"); his "Of Being Numerous" opens, "There are things/We live among 'and to see them/Is to know ourselves,'" while "Some San Francisco Poems" observes, "Obscurely 'things/And the self'/Prosody/Sings"—these lines coming from part 5, with its almost Stevensian title, "The Translucent Mechanics" (*NCP* 38, 163, 227).

But what happens when we compare late Stevens and late Oppen side by side? Stevens' "Note on Moonlight," from *The Rock*, opens as follows:

> The one moonlight, in the simple-colored night,
> Like a plain poet revolving in his mind
> The sameness of his various universe,
> Shines on the mere objectiveness of things.
>
> (*CPP* 449)

The lineation of lines 2 and 3 offers an Oppen-like ambiguity: Is the "one moonlight" like "a plain poet revolving in his mind"? Or is it rather, as line 3 qualifies, "Like a plain poet revolving in his mind/The sameness of his various universe," where the "sameness" and "one moonlight" are likened? Stevens carefully avoids a comma after "mind," which would have formed two distinct clauses. Thus, his lineation opens both possibilities for the simile, at least on first reading. Note also how Stevens' poetry of mind here intersects with a world that "Shines on the mere objectiveness of *things*" (emphasis added).

To be sure, the poem does not sound or look like anything Oppen would write in the 1960s. But, as we shall see, Oppen does share a repetitive diction that refracts "being" in a manner akin to Stevens' own investigations into existence and experience. As "Note on Moonlight" continues:

> It is as if being was to be observed,
> As if, among the possible purposes
> Of what one sees, the purpose that comes first,
> The surface, is the purpose to be seen, ...
>
> (*CPP* 449)

This poetic "note" is less provisional than those of "Notes Toward a Supreme Fiction" (1942). It is insistently present. Stevens favors "It is as if" rather than his more customary "It was as if"—recall "Not Ideas About the Thing But the Thing Itself" with its teasing last lines: "It was like/A new knowledge of reality" (*CPP* 452). But the present and past (or hypothetical) also blend here as the line reflects on "being" that "*was* to be observed": the "possible purposes/Of what one *sees*, the purpose that *comes* first,/The surface, is the purpose to be *seen*" (emphases added). Note also the evocative sibilance of "surfa*ce*" and "purpo*se*" that aurally unites the dilemma of the self responding to surface appearances through the lens of its own purpose or activity—its seeing self.

Such repetitions in late Stevens often conjure "the poem" or "poetry" as attentive prisms through which experience is refracted. "*The Poem as Icon*," the second part of "The Rock," opens:

> It is not enough to cover the rock with leaves.
> We must be cured of it by a cure of the ground
> Or a cure of ourselves, that is equal to a cure
>
> Of the ground, …
> …………………..
> The fiction of the leaves is the icon
>
> Of the poem, …
>
> (*CPP* 446)

In Oppen's "Semite," from *Myth of the Blaze* (1972–75), the poem shifts from considering "distances" and "the sky" to a similarly repetitive and self-reflexive idiom in which poems suddenly feature:

> the sky the low sky
>
> of poems precise
> as the low sky
>
> (*NCP* 251)

This poem also alludes to Stevens' "The Planet on the Table" in a characteristically Oppenesque maneuver where thoughts of atrocity and survival—prompted here by the Holocaust—accentuate the fragility of a domestic safety suddenly punctuated by the vitality of the poem itself:

Think

think also of the children
the guards laughing

the one pride the pride
of the warrior laughing so the hangman
comes to all dinners Aim

we tell each other the children cannot be
    alone whereupon murder

comes to our dinners poem born

of a planet the size

of a table top

(*NCP* 252)

"The Planet on the Table" marks Stevens' retrospective on his own poetic career, at least as represented by the impish Ariel: "Ariel was glad he had written his poems" (*CPP* 450). "What mattered" for Stevens' poem is that those poems bear a trace of "the planet of which they were part" (*CPP* 450). The planet on the table for Stevens is thus the poem itself, which is undeniably part of the larger planet, informed by it experientially. Oppen's poem "born/of a planet the size/of a table top" is both more minute and a potentially tragic inversion of Stevens. Stevens' planet on the table is a poem that makes its own evocative world and evokes the world of which it is part. But if Oppen's poem issues from a *planet* the size of a "table top," it is both productively and tragically small compared with the larger reality of "murder" that "comes to our dinners" (either directly or overheard on the news while eating TV dinners). Both poets countenance only a poetry that is vitally part of, or issues from, the world: *the* test of poetry's viability and credibility. Both poets recognize also how poetry has to stare down atrocity, even as it encounters the limitations of its minute powers, which are, productively and tragically, *definitive* (as the Stevens of "Esthétique du Mal" would agree). But there is an ethical trouble of scale for Oppen in his "poem born/of a planet the size/of a table top" that sits uncomfortably alongside Stevens' less imaginatively troubled, if modest, hopes for his poems in old age, at least as encountered in "The Planet on the Table."

Unlike Stevens, Oppen also elongates his repetitions, frequently reusing and rewriting lines across poems. In "To the Poets: To Make Much of Life," also from *Myth of the Blaze*, we read:

> no need to light
>
> the lamps in daylight *that passion*
> *that light within*
>
> *and without*   (the old men were dancing
>
> return
> the return of the sun)   no need to light
>
> lamps in daylight working year
> after
> year the poem
>
> discovered
>
> in the crystal
> center of the rock image
>
> and image the transparent
>
> present ...
> ....
> the fathers said we are old
> we are shrivelled
>
> come.
> (*NCP* 260)

The pressure of this poem partly issues, as in Oppen's "Semite," from an awareness of suffering communicated through the media: "we speak of the abyss/of the hungry we see their feet their tired/feet in the news" (*NCP* 260). Oppen will go on to repackage this poem in "To Make Much," from his last collection, *Primitive* (1978):

> of the world of that passion
>
> *that light within*
> *and without*   no need
>
> of lamps in daylight writing year
> after
> year the poem
>
> discovered
>
> in the crystal

center of the rock   image

and image   the transparent

present tho we speak of the abyss
of the hungry we see their feet their tired

feet in the news ...
... as in universal

storm the fathers said we are old
we are shrivelled

come

(*NCP* 271)

Admittedly, Oppen's lineation and syntax are more radical than even the Stevens of "The Man with the Blue Guitar." Oppen is also clearly more attuned to the "universal/storm" of atrocity—made particular "in the news"—than Stevens typically was in his poetry. Oppen's perhaps literary "fathers," moreover, do not obviously involve Stevens. Oppen seems to allude to the Eliot of "Preludes," with its plaintive "And then the lighting of the lamps" (23), transformed in Oppen to a redundant illumination, shedding no light on the real labor of achieving "the poem" discovered. Eliot also influences the last poem of *Primitive*, "Till Other Voices Wake Us," where Oppen reflects on "adolescence with my father/in France" and his early career as a poet inheriting Eliot's Modernism: "writing/thru the night (a young man,/Brooklyn, 1929)," creative work assisted by *necessary* lighting (*NCP* 286). The poem obviously tropes the conclusion of "Prufrock," which inspired its title, with Oppen taking solace in "a music more powerful/ than music/till other voices wake/us or we drown" (*NCP* 286). And is it to Coleridge's "Dejection: An Ode" that Oppen alludes with "that passion/*that light within/and without*" (in the later poem only partially italicized), considering Coleridge's "The passion and the life, whose fountains are within" (351)? What counts for allusion in Oppen is, I admit, slippery.

   Yet if Oppen is *not* Stevensian in the way Ashbery or Merrill sometimes were, the primacy of "the poem" and the creative repetitions conveying "being" are undoubtedly features Oppen and Stevens share (though Oppen rarely favors Stevens' taste for paronomasia). One should also not forget how Stevens can be as direct as Oppen in stressing the vitality of perception, as in the plainly titled "Looking Across the Fields and Watching the Birds Fly." This poem rejects

Stevens' prior rhetoric of "major man," but still adopts the language of "parts" from *Parts of a World*:

> Not one of the masculine myths we used to make,
> A transparency through which the swallow weaves,
> Without any form or any sense of form,
>
> What we know in what we see, what we feel in what
> We hear, what we are, beyond mystic disputation,
> ....
> And what we think, a breathing like the wind,
> A moving part of a motion, a discovery
> Part of a discovery, a change part of a change,
>
> A sharing of color and being part of it.
>
>   (*CPP* 439–40)

If Oppen might have queried Stevens' capability of "being part of it"—note the rhetorical remove in which this poem stems from "the more irritating minor ideas/Of Mr. Homburg" (*CPP* 439)—nevertheless these poets share an incantatory poetics that seeks to establish how, as Stevens has it, "The spirit comes from the body of the world" (*CPP* 440). As Oppen marvels, "The self is no mystery, the mystery is/That there is something for us to stand on," these lines coming from the incantatory "World, World—," which sounds distinctly Stevensian in its close: "The act of being, the act of being/More than oneself" (*NCP* 159).

Finally, before I turn to Glück, Oppen's poetics nails its flag to the mast of an integrity and authenticity in which every word is won (Oppen being a tireless reviser, who claimed an "inexhaustible" ear [Englebert and West 11]). As such, Oppen privileges the "honorable" over nobility, but teeters on rehabilitating Stevens' term as explored in "The Noble Rider and the Sound of Words" (1942). As part 31 of "Of Being Numerous" reads:

> Because the known and the unknown
> Touch,
>
> One witnesses—.
> It is ennobling
> If one thinks so.
>
> If to know is noble
>
> It is ennobling.
>
>   (*NCP* 182–83)

This rare instance of paronomasia ("know"/"noble," implicitly touching what is knowable) chimes with what Oppen calls, in his poem "West," "The rare poetic/ Of veracity" (*NCP* 215).[4] Such veracity was Oppen's poetic *credo*. As "Blood From the Stone" asserts, "Answer./Not invent—just answer—all/That verse attempts" (*NCP* 52). What Oppen's verse realizes is a music written *after* Stevens, at least for the reader familiar with Stevens who hears Oppen address "the center of the thing" or "the armed man/At the root of the thing" or, in his repetitions, conjures a Stevensian obsession with the here and now: "To say again: the massive heart/ Of the present" (*NCP* 112, 145, 136). Late Oppen at least *sounds* similar to late Stevens in its repetitions and themes: "River of the substance/Of the earth's curve, river of the substance/Of the sunrise, river of silt, of erosion, flowing/To no imaginable sea. But the mind rises/Into happiness, rising/Into what is there" (*NCP* 155).

***

Louise Glück writes in her essay "Invitation and Exclusion," "It never occurred to me that I wasn't going to write poetry until I read Wallace Stevens" (*PT* 113). If, for Glück, absorbing Shakespeare, Blake, Keats, Yeats, Eliot, and Pound "strengthened an existing sense of vocation," her wry candor as to Stevens is revealing: "Reading Stevens, I felt I would never write, and because I didn't want this to be true, I had to look more closely at those early experiences ... to find the source of the verdict" (*PT* 113). Glück contrasts Stevens with Eliot:

> Stevens' meditative poems are not addressed outward; they are allowed to be overheard. That is the nature of meditation: the speaker and the listener are one. But to overhear is to experience exclusion; reading Stevens, I felt myself superfluous, part of some marginal throng ... The difficulty to the reader is a function of the poem's mode, its privacy: to be allowed to follow is not to be asked along. Think ... how full Eliot is of invitations, of pleas, of questions. And of constraints.
>
> (*PT* 115)

That qualification, "constraints," is crucial. For Glück is acutely aware that the "issue is not the presence, or degree of presence, of the personal. Eliot's masks and Stevens' sublime monologist suggest parallel restraints: neither poet seeks to make of himself a recognizable figure" (*PT* 115).

Glück mainly considers here "The Idea of Order at Key West," but draws on much wider experience of Stevens. While conceding that "Unlike Eliot, Stevens is not alarmed by diversity" (*PT* 118), Glück *is* alarmed by the degree to which she feels excluded by Stevens. No doubt with Stevens in mind, she concludes ambivalently, "The poems from which I feel excluded are not poems from which I can learn. Neither are they poems I can ignore" (*PT* 123). In a revealing metaphor, she adds, "Those poems we passionately admire but never fully occupy have to be converted into tenanted space; they must be occupied to be points of departure." However, for Glück, "conversion is dogged imitation," the derivative recreation of a "monument" that may prove an "obstacle." She concludes that "the poems we write in this state are the dead products of fear and inhibition; they have no author at all" (*PT* 123). Stevens, therefore, appears to Glück a poet of debilitating "astonishments" as another essay, "Education of the Poet," observes (*PT* 9).

But what of the Stevens in Glück's poetry? And has Stevens had an unwitting influence on Glück, if not in diction then as an exemplar, however negative? In her poem "Four Dreams Concerning the Master," which features her teacher Stanley Kunitz and is reproduced in "Education of the Poet," the first dream reads:

> S. is standing in a small room, reading to himself.
> It is a privilege to see S.
> alone, in this serene environment.
> Only his hand moves, thoughtfully turning the pages.
> Then, from under the closed door, a single hazelnut
> rolls into the room, coming to rest, at length,
> at S.'s foot. With a sigh, S. closes the heavy volume
> and stares down wearily at the round nut. "Well," he says,
> "what do you want now, Stevens?"
>
> (*PT* 13)

"S.," Glück informs us, is Kunitz. The "serene environment" where he reads a "heavy volume"—recall Stevens' fondness for solitary readers in his poems—is disturbed by the seemingly incongruous "hazelnut," which is "single," unaccompanied. Kunitz closes the book once the hazelnut "comes to rest" at his foot (there is no contact between "S." and the nut). This prompts the book's closure and the weary stare downwards before that astonishing, identifying question, as if addressed to a bothersome child: "Well, what do you want now, Stevens?" Stevens was both rotund and idiosyncratic—hence perhaps, ironically, a "round nut." Or is this the bewildering "empty hazelnut," the chariot in which Mercutio places the dream-manipulating Queen Mab in *Romeo and Juliet* (Shakespeare 342)?

This dream is subtitled *The Supplicant*, but who is pleading with whom? Is it Kunitz who wants to be left alone reading (as a quasi-solitary Stevensian reader, or otherwise) or Stevens who begs for attention? The fourth dream involves Eliot, at least comparatively. Entitled *Conversation with X.*, this last part of the poem reads:

> "You," he said, "you're just like Eliot.
> You think you know everything in the world
> but you don't believe anything."
>
> (*PT* 14)

Whatever the importance of this poem for Glück, her essays *are* occasionally Stevensian. She writes, seemingly nodding to Stevens' death-of-the-gods motif in which "the great poem of the earth remains to be written" (*CPP* 730): "The impulse of our century has been to substitute earth for god as an object of reverence" (*PT* 21). She tropes the last line of "The Snow Man" in another essay, where the poet may "become, briefly, nothing that is not that work (as Stevens might have had it)" (*PT* 89). She makes a virtue of figurative and emotional *impoverishment* "unique in its capacity to renew"—that it may deliver a "passionate openness which in turn re-invests the world with meaning," similar to Stevens' renditions of productive "poverty" (*PT* 134).

To be sure, Glück is critical of Stevens, interestingly in contrast with Oppen. She celebrates these lines from Oppen's "A Language of New York": "Possible/ To use/Words provided one treat them/As enemies ... /If one captures them/ One by one proceeding/Carefully they will restore/I hope to meaning/And to sense" (*NCP* 116). Glück observes, "This is Oppen's definition of substance and integrity. This particular ideal of service to language carries with it a high valuation of communication. Very different from the service done, say, by Stevens, with his taste for rarities, his autoerotic sensuousness. Words restored ... make a language available for common use, not a hermetic patois" (*PT* 31). But does Stevens solely represent for Glück an aloof, linguistically exclusive artist, especially when one reads across her career?

"The Winged Horse" from *Vita Nova* (1999) channels the notion of abstraction as follows:

> Here is my horse Abstraction,
> silver-white, color of the page,
> of the unwritten.

Come, Abstraction,
by Will out of Demonic Ambition:
carry me lightly into the regions of the immortal.

I am weary of my other mount,
by Instinct out of Reality,
color of dust, of disappointment,
notwithstanding
the saddle that went with him
and the bronze spurs, the bit
of indestructible metal.

I am weary of the world's gifts, the world's
stipulated limits.

And I am weary of being opposed
and weary of being constantly contradicted by the material, as by
a massive wall where all I say can be
checked up on.

Then come, Abstraction,
take me where you have taken so many others,
far from here, to the void, the star pasture.

                                                                    (*Poems* 393)

The weariness and "massive wall where all I say can be/checked up on"—
monitored, written up—recall Glück's prior distaste for the "monument" or
"obstacle" in "Invitation and Exclusion." She apostrophizes large abstract
nouns, including "Abstraction" itself. Even the embodied *horse* Abstraction
has only a brief chance to be "silver-white" before representing not its body
or mane but the "color of the page" and the shadowy "unwritten." The poem
is burdened by the desire for escape from influence or worldly concerns—
those "stipulated limits"—despite the allure of the material of that "saddle,"
the "bronze spurs," and, in an Oppen-like phrase accentuating actuality,
"the bit/of indestructible metal." In fact, the notion of being "opposed" and
"constantly contradicted" by "the material"—whether poetry or the physical
world—suggests a problematic relationship between this poet and the world,
going beyond Oppen's sense of the primacy of *The Materials*, as his 1962
volume is named. Hence the desire for some Parnassian "star pasture." We
should also note Glück's awareness of Abstraction's powers to "take me where

you have taken so many others," which, if not exactly an allusion to Stevens, does accentuate the allure of this attractive "horse" and the aforementioned "pasture" to which numerous artists or other poets have been implicitly conveyed.

Stevens' "noble rider" represents "Plato's pure poetry," refracted through Coleridge; but the rider also represents a bathetic return to earth in which the "figure becomes antiquated and rustic" (*CPP* 643). It is the "emblem of a mythology" superseded, and yet, for Stevens, the figure still enables its audience to recognize the "robust poet," even if the combined figures (noble rider/poet) are not ones to which we can yield: "We cannot. We do not feel free" (*CPP* 643, 644, 645). Stevens explains how his "noble rider" requires an imagination that swings dangerously free from reality: "The imagination loses vitality as it ceases to adhere to what is real" (*CPP* 645). Other horses and riders famously populate Stevens' essay: from Verrocchio's equestrian statue of Bartolommeo Colleoni (representing a positive "nobility") to Clark Mills's statue of Andrew Jackson (a work of Coleridgean "fancy"). Stevens admits, "About nobility I cannot be sure that the decline, not to say the disappearance of nobility is anything more than a maladjustment between the imagination and reality" (*CPP* 663), a formulation that nonetheless allows the possibility that such a maladjustment may, by the early 1940s, be incorrigible.

Glück seemingly takes a lead from Stevens' equation of the imagination with nobility as facilitating "self-preservation"—that "violence from within that protects us from a violence without" (*CPP* 665). "The Winged Horse" harnesses Abstraction—despite its dangers—as a violent preserver in face of her "other mount," which emerges through "Instinct out of Reality." The poem concludes, "Bear me quickly,/Dream out of Blind Hope" (*Poems* 393), where "Dream" is likely another noun (Glück being careful not to capitalize beginnings of lines, unless they commence sentences). This dream, itself an abstraction, is meant to counter the "Blind Hope" that may be a product of "Demonic Ambition," the hope perhaps for recognition that may divert the writer from her true gifts while dangerously capitulating to "the world's gifts."

Of course, to apostrophize abstraction does not a Stevensian poem make. My point, however, is not that Glück is alluding to Stevens, but rather that she marshals abstraction in a poetry wary of influence written in light of Stevens. Glück's sense of abstraction follows a Keatsian and Stevensian notion of imaginative preservation (also consistent with the void-filling tendencies she detects in Eliot; see *PT* 20–21). In "Exalted Image," from *The Seven Ages*, the question "With what do you fill an empty life?" renders the implicit answer:

> Amorous figures, the self
> in a dream, the self
> replicated in another self, the two
> stacked together, though the arms and legs
> are always perfectly shaded
> as in an urn or bas relief.
>
> Inside, ashes of the actual life.
> Ashes, disappointment—
> (*Poems* 429)

If the ashes represent "disappointment," they recall the "dust" and "disappointment" of "The Winged Horse." Glück resurrects Keats's "Ode on a Grecian Urn," which abstractly conceives the lovers preserved in that artifact who will never know change; or, as Glück has it, "the moment/of consummate delight, of union, able to be sustained" (*Poems* 430). The male figure in her poem thus realizes in "his apparent abstraction"—one "neither distracted nor frightened"—an understanding that "restored it all." This seemingly preserves the "exalted figure of the poet, figure of the dreamer" so vital to Glück (*Poems* 430).

Where Stevens undeniably appears in her poetry is the ambivalent "Ceremony" from *Meadowlands*. This darkly humorous piece captures a domestic dispute between two first-person speakers. Challenging the charge "One thing I've always hated/about you: I hate that you refuse/to have people at the house"—with its comical dig "Flaubert/had more friends and Flaubert/was a recluse" (*Poems* 310)—the other speaker counters:

> If you're so desperate
> for precedent, try
> Stevens. Stevens
> never traveled; that doesn't mean
> he didn't know pleasure.
> (*Poems* 311)

To which the first voice responds, "Pleasure maybe but not/joy."

In the Stevens household, the precedent set was indeed to "refuse/to have people at the house," largely but not exclusively because of Elsie. Stevens *did* travel in his younger life, early professional career, and, occasionally, between New York and Connecticut; but, outside the United States, never really made it further than Canada and Cuba. Initially, it seems curious that the speaker who is accused of being a recluse and leading a habitual life—"chicken Monday, fish Tuesday"—should accuse his or her accuser of being "so desperate for precedent" (*Poems* 310-11). But the voice that suggests "try/Stevens" humorously takes the reclusive Connecticut poet as a literary precedent to imply that to act on *ceremony*, to accept the social precedent of having "to have people at the house," may itself amount to nothing more than a convention equally habitual, whether embraced or grudgingly endured.

However, just as Glück resists a Stevens whose poetry she finds habitually "exclusive," the uneasiness we feel in reading this intimate yet distant poem is also colored by the danger of taking literary precedents—Flaubert, Stevens—as literal guides about how to live, what to do (in the language of a Stevens poem; see *CPP* 102). Certainly, there is pointed irony in suggesting someone who wants to set a social precedent for entertaining should seek *this* literary solution: "try/ Stevens. Stevens." The poet's name appears twice on the same line, separated only by a full stop. Implicitly, there is no immediate communal pleasure in "trying" Stevens (not that "joy" is necessarily communal). Moreover, Glück seemingly suggests one cannot *really* "try/Stevens"—at least not exactly as one might "try" the artichokes with which the poem begins and which become a token of rejection in the first speaker's concluding dig: "When you make artichokes,/ make them for yourself" (*Poems* 311). Perhaps the point of "Ceremony" is that for the socially expansive speaker Stevens remains an acquired taste, if he can be absorbed at all, a figure who represents solitary pleasure/consumption, whether of food or literature or reflection.

There is in Glück always a sense of the poet's vocation and life intersecting, however challengingly, in poems written in light of Stevens, even if it is a poetry seeking shade from this harassing master. Considering Oppen's later work with its attention to the primacy of poetry negotiating "things/And the self"—poems written in an incantatory music that chimes with Stevens—and considering Glück, who resists Stevens while harnessing abstraction, it is clear that the currents in which poetry has been written *after* Stevens often take surprising and revealing turns. These not-so-noble riders have traversed poetic terrains that are still, to some extent, in the making—as Modernism and Postmodernism are mapped and remapped—not least in the sound of words: their daring gestures *as* sonority, allusion, lineation, narration, and repetition.

Notes

1   In parentheses throughout this chapter, Oppen's *New Collected Poems* will be abbreviated as *NCP* and his *Selected Prose, Daybooks, and Papers* as *SP*, while Glück's *Poems 1962-2012* will be shortened to *Poems* and her *Proofs and Theories* abbreviated as *PT*.

2   The Objectivist Rakosi, like Oppen, also experienced a significant silence, which no doubt captured Oppen's attention in assessing Rakosi *v.* Stevens. Marjorie Perloff has discussed Stevens' influence on Rakosi (see Perloff).

3   There are two highly ambiguous notes concerning Stevens in Stephen Cope's selections from Oppen's *Daybooks*. One entry begins, "History of art: clearly Stevens [*sic*] interest could disappear. And Williams. I do not think Rilke or Blake could disappear." However, it is unclear whether Oppen alludes to Rilke/Blake or Stevens/Williams when he then comments, "but they are part of the history of perception" (*SP* 158). Another observes in italics, "Thru Pound and Williams the young men have found a breaking of conventional forms … which in the end will leave them outside the shelter of cliche [*sic*]. And that will lead them eventually to a reappraisal of Stevens and Eliot of the Quartets. For Pound and Williams are without *intellectual* interest" (*SP* 193). Oppen's comment neither necessarily privileges Pound and Williams over Stevens and Eliot nor vice versa. But Oppen does associate Stevens with "intellectual" content, a feature coinciding with his own poetry. It may be this similarity that occasioned Oppen to resist Stevens.

4   Oppen also writes in "The Mind's Own Place," "It is possible to find a metaphor for anything, an analogue: but the image is encountered, not found; it is an account of the poet's perception, the act of perception; it is a test of sincerity, a test of conviction, the rare poetic quality of truthfulness" (*SP* 31–32).

Works Cited

Coleridge, Samuel Taylor. *Poems*. London: Dent, 1993. Print.

Eliot, T. S. *Collected Poems 1909–1962*. London: Faber, 1965. Print.

Englebert, Michel, and Michael West. "George and Mary Oppen: An Interview." *American Poetry Review* 14.4 (1985): 11–14. Print.

Glück, Louise. *Poems 1962–2012*. New York: Farrar, 2012. Print.

Glück, Louise. *Proofs and Theories: Essays on Poetry*. New York: Ecco, 1994. Print.

Maritain, Jacques. *Creative Intuition in Art and Poetry*. New York: Pantheon, 1953. Print.

Nicholls, Peter. *George Oppen and the Fate of Modernism*. Oxford: Oxford University Press, 2007. Print.

Oppen, George. *New Collected Poems*. Ed. Michael Davidson. New York: New Directions, 2002. Print.

Oppen, George. *Selected Prose, Daybooks, and Papers*. Ed. Stephen Cope. Berkeley: University of California Press, 2007. Print.

Perloff, Marjorie. "Looking for the Real Carl Rakosi: Collecteds and Selecteds." *Journal of American Studies* 30.2 (1996): 271–83. Print.

Shakespeare, William. *The Oxford Shakespeare: The Complete Works*. Ed. Stanley Wells and Gary Taylor. Oxford: Clarendon, 1988. Print.

Shoemaker, Steve, ed. *Thinking Poetics: Essays on George Oppen*. Tuscaloosa: University of Alabama Press, 2009. Print.

Stevens, Wallace. *Letters of Wallace Stevens*. Ed. Holly Stevens. Berkeley: University of California Press, 1996. Print.

Stevens, Wallace. *Wallace Stevens: Collected Poetry and Prose*. Ed. Frank Kermode and Joan Richardson. New York: Library of America, 1997. Print.

10

The Stevens Wars

Al Filreis

In the house the house is all
house and each of its authors
passing from room to room

Short eclogues as one might
say on tiptoe do not infringe
                    —Susan Howe, "118 Westerly Terrace"

Susan Howe's poem, its title bearing Wallace Stevens' suburban street address, takes us as far as one can imagine from the Stevens whom we (up through at least 1972) thought barely hid his secret French Symbolist identity and who in the poems would always apparently rather be elsewhere.[1] Collected in *The Souls of the Labadie Tract* (2007), Howe's thirty-six-page homage to Stevens appears there with an intent that bespeaks the Stevens she reveres: native to, not alienated from, an American psychic past of utopian Quietist sects, Jonathan Edwardism, and "history qua history"; dwelling upon instead of repressing a poetics that meets at "antithetical crossroads" and produces the "loose ramshackle/extract poem" rather than merely the ironic ditty that leaves its traces only as a passing early phase of Anglo-American Modernism (53).

Any consideration of what has happened to Stevens since the mid-1970s must eventually return to Howe, but for now it suffices to say something about the way "118 Westerly Terrace" culminates a general though disorganized project: many poets, including some otherwise unlike Howe, who are devoted readers of Stevens, see historical magic in the poetics of everyday life—the quiet house on a weekday evening, the reader in his chair, the large man made out of words, the sullen Old School Modern sitting at the end of his bed in the vestige of dream, the figure of capable imagination bathed in the ordinariness that can induce the quiet suburban night to rear up suddenly in "A Rabbit as King of the Ghosts." That edge space he tried to write into writing—between dawn and day as between language and being, between thinking and composing, between irony and rumination, between being here (in the poem) and being displaced—is often, in the stanzas, a description of the scene of composition that serves as the starting point for fecund flights of what Stevens in the 1940s and Stevensians from 1950 through the mid-1970s incessantly called "the imagination" (as supposedly distinct from "reality"). Radical feelings of dislocation can arise from situatedness. Dennis Barone, an experimental prose writer and poet who happens to live in West Hartford, where Stevens did, has reproduced this sense in the words and phrases he chose for his own poem "An Ordinary Evening" (2007), modeled on Stevens' great late poem of slow seriatic style, "An Ordinary Evening in New Haven" (1949). Here are some of Barone's words: "empty," "Quiet," "large," "slightly," "nothing remains," "dried out," "sits," "awaits," "Dreams," "Stretches forth," "distant," again "Slightly" (*VW* 7–8).[2] Most of the poems written by contemporary poets that overtly pay homage to Stevens comprehend a disaffected intensity—somewhat itself a typical Modernist tone—and frame and formalize it with the sheer verbal excitements of admitting into the poem traces of the domestic space in which the act of writing occurs, the latter a postmodern mode Stevens perfected a few years before John Ashbery began writing maturely and a generation before Lyn Hejinian's *My Life* disjunctively rendered the American home.

Notwithstanding these later effects, the Stevensian disaffection has been a marvel, since it tends to prohibit definitive legacy. Had such a stance not thwarted obvious influence, I suspect the field would never have become so wide open that Howe could now, after all these years of admiration, place Stevens onto the Labadie tract uncontroversially. Stevens after 1975 has been, to be sure, a going concern, yet his effect on poetics has been diffuse and nearly unidentifiable on the whole. The figure of the man in the room in the house, or striding arhythmically to the office, or sitting in the park, is itself sufficiently unfocused in an affection for mundane things—yet at once distrusts thingy poets as merely social and clings with surprising partisanship to abstraction—as to enable poetic identities across the literary-political and theoretical landscape. Reading poetry magazines, blogs, and reviews, one feels Stevens is everywhere but also nowhere. Modernist claims about locality, in, for instance, poems like "Description Without Place" and "An Ordinary Evening in New Haven," make an act much harder to follow than, say, William Carlos Williams' *Paterson*:

noncollaged, all series and no essence, abstract yet full of referential bric-a-brac, radically displaced yet apparently eschewing political position.

If Stevens can seem anything to everyone, perhaps that is as it should be—the style generative, the figurations of the poet various. I can locate the posthumous Stevens as the tragic composer (in David St. John's poem "Symphonie Tragique" [*VW* 115–18]), as the impressionistic landscape colorist (in Charles Tomlinson's "Suggestions for the Improvement of a Sunset" [*VW* 132]), as once again the man made of words (in R. S. Thomas' "Homage to Wallace Stevens" [*VW* 130–31]), as the avowed urbanist (in Lewis Turco's "An Ordinary Evening in Cleveland" [*VW* 133–35]), and as the meditative midnighter by the suburban window hearing in night's voices "All the oblique ruins of the unsaid" (in Ann Lauterbach's "Annotation," a brilliant replication of Stevens' diction [*VW* 73]). "The room behind the room," writes Lauterbach,

> Has lost its particularity, a tent
> In a field of tents.
> These are like the endings of words
> As rooms resemble the beginnings.
> (*VW* 73)

Morri Creech's Stevens leads him to a room, too—to the bed in which, in the Dantesque terza rima stanza of "The World as Meditation," Stevens imagined the subject position of Penelope sleepily and passionately imagining Ulysses' return, which she (and he—Stevens) can conjure only through a half-waking state. Creech, a formalist in the manner of Anthony Hecht (he was the first recipient of the Hecht Award) and much praised by poetic conservatives, rewrites through "The World as Meditation" Primo Levi's reminiscence of "The Canto of Ulysses" in Auschwitz, recalled from the survivor's bed back home in Turin. Stevens' Penelope awaits Ulysses, but meantime the "patient syllables" of the poem itself enable her to survive alone, just as syllabic reductions of love can console us (*CPP* 442); on the other hand, Creech's Levi dreads and needs the return of the poem of Ulysses at Auschwitz as the linguistic gesture that once saved him but now dooms him, while Stevens' fictive frame must provide the dreamy domestic bed scene (see Creech 21–22).

The Stevens in Robert Bly's heroic poem "Wallace Stevens' Letters" is a man hard to love, and *thus* beloved: "stiff and stern and almost like a hero" (*VW* 11). Stevens after Stevens is also sometimes merely an antipoetic influence to be awed, as in Richard Eberhart's verse-memory of drinking pitchers of martinis with the big poet in his habitual lunchtime inn ("At the Canoe Club"), in which the recollected "jaunty tone, a task of banter, rills/In mind, an opulence agreed upon" of such drunken two-hour repasts is found absolutely nowhere in the poetics of the homage itself (*VW* 31). (Talk about disaffection! Talk about anxiety of influence!) We also often find the businessman-poet who enjoyed a good income but then also contemplated money's strangely rich idiomatic life, as in Dana Gioia's clever synonym-generating satire called "Money," a formalist's riff on Stevens' politically indecipherable mantra "Money is a kind of poetry" (*VW* 41; *CPP* 905).

The Stevens we discern in homages and imitations ranges from the Hopperesque purveyor of hard flat American shapes and surfaces (in Tony Quagliano's "Edward Hopper's *Lighthouse at Two Lights*, 1927" [*VW* 103]) to the theorist of nothingness who makes us think with fecundity (in Jerome Sala's "A Model Summer" [*VW* 119]),[3] from the fussy middle-aged man with the tropical imagination (Lisa Steinman's "Wallace Stevens in the Tropics" [*VW* 125])[4] to the atomistic language philosopher in Michael Palmer's lyric on "Linear Inquiry" (*VW* 96). Palmer's preferred Stevens is the purveyor of logical-philosophical propositions, the deliberately unrigorous Wittgenstein of "Connoisseur of Chaos": "A. A violent order is disorder; and/B. A great disorder is an order. These/Two things are one. (Pages of illustrations.)" (*CPP* 194). Here is Palmer:

> [Let *a* be taken as ...]
> a liquid line beneath the skin
> and *b* where the blue tiles meet
> body and the body's bridge
> a seeming road here, endless ...
> (*VW* 96)

This homage is at once a philosophical investigation—that is, into the poetic language of philosophy—and a love poem, a final soliloquy with an interior paramour. Its words are the result of "the project of seeing things" in the *Ding an sich* manner of *Parts of a World* (1942), poems like "The Poems of Our Climate," "Prelude to Objects," and "Study of Two Pears." Palmer's Stevensian epistemology runs this way:

> things seen
>
> namely a hand, namely
> the logic of the hand
> holding a bell or clouded lens

the vase perched impossibly near the edge
obscuring the metal tines.

(*VW* 96)

Charles Bernstein has rewritten "Loneliness in Jersey City" (1938) as "Loneliness in Linden" (2008), reconstituting the prewar immigrant-filled American city with more direct foreboding of the coming annihilation of these people's Old Country relatives. In Stevens, "Polacks … pass in their motors/And play concertinas all night./They think that things are all right" (*CPP* 191). Bernstein does not contradict so much as point up the irony of such playfulness through another layer of irony pulling at Stevens' apparently political unconscious, Linden being a place "Where Jews do Jewish things" and "No one pretends to understand" what happens "When the fear and the hum are one" (112). Bernstein plays upon the difference/not-difference between two industrial working-class New Jersey cities, such that readers will not easily perceive the extent to which the satire is set against the ideologically savvy yet anti-Semitic Stevens; and the poem is either literally or literally *and* aesthetically "*After* Wallace Stevens" (112).

Lytle Shaw has the distilled cadences of Stevensian rhetoric in his head as Bernstein does. A devotee of Frank O'Hara who sensed that "the epistemological dilemmas that [Stevens'] work as a whole explores (of which 'The Snow Man' is one of the best examples) get replayed in a bit of an overly consistent way,"[5] Shaw has written through the utterly familiar diction and cadence of that set piece in a prose poem called "The Confessions 2" (2002), in which, as Stevens' "mind of winter" (*CPP* 8) becomes "mine of copper," the geopolitical setting changes while all rhetorical traces are followed: "One would have to have a mine of copper, and have been cold to the union's safety and wage pleas for a long while, and perhaps have amassed a cabinet of classical artifacts in a sound proof basement displayed on custom aluminum mesh grids, or have run for several city offices …" (30). As with Bernstein, the poem seems to offer an ironic reversal of Stevensian social positioning while perfectly and respectfully rhyming Stevens' rhetoric in such a way as to affirm his politics of form.

In today's Stevensian poetry, one too frequently discerns Stevens the Modernist who has gotten so completely under the later poet's skin that pure satire, for instance in Mark DeFoe's "Thirteen Ways of Eradicating Blackbirds," seems the only poetic recourse, a dead end. Here is DeFoe's seventh epigram:

Dye yourself black. Whirl about wildly, thrash,
flap, chirp, and tweet like a demented lark.

(*VW* 17)

Such parodies (I could quote a dozen) tend to riff on a single poem, quick-take attempts at posing in a particular ironic position, one abandoned as quickly as assumed. These satires convey a Stevensian manner and do not entirely lack interest, but ultimately the measure of Stevens' sustained effect is better assessed in the writing of poets who seek to contemplate *"The Whole of Harmonium"* (*L* 834), a term he used to support an insistence that his work was a single worthy but finally doubtful project, a *Cantos* under many titles, a flawed and not finally constructed edifice, a "greenhouse [that] never so badly needed paint," a "great structure ... become a minor house" (*CPP* 428). In "Thinking of Wallace Stevens," Robert Creeley, a strong poet if ever there was one, faced a predecessor whose overall aesthetic sensibility was so rhetorically overwhelming that one could not help but fall into a demotic yet abstract Stevensian vocabulary, thus "mak[ing] all acquiesce to one's preeminent premise" (*VW* 16). There is an almost Bloomian anxiety of influence affecting Creeley here, awakened frighteningly, I think, in a writer whose ample fierceness is rarely reserved for others among the poetic company and who explicitly—along with Jerome Rothenberg—despised Harold Bloom's Romantic-psychoanalytic theory of agony in the literary community. Yet here Creeley protests too much, in uncharacteristic verse: "No one can know me better than myself" (*VW* 16). Such a negatively imagined disaster of poetic selfhood is followed by meditative unrhymed couplets right out of the late Stevens, where slowness, dullness, age, and an "almost ancient proximity" (Creeley's phrase) lead to the exhilarating near-final realization that (in Stevens' formulation) "the absence of the imagination had/Itself to be imagined" (*VW* 16; *CPP* 428). Here are two of Creeley's Stevensian couplets:

> The candle flickers in the quick, shifting wind.
> It reads the weather wisely in the opened window.
>
> So it is the dullness of mind one cannot live without,
> this place returned to, this place that was never left.
>
> (*VW* 16)

When Creeley is "thinking" of this figure, he fails to choose between a languagey Stevens and a meditative Stevens, such that one never really knows what the "preeminent premise" is. Is it that linguistic identity constructs human subjectivity, that the "c" precedes both chorister and choir (to use the trope of "Not Ideas About the Thing But the Thing Itself")? Or is it that the figure in the poems is part of nature and thus, also, in that sense, a part of us—a person, a human figure operating behind the poem, writing to us in various yet wholly associated states and moods, insistently "alive" and "At a table" ("The Man with the Blue Guitar" [*CPP* 142]), telling us of a life consistently lived just at the point when we have begun to doubt such wholeness?

The poems of Stevens do not come down on one side of this question, and yet it is the question that has dominated poetics in the past three decades. The various explanatory gestures in Stevens' poems, essays, and lectures, and in memos and letters about the Supreme Fiction and other such concepts, seem of little direct help to us now. Reading across a hundred recent poems following from or inspired by him, I see that his style, reckoned in the era after which affiliation with social problems made a productive peace with process-oriented writing, functions variously but, again, inconclusively. And so again advocates of Stevens' relevance to contemporary poetics have seemed disorganized—have not for the most part felt the need to form *that* community among so many others that serve the purpose of asserting the lineage back through Modernism. It is not necessary that they break or be broken into camps. Indeed, were the Stevensian mode to function in contemporary poetics as the Poundian has from around 1950 until recently, the polarization might contradict its greatest effects. Still, the only useful function of the critic in this situation is to give some broad shape to the sides in an argument that is not being waged except here and there through skirmishes in which the antagonists can thus claim that other matters are at stake. The lack of contestation ipso facto means that one side has won the argument; the indifferent aspect of the discussion itself tends to permit the meditative, unagonistic Stevens to carry the day.

Preparing to write this chapter, I gathered together 120 poems operating in some way under the sign of Stevens; the majority are explicit responses (see Barone and Finnegan). I then forced myself to divide them into two rude yet perhaps indicative categories. The first Stevens discernible here is the ruminative poet, essentially Romantic although often cleverly dubbed "post-Romantic." The subject's pronoun can be vague—a plural "we" or a dissociative "one," sometimes the third-person personal "he" as the speaker—but is always consistent. The speaker is a poet-figure evolving over the course of poems: a modern person always on the verge of, but finally doubtful of, natural description; a Romantic situation observed at the point where subjectivity qualifies realism. For many who admire the meditative-lyric Stevens, the sensibility is post-Christian; "Sunday Morning" is a poem for starters. When biography is engaged, George Santayana's influence becomes a reference point. Additionally or alternatively, "Notes Toward a Supreme Fiction" (1942)—arguably Stevens' major programmatic poem—if read in a certain way, presents the developed idea (that in modernity the aesthetic has replaced divinity). A much later poem, "Not Ideas About the Thing" (1954), can be said to express the final subjectivist's regret as the sound of the world out there is, in the end, prelinguistic and externally real. Language is not the final thing; the thing itself is. The late sedentary poems are an allure, as power-of-imagination lyrics, such as "The World as Meditation," "Questions Are Remarks," "A Postcard from the Volcano," and "The Men That Are Falling." Poems of recollection, for instance "The Poem That Took the Place of a Mountain," are not so much deemed metapoems, poems about poetics, as Romantic high-view retrospectives of the personal landscape the poems form, a footing or purchase gained on a life observed. His effect is conservative—as a conservator of values associated traditionally with lyric. "His major poetry," wrote John Hollander—that "elegant romantic" who on Stevens' birthday in 1975 was said to have "one distinguished American predecessor: Stevens" (Davie 30)—"energetically engaged the task of preserving our cardinal nobilities from decay into trivialization and into mockeries of what they had been" ("Reinvent" 14). Stevens becomes a conservative Modernist standing against Modernist excess. If Stevens was "one of the very greatest of our poets in a century during which the loudest of assertions had started to ring false" (14), then the truth would sound in the "reverberating" lyricism of "The Creations of Sound"—verse that does not make truculent, discordant claims but rather, as that poem would have it, "eke[s] out the mind," forming the "particulars of sound" (*CPP* 275). Thus for advocates of the meditative-lyric Stevens, the key poetic unit is the line.

Distinct from all this is what might be roughly called a languaged Stevens: theoretical, serial, and nonnarrative, metapoetically radical, sometimes satirical (and *anti*narrative), always obsessive about the state of poetics, and insisting on consciousness of the compositional mode as itself a pressure inducing the poem to be composed. This Stevens offers a theory of rhetoric in which the poem does the work that the poem generally contends such a poem should or must do. The poems speak in a rhetoric *of* rhetoric while enacting rhetoric's general centrality. Stevens here is no conservator of lyric tradition, no defender against decay, trivialization, or mock. The serial or seriatic style—early in "The Man with the Blue Guitar," more maturely in "Notes," "Description Without Place," "Esthétique du Mal," "Things of August," "The Auroras of Autumn," and "An Ordinary Evening"—actually befits rather than rejects the cyclonic Modernist historical modes adopted early and briefly by Eliot, grandly and insistently by Pound, and later by Williams. The work of reading history in the post-*Pisan* cantos and in Stevens' longer poems of the mid- and late 1940s involves a surprisingly similar critical reading activity. That Stevens offers a way of understanding a particularly American kind of poetic historiography or philosophical concept of what it is to be historical is, I think, the primary cause of Howe's great devotion to him, as most clearly disclosed in "118 Westerly Terrace." Many, although not all, contemporary poets who are coming to admire the languaged Stevens—not Howe in this particular aspect; but Bernstein, yes—commence their affection with the antic, parodic, and self-parodic poems of *Harmonium* and other works in that mode that appear again, with a bit more gloom under the satire, in the mid- and especially late 1930s (e.g., "Loneliness in Jersey City," "Anything Is Beautiful if You Say It Is," and "Cuisine Bourgeoise"). This poetics is contingent but not psychological—unrevelatory. The poem is the mind in the act of finding what will suffice, but what will suffice is not mind but language. The man made out of words is words. And the words (stanzas in unconsecutive series) seem to move in their own direction.

In recent years, Stevens' long poems have been permitted the reputation of their directionlessness, but this had not always been so. In the mid-1960s, avant-garde poets who might have included Stevens in their advocacy of serial writing did not merely leave him unmentioned but believed in a conservative anti-Modernist academic conspiracy to possess the soul of the Stevensian poetic. For three minutes in the middle of Jack Spicer's second of three famous June 1965 lectures in Vancouver—this second talk was about the concept of the serial poem, and gave Spicer a platform for commending such a method arising out of the Spicer/Blaser/Duncan confabulation—a surprising discussion about Stevens interrupted the flow. An audience member asked Spicer if he considered "Notes Toward a Supreme Fiction" a serial poem. Spicer, after hesitating quite a bit, thought not: Stevens had had a plan and had stuck to it, even if he had allowed himself to wander in the middle. But, the questioner observed, Stevens at various times had said about that poem just what Spicer was now saying about the serial poem generally. "If you have a nice map," was Spicer's rejoinder, "and you want to get from here to the north tip of Vancouver Island, then it sort of isn't the same thing as if you just sail out there and don't know where you want to go, and let the wind carry you." The questioner persisted, though, asking about "The Man with the Blue Guitar." Spicer began to take the point. Stevens *did* write serially, and Spicer conceded that the poems of *Transport to Summer* might at least be considered "*edited* serial" poetry. But then a second thought and a turn toward a vague but powerful institutional rationale for Stevens' absence from such avant-garde talk: "I don't know," said Spicer after another moment.

The awful thing about Stevens is that everybody in English departments who hates poetry, which is just about everybody [laughter], loves Stevens [more laughter]. You know it really ... I liked Stevens a great deal more before I saw that ... There's just a real hatred. They always like Stevens. All of these people. The more they hate poetry [the more] they like Stevens, so although Stevens moves me I've gotten more distrustful of him.[6]

Today's much-admired meditative Stevens descends in part from the anti-Modernist academic assimilation of the Stevens whose Modernist language and epic wandering are suppressed in such a move—the move Spicer deeply distrusted. That hegemonic stream joined the faction of those in the academic poetry world who wanted their modern poets in a lineage directly running from Romanticism but did not want to engage the Modernist/anti-Modernist battle. What Spicer was doing in 1965 was expressing a willingness to cede the entire ground to such readings—an error, as at least some in Spicer's audience already understood, but one credentialed and well reasoned on the quasi-anarchic poetic left. By 1998, when Peter Gizzi transcribed, edited, and annotated Spicer's Vancouver lectures and expressed his total admiration for the Spicerian project, half the Stevens ground had been taken back. That by then the field had opened is indicated in many ways; one is surely that Gizzi, an energetic advocate of the Stevensian mode as befitting rather than blocking experimental poetics, could accommodate Spicer's Vancouver advocacy into his aesthetic world without fear of contradiction (or, for that matter, of academic co-optation or, on the contrary, of exile from the avant-garde company).

Gizzi is one of our most important contemporary Stevensian poets, yet he is adamantly nonideological about it. *Periplum and Other Poems* gathers early work from 1987 to 1992, and Stevens is everywhere, although in the background. Epigraphs from Emily Dickinson, Spicer, James Schuyler, George Oppen, Ashbery, Rainer Maria Rilke, Rosmarie Waldrop, and Keith Waldrop assert the preferred literary company and do not so much suppress the presence of Stevens as express a remnant of outmoded embarrassment (Stevens and *Dickinson?* Stevens and *Oppen?*) and a debt more pervasive than dedications can allow. The great sequence "Music for Film," written in Provincetown in August 1990, looks and sometimes reads like the Oppen of *Discrete Series* but is more interestingly Gizzi's attempt at his own "Variations on a Summer Day" (1940), floating, chartless, using weather as device for directionlessness and (momentary) lack of poetic ambition.

Some Values of Landscape and Weather (2003) is Gizzi's most Stevensian volume. Again the landscape-and-weather trope provides a means of laconic improvisation, a going which way the wind blows, a subject as a cloud, "imitation[s] of life" that can use terrestrial being as an excuse for impersonality and dislocation (11). Gizzi here is in Stevens' floating middle period: "Landscape with Boat," "Of Bright & Blue Birds & the Gala Sun," "The Search for Sound Free from Motion," "Forces, the Will & the Weather," "Debris of Life and Mind," even the dour "Yellow Afternoon." The ironic word-level sonority of "A History of the Lyric" has *Harmonium* in it, however:

> there are beetles and boojum
> specimen jars decorated
>
> with walkingsticks, water striders
> and luna moths
>
> a treatise on rotating spheres
>
> (*Some* 4)

Gizzi's whole project might be captured in that phrase: "a treatise on rotating spheres"—what Jordan Davis calls a "shorthand sublimity"[7] at the level of the line combined with a knowing engagement with the pathetic fallacy for the purpose of pushing the human to the top of abstraction and thus away from sentiment.

Artificial Heart (1998) is the book in which Gizzi came into his own poetically. Here the pronominal address is often generalized; it points to the poet (even in the first-person plural "we"), an unidentified she—as in "The Idea of Order at Key West," a muse or paramour a bit damaged over time but still ready for verse, a version of the subject: "She sang unwrapping her bandages" (45). Articles refer to general impersonal states of being ("The body remembers joy"; "The day static with stuck weeds" [45]), and a communal, funereally functioning "they" who arrive at the end of poems—Ashberyian in this sense—to bring stories that were not told in this poem but might have been told had we not done our work of telling about something else. Gizzi's "Will Call" ends:

> It was an average day.
> An arrangement of place. A state of report
>
> or a state of grace. For centuries weeds have hidden it.
> Now autumn. Silence is what we make
>
> of eyes, trees and growing vine. It pierces.
> And these are the stories they will bring in boxes.
>
> (*Artificial* 53)

The *ut pictura poesis* of "Utopia Parkway," dedicated to the New York School-affiliated poet-painter Trevor Winkfield, is written out of Stevens' poems about paintings (especially in *Parts of a World*) and his 1951 MoMA talk, "The Relations between Poetry and Painting," which in its turn had influenced O'Hara, Ashbery, Kenneth Koch, and Schuyler from the start.

There is not much doubt that Stevens' survival through the New American Poetry is owing largely to Ashbery, whose very earliest verse at Harvard could be said—only now that we can look back on it, for it would have been invisible to caretakers of the Stevens aesthetic then—to be the purest early postmodern legacy of this poet. We know that Ashbery's college friend O'Hara learned his Stevens directly from F. O. Matthiessen in the classroom; O'Hara wrote a thesis for Matthiessen on "Chocorua to Its Neighbor" (see Filreis 14). Such a choice, in an era when the Stevens taught, if he was taught at all, was "Sunday Morning"— standard lyric, post-Christian "Modernism," but really just Modernist sensibility smoothed into a Keatsian line—must have struck O'Hara's other lit teachers as odd, willfully obscure, and "contemporary": late, seriatic, post-Romantic, implicated in inexplicable ways with the pragmatic (northern New England) end of the Emersonian and Thoreauvian transcendental ethos. Ashbery's Stevens at Harvard more likely was absorbed through the remnant of the *Advocate*-affiliated salon-style (and implicitly gay) evenings of talk with donnish descendants of Santayana, the crypto-Catholic milieu Stevens himself at Harvard drank in and which helped produce his over-the-top florid, "Comedian as the Letter C" style, in which words like "green" and "blue" seem to be more on-the-grid symbols of the fertile imagination whose avatar is the Modernist ephebe the young Ashbery doubtless wanted to be when he wrote poems such as "Some Trees." Ashbery fifty years later returned to his and Stevens' alma mater to accept, modestly, the Charles Eliot Norton Chair (the same that Stevens had turned down, having summoned even more embarrassment and irritation at the invitation than Ashbery; see Richardson 300). What Ashbery said in a series of lectures there, published as *Other Traditions* (2000), provides a map back from the New York School to Stevens, even though Stevens is not the subject of any of the lectures. Ashbery was intent on saying nothing that was obvious about his forebears and favorites, but his polite insistence that a nature poet could be Modernistic (in describing *everything*—John Clare), that there were Surrealists we have forgotten (David Schubert, whom Ashbery learned to admire because Stevens did), that early Modernism needed to be rethought (Laura Riding), and that Harvard and radicalism on one hand and Modernism on the other did sometimes converge (in John Wheelwright) has helped to rewrite the story of the development of Ashbery's lifelong rueful adieu to experience, now so famous as to have become ahistorical. Recent books such as *Your Name Here* (2000) have made Stevens' importance to Ashbery's language more profound than ever. After reading all the poems in such a book, one has the impression that *this* is where Stevensian Modernism was heading all along: an occasional poem that never arrives at its occasion; conventional wisdom, rendered in idiomatic speech, which thus becomes new; the search for a supreme fiction in the way we live our days, as a parable of reality in addition to being meaningful in itself; objects, names, titles, sexy bric-a-brac, unimportant except as words and memories of old words now out of circulation; the erasure of all difference between first-, second-, and third-person address as (even) between singular and plural; and the floating indexical pronoun (the rhetorical device *polyptoton*). If the pure Stevensian verse of "Some Trees"—a perfect imitation of the Stevens love poem, with a slight homosexual inflection—marks the starting point of Stevens in the New York aesthetic a half century earlier, a minor poem like "A Postcard from Pontevedra" in *Your Name Here* clinches Stevens' relevance to contemporary postmodern poetics.

Two figures, apparently new to each other, meet under some trees, but the location cannot be located except by the measure of how far these two—are they prospective paramours? are they poet and new muse?—mark off the extent of their agreement with "the world"; greater disagreement with "the world" means the poem has moved far afield, but the two have arrived at that not-place together, "Arranging by chance/To meet" (*VW* 4). The trees have a language and tell them just to be there, to touch accidentally, as trees do. "Some Trees" veers from nature poetry, as from love poetry, as accident becomes "accent," the stresses of the words on the page, the patient syllables of lyric lines that otherwise do not make complete sense, words "put on" as on a canvas with strokes effecting painted-on leaves. "Some Trees" is pure natural artifice; its accents "seem their own defense," requiring no experimental reality check. The askew hierarchy of love's actions—first we "touch," then we "love," *then* we "explain"—expresses hope that beyond love, greater even than love, is the performance of speech (*VW* 4). Written at about the time of Stevens' "Final Soliloquy of the Interior Paramour," this is Ashbery's first such soliloquy, a poem about a direction in which the poems might move, measured by estrangement "from the world" and a new kind of affection for the disaffected Other: their accidental quality, their commitment to description without place, and their lyric elevation of explanation (poetics) above lyricism (the poem itself). "Some Trees" is a beautiful Stevensian set piece, almost didactic as such, yet formative for Ashbery in an era in which he had to contend with and maintain distinction from emergent Beat claims of natural writing, spontaneity, digression, and their own very different version of disaffection.

Yet, as I have suggested, I deem the Stevensian Ashbery of recent years more significant. A poem such as "A Postcard from Pontevedra," seeming at first to be one of those easy writes, a paratactic toss-off—chatty, demotic, randomly referential ("I was waking up/at the Maison Duck you see")—ends up embodying the problem of how we can live abstractly, aptly dislocated, yet still be of the world, how one can be a terrestrial being bearing a social language, leaving a legacy of poems that form what Stevens movingly called a planet on the table. If later generations, "picking up our bones," will never have known that the body once holding these bones together had made something—a human edifice, the built environment—then these later ones will "speak our speech and never know" that their language is unnatural, that our meaningfulness was *made* (*CPP* 128–29). The poem expressing this "Cries out a literate despair" itself; its status as lyric must console the poet-speaker with having made "A dirty house in a gutted world" that is nonetheless "Smeared" with the natural, "the gold of the opulent sun" (*CPP* 129). That is Stevens, writing about poetic legacy in the ironically titled "A Postcard from the Volcano," a little verse-message sent to us from an impossible place. It is a poem in which the speaker, despite his instincts to preserve his speech and to make a definite impact, goes along for the ride—permits the wearily observed "literate despair" to become itself the writing. The final opulence, reversing despair, is standard Stevensian Modernism: the absence of the imagination had itself to be imagined, a positive emergence at the last moment from the negative out of the realization that emptiness at least must be conceived as such. "A Postcard from Pontevedra"—an actual, yet for the poet wholly invented, seaside place—demands of Ashbery's speaker, living in this postindustrial situation, that he not know where he is situated, that it not matter, that he be deprived of a sense of place. Knowing, rather than not knowing, is generative. The speaker is dislocated, but the questions that develop out of the certainty he does not feel—certainty being an obviously inappropriate stance here—lead us to the most basic earthly song, originary sounds produced in the ultimate open-ended place (the ocean), in verse aswim at the very end of the contemporary imagination:

> I was waking up with this humming in my ears—
> sound of the sea, of a basket of nettles.

It's O.K. to ride, to not go along. I'm not sure
where Pontevedra is. If I was I'd have to ask myself

so many other questions, ones you never
taste in the brightness of your day,

though they answer me
like the risen sea.

(74)

Where the early Stevensian Ashbery set out a viable poetic program and charmingly asserted his counteraesthetics, the later Stevensian Ashbery is real. His other-worldly line-by-line logic, his antic semi-Surrealism, is of our world. We know this as we read. Later Ashbery talks of an almost imponderable contemporary social situation that, when Stevens pondered them in his time—talking and writing about war, the demise of newspapers, what we would today call "sprawl," the bodily numbness produced by modern office work, the absence of suburban street life, the new political geography caused by radio, and so on—induced a myth of disintegration about the great poet whose "personal life," and even whose essays and other prose statements, stood separate from the lush poetry. Ashbery reminds us that the poem is the life. We did not and perhaps still do not believe in Stevens' Pascagoula, his Havana, his Tehuantepec, his Oklahoma, or his Tennessee, but Ashbery's postcard from Pontevedra speaks of reality, notwithstanding (or rather because of) its devotion to the rhetoric of the unreal.

John Hollander, a poet who as a critic is keenest about Stevens' music (see Hollander, "Sound"), believes absolutely in the necessary veracity of those places. In the Frostian sense, they are discernible poetic destinations, to be (once) beheld and then excitedly recalled. It is *not* okay to ride and not go along. Hollander's 2003 book, *Picture Window*, struck reviewers and critics as a renewed case for the mode of Stevens. One critic saw in *Picture Window* that the poems' speaker "ponders our habits of perception" in the manner of Stevens and Coleridge (Seaman 1633). A reviewer noted that Stevens and Auden were in these poems, as Hollander "combines a reader-friendly alertness with intellectual sophistication"; Stevens via Hollander "develop[s] an instantly recognizable take on 'the mind's/Complicating, fragile reflectiveness.'"[8] Clearly (keeping to my rude binarism), Hollander is to the meditative post-1975 Stevens as Ashbery is to the languaged. While *Picture Window* can and probably should be read on its own terms, the late style of a poet richly and variously reexpressing an important early influence, I am tempted to read it as a lyric contribution to the literary-political battle over one still undecided aspect of Modernism's influence on the contemporary—for poetic but also canonical, theoretical, and institutional reasons, a return to Stevens as if to the point where the young Stevensian entered the field (Hollander's first book appeared in 1958) just as the New York School and more generally the New American Poets, with their paratactic, anti- and nonnarrative, postlyric, antic or unrestrained, antiformalist, and serial styles, were being summoned and consolidated, minus Hollander to be sure. *Picture Window* is to my mind the strongest instance, from the meditative/(post)-Romantic side of the Stevens Wars, of the effort to reset the program, to "ponder our habits of perception" again in a 1950s poetic, restoring the moment when the direction after Modernism was not yet clear. With a few notable exceptions, the poems of the 2003 volume could have been written in 1958, and not badly, I might add. Deliberate innocence can be a viable mask. In this narrow sense I believe the remarkable poem "Those Fields" to be a deliberately innocent rewrite of "Some Trees," as if to say: *this* is how Stevens ought to play out in our poems.

"Those Fields," in unrhymed three-stressed quatrains (like "Some Trees"), begins in a field. It is a nature poem with simple pathetic fallacies ("kindly lichens"), until we come upon the phrase "among which ..." and then the emergence of "someone" (6). This "someone then/was picking out a path/and heading for ..."—*for what?* For a destination somewhere in those fields, an object that the grammar of the lyric withholds from us by qualified language, short enjambed lines, and an accumulation of logically confusing or distancing prepositional phrases. At this point "Some Trees" and "Those Fields" are siblings operating under the sign of Stevens. But in "Those Fields" the lone reflective figure makes meaning not by "picking out a path" through relationships that happen to be right there (in *those* fields) but by remembrances of elsewhere—by waiting, through qualified Stevensian phrasing, until the Romantic revelation predictably arrives. And the peaked recollection during what is otherwise a tranquil scene is come upon at the end:

> this quickened moment
> of the wild recalled
> from early solitude,
>
> here at a late place where,
> spotted with rocks of
> fact, regathered fields
> arise in a calm room

in lamplight and its soft
shadows that give shape
to what the low sound
of *now* has come to mean.
(*Picture* 6–7)

This is late Stevens ("A Quiet Normal Life," "An Old Man Asleep," "The Plain Sense of Things," "Large Red Man Reading," "The Poem That Took the Place of a Mountain") rendered in a recalled early derivative style by a poet writing a late poem about "early solitude" made meaningful "at a late place." But whereas in "Some Trees" the two figures (poet and muse? speaker and reader? versions of the subject? two people newly in love?) "Are suddenly what the trees try/To tell us we are:/That their merely being there/Means something" (*VW* 4), the lone walker through the field in Hollander is "heading for what/can no more now be/determined than what tones/of sleep the overcast/sky had contrived to/vary its blank with," and "all certainty" has "now" been "confined to knowledge/of a remembered/red" and other colors and recalled images (6). "Some Trees" is less about a human relationship (it is not really a love poem) than the very idea of relation: two (or more), including whatever quantity the word "some" signifies, come to "mean something" in relation, the context created; merely being in relation (to nature or to selves) generates the meaning, thus accidentally in the case of poems whose words are *themselves* "Arranging by chance/To meet" in the poem's language (*VW* 4). The accents of the poem are their own defense. This is Ashbery's post-Stevens Defense of Poetry, while Hollander's "Those Fields" is a personal assertion of belatedness. Despite its insistence on "now," it has set its direction toward "what/can no more now be/determined."

If Hollander returns to the poet's house and room in order to reassess the lyric's lineage up through the present speaker, then it is a poem about poetry in that narrow sense. Susan Howe, in "118 Westerly Terrace," dwells upon the same room with an entirely different result. The room is the source of New World facticity, where "predecessors" contemplated bringing a passionately utopian sense of the quotidian.

Face to the window I had
to know what ought to be
accomplished by predecessors
in the same field of labor

> because beauty is what *is*
> What is said and what this
> *it*—it in itself insistent *is*
>   (97)

The poet's predecessors, and thus Howe's too (she sees herself in a uniquely unrendered American line that runs from Thoreau through Stevens), intone "The tone of an oldest voice" (92). They inhabit a space where the imagination is housed, a set of facts told in this almost concrete poem about the fact of living. For Howe, Stevens' obsessive dwelling upon the problem of imagination and reality is a literal *dwelling*. What happens thus in the house, in which the largest American red man is reading and writing, is that the passage—the key linguistic element of Howe's historical collage style in *Pierce-Arrow*, *The Non-Conformist's Memorial*, and elsewhere—becomes a space through which one must physically pass, on the way from sleeping to waking, bedroom to desk, imagination to reality, dawn to day. Through the literalization of the passage, Stevens' singular dedication to the life of the imagination can be grounded in New World utopianism, each word reinvested with a spirit we thought we had lost when, from "Sunday Morning" on, Stevens seemed to have declared the end of theology, and his version of post-Christian Modernism was born in *Harmonium*'s tremendous influence.

> It was the passage I always
> used at first fall of dusk so
> the thought of it hangs like
> a bright lamp in the realm
> of spirit where each word is
> consent to being or consent
> to partial being on its own
>   (98)

Belladonna Press published Howe's poem separately in 2005, and that was the year Knopf published Hollander's "Those Fields," yet how very different are the shadows cast by the domestic Stevensian lamplight. One bathes in the soft calm of a room in which an old personal intensity is recollected. The other portends a "spirit storming in blank walls" ("A Postcard from the Volcano" [*CPP* 129]) with the almost magical energy of which an American language has constituted itself.

Notes

1   The project to make Stevens French culminated in Michel Benamou's *Wallace Stevens and the Symbolist Imagination*. The current chapter is a slightly updated revision of my earlier essay of the same title published in a special issue of *boundary 2*, edited by Charles Bernstein, on "American Poetry after 1975" (36.3 [2009]: 183–202). I am grateful for the opportunity to revisit my essay here and happy to acknowledge its earlier publication.

2   In covering the field of poetic responses to Stevens since the mid-1970s, I was greatly aided by the excellent gathering edited by Dennis Barone and James Finnegan, *Visiting Wallace: Poems Inspired by the Life and Work of Wallace Stevens*, for which I wrote the foreword. All poems quoted from this anthology will be referenced by means of the abbreviation *VW*; poems not or only partly included there will be referenced separately. I list the following poems cited from *Visiting Wallace* in the order in which I discuss them in this chapter to note their original publishers: Dennis Barone, "An Ordinary Evening," *Wallace Stevens Journal* (Fall 2007); David St. John, "Symphonie Tragique," *Wallace Stevens Journal* (Spring 1993); Charles Tomlinson, "Suggestions for the Improvement of a Sunset," *Collected Poems* (Oxford University Press, 1985); R. S. Thomas, "Homage to Wallace Stevens," *Collected Later Poems, 1988–2000* (Bloodaxe, 2004); Lewis Turco, "An Ordinary Evening in Cleveland," *Fearful Pleasures: The Complete Poems, 1959–2007* (Star Cloud, 2007); Ann Lauterbach, "Annotation," *Clamor* (Penguin, 1991); Robert Bly, "Wallace Stevens' Letters," *Gratitude to Old Teachers* (BOA, 1993); Richard Eberhart, "At the Canoe Club," *Collected Poems, 1930–1976* (Oxford University Press, 1976); Dana Gioia, "Money," *The Gods of Winter* (Graywolf, 1991); Tony Quagliano, "Edward Hopper's *Lighthouse at Two Lights*, 1927," *Wallace Stevens Journal* (Spring 1993); Michael Palmer, "The Project of Linear Inquiry," *Notes for Echo Lake* (North Point, 1981); Mark DeFoe, "13 Ways of Eradicating Blackbirds," *Epoch* (Spring 1978); Robert Creeley, "Thinking of Wallace Stevens," *The Collected Poems of Robert Creeley, 1975–2005* (University of California Press, 2006); John Ashbery, "Some Trees," *The Mooring of Starting Out* (Ecco, 1997).

3   Jerome Sala's "A Model Summer" was composed in 2008 for Barone and Finnegan when they put together *Visiting Wallace* and first included there.

4   Lisa M. Steinman's "Wallace Stevens in the Tropics" was likewise first included in Barone and Finnegan's *Visiting Wallace*.

5   Cited from a web page I made some years ago that quotes from Lytle Shaw's email correspondence with me; see http://www.writing.upenn.edu/~afilreis/88v/lytle -explains.html.

6   I have transcribed these comments directly from the PennSound recording of the June 15, 1965, lecture in Vancouver: http://writing.upenn.edu/pennsound/x/

Spicer.html. Gizzi's edition is: Jack Spicer, *The House That Jack Built: The Collected Lectures of Jack Spicer.* Ed. Peter Gizzi. Hanover: Wesleyan University Press, 1998.
7   See the book jacket of *Some Values of Landscape and Weather.*
8   Anon. Rev. of John Hollander, *Picture Window. Publishers Weekly* 250.20 (2003): 67.

Works Cited

Ashbery, John. *Your Name Here.* New York: Farrar, 2000. Print.

Barone, Dennis, and James Finnegan, eds. *Visiting Wallace: Poems Inspired by the Life and Work of Wallace Stevens.* Iowa City: University of Iowa Press, 2009. Print.

Benamou, Michel. *Wallace Stevens and the Symbolist Imagination.* Princeton: Princeton University Press, 1972. Print.

Bernstein, Charles. "Loneliness in Linden." *Conjunctions* 50 (2008): 112. Print.

Creech, Morri. *Field Knowledge.* Baltimore: Waywiser, 2006. Print.

Davie, Donald. "Gifts of the Gab." *New York Review of Books.* October 2, 1975: 30–31. Print.

Filreis, Alan. *Counter-Revolution of the Word: The Conservative Attack on Modern Poetry, 1945–1960.* Chapel Hill: University of North Carolina Press, 2008. Print.

Gizzi, Peter. *Artificial Heart.* Providence: Burning Deck, 1998. Print.

Gizzi, Peter. *Some Values of Landscape and Weather.* Middletown: Wesleyan University Press, 2003. Print.

Hollander, John. *Picture Window.* 2003. New York: Knopf, 2005. Print.

Hollander, John. "The Sound of the Music of Music and Sound." *Wallace Stevens: A Celebration.* Ed. Frank Doggett and Robert Buttel. Princeton: Princeton University Press, 1980. 235–55. Print.

Hollander, John. "To Reinvent Invention: John Hollander on Wallace Stevens." *American Poet* 17 (2000): 14–15. Print.

Howe, Susan. *Souls of the Labadie Tract.* New York: New Directions, 2007. Print.

Richardson, Joan. *Wallace Stevens: The Later Years, 1923–1955.* New York: Morrow, 1988. Print.

Seaman, Donna. Rev. of John Hollander. *Picture Window. Booklist* 99.18 (2003): 1633–34. Print.

Shaw, Lytle. *The Lobe.* New York: Roof, 2002. Print.

Stevens, Wallace. *Letters of Wallace Stevens.* Ed. Holly Stevens. Berkeley: University of California Press, 1996. Print.

Stevens, Wallace. *Wallace Stevens: Collected Poetry and Prose.* Ed. Frank Kermode and Joan Richardson. New York: Library of America, 1997. Print.

11

Stevens' Musical Legacy:
"The Huge, High Harmony"

Lisa Goldfarb

"At the earliest ending of winter,/In March" (*CPP* 451), five years ago in New York, a number of poets gathered to discuss what they admire in Stevens and to identify poems of their own in which they see themselves conversing with him, poems that show the mark of Stevens' influence. "What we all do with Stevens," Matthew Rohrer mused, "is find our calling in him. There are so many Stevenses in his work" (126). Rohrer proceeded to trace his own engagement with Stevens, and, as many other poets did, he drew attention to Stevens' musicality. The repetitions in "Gubbinal" ("The world is ugly,/And the people are sad" [*CPP* 69]) became the last line in his poem "To a Croatian Poet," for the "mysteriously emotional" power that Stevens' repetitions convey (Rohrer 126). Citing "The Emperor of Ice-Cream" as Stevens' "best poem by far," Rohrer summed up, "The poem is also just a gallery of poetic music" (127). During that evening, one poet after the other similarly pointed to aspects of Stevens' musicality as a shaping spirit in their development. When Eamon Grennan read from "A Fish-Scale Sunrise," his foot tapped to the rhythm of Stevens' sentences ("Melodious skeletons, for all of last night's music/Today is today and the dancing is done" [*CPP* 130]). When Elizabeth Willis discussed Stevens' representations of snowy landscapes—from "The Snow Man" to "A Quiet Normal Life"—she summoned Stevens' musical language in her description of what snow does to the voice: "Like the damper pedal on a piano, it doesn't just soften sound but sustains it" (137). Of all the poets who spoke that evening, Maureen McLane was the most expansive in her tribute to Stevens' musicality. Her comments addressed his "flagrant linguistic play in poems like 'Bantams in Pine-Woods' or 'The Emperor of Ice-Cream'" (117) and the way "his aviary sounds forth" (118), to his more abstract music, the complex "legacy of minstrelsy" (119) that she finds in "Notes Toward a Supreme Fiction" and more broadly in his work. For McLane,

Stevens is "the poet who best exemplifies Thomas Carlyle's definition of poetry as musical thought" (118).

Given how all-encompassing Stevens' musical project is—John Hollander named it a "master trope" in 1980 (235)—it is only fitting that his poetic music looms large in poets who have come after him. It is Stevens' musical legacy that I address in this chapter, focusing on poets who themselves identify Stevens as important to their formation and practice. The chapter unfolds in three sections. In the first, I briefly review the contours of Stevens' musical narrative. Next, I work with Dennis Barone and James Finnegan's beautiful anthology, *Visiting Wallace: Poems Inspired by the Life and Work of Wallace Stevens*, to discuss some of the ways poets have tapped into various aspects of Stevens' musical practice. In a recent *Paris Review* interview with Maureen McLane, Susan Howe asserts that her "favorite twentieth-century poet is Wallace Stevens" (166). To close, in Section III, I focus on Stevens' more abstract music and speculate on the way both his pronouncements about sound and his experiments with sound have influenced a poet such as Howe, whose work we most often connect to other poetic traditions and lineages seemingly far from Stevens.

I

What is most distinctive about Stevens' musicality, and its afterlife in the work of poets who follow him, is how multidimensional his practice is: sound-play, birdsong, musical figures and structures, auditory images, all contribute to the musical universe of his verse. At the heart of Stevens' musical practice is a project to reinvent or reinvigorate modern poetic language in nearly every poem and throughout his writing life. Stevens dynamically enacts a transformation from language to "a kind of music" (Rosu 14) throughout the *Collected Poems*, and he presents us with a narrative of sorts that traces the movement from "The words of things [that] entangle and confuse" (*CPP* 33) to sounds and rhythms that contribute to a "huge, high harmony" which intermittently sounds through the volumes and punctuates his work (*CPP* 378). I lean on the word "intermittent" here, because it is important to emphasize that the tale that emerges from reading Stevens' work across poems and texts is not a linear one carrying us from "preparation" (*CPP* 128) to a final accomplished harmony or a transcendent music. Rather, this musical rejuvenation of language—Stevens' wrestling with and harnessing of the raw noise of the world (natural, human, exterior, and interior) into a poetic language "subtler than we ourselves" (*CPP* 128)—is ever-present and a process that the poet reenacts at all stages of his career. Stevens carries us into a poetic world in which, at one moment, we hear the raw noise of nature (the sound of the bucks that "went clattering" [*CPP* 3]), and, at the next, a sound that seems to promise something larger—it could be the "Rou-cou" of the dove in "Song of Fixed Accord" (*CPP* 441) or the "tink-tonk/ Of the rain in the spout" in "An Ordinary Evening in New Haven" (*CPP* 406). At times, such promises or utterances converge to produce "many majesties of sound" (*CPP* 103) that confirm and celebrate our human sense and presence in the natural world. Yet, all along the way, in early and late poems, Stevens points to the difficulty of the musical-poetic transformation that he seeks. From time to time, he describes the arc of his poetry; he continues to try to catch hold of "A mountainous music" that "always seemed/To be falling" and "to be passing away" (*CPP* 147). As he writes of the "existence of the poem" in "A Primitive Like an Orb," Stevens' music "is and it/Is not and, therefore, is. In the instant of speech,/The breadth of an accelerando moves,/Captives the being, widens—and was there" (*CPP* 378).

II

Certainly, we can hear echoes of Stevens' distinctive sound-play—the sounds of the present in "Mozart, 1935," "its hoo-hoo-hoo,/Its shoo-shoo-shoo, its ric-a-nic" (*CPP* 107)—in later poets. A few examples should, as Stevens would say, suffice. Theodore Roethke, writing the generation just after Stevens' own, composes the lighthearted "A Rouse for Stevens," parenthetically and comically "To Be Sung in a Young Poets' Saloon," a poem that pays explicit tribute to the earlier poet's sound-play, employing compound words more important for their sound than their meaning: "Wallace Stevens, what's he done?/He can play the flitter-flad;/ ... /He can plink the skitter-bum" (*VW* 110).[1] Yet, at the same time Roethke strikes sounds reminiscent of Stevens (the "hoo-hoo-hoo" etc.), he also summons many dimensions of Stevens' musicality. His "Rouse for Stevens" reminds us that musicality extends to the poet's experimenting with sounds and words other than those we hear in English. Just as Stevens incorporates French words and sounds into his verse to demonstrate that "French and English constitute a single language" (*CPP* 914), Roethke whimsically draws German into his poem: "*Wallace, Wallace, wo ist er?*" (*VW* 110). He also crucially casts the poem as a dialogue, a song that asks for our participation, summoning Stevens' idea of a poetry that engages speaker and reader in intimate conversation: the poet delineates verses for the poetic speaker (stanzas 1, 2, and 3), for the speaker and the audience (stanza 4), and for the audience alone (stanza 5). The tone is jocular throughout, yet Roethke closes the poem movingly, ending with an unambiguous answer to a question about Stevens' legacy: "Wallace Stevens—are we *for* him?/Brother, he's our father" (*VW* 110).

Although they gesture to different dimensions of Stevens' musicality, there is hardly a poet represented in *Visiting Wallace*, whether closer to Stevens' generation or contemporary, who does not evoke some aspect of Stevens' sound-play or summon his musical vocabulary. We see a poet like Dick Allen, who in "Memo from the Desk of Wallace Stevens" laces his language with a musical vocabulary reminiscent of Stevens. His speaker imagines a postcard "Luscious or smashing for/Nightmares or psalm-sings and/Scribbles of pencils" to be mailed from "beaches where/Waves look like forestry/Ghosts in their gullies that/Waltz in the shadows" (*VW* 1). In "The Hierophant of Hartford," Kurt Brown summons a Stevensian aviary, "A polychrome of swans and peacocks, owls and doves" with "Golden-eyed macaws" that "made music in the boughs" (*VW* 13). James Merrill, in his stunning poem "The Green Eye," recalls Stevens' insistent repetitions (as in "Credences of Summer"), as if the mere repetition of the word "green" could effect the imaginative transformation he seeks: "Green to the orchard as a metaphor/For contemplation," "green/Of orchard sunlight," "A mosaic of all possible greens" (*VW* 84). Even as John Berryman levels a critical eye on Stevens in his elegy "So Long? Stevens," struggling to define "something … something … not there in his flourishing art," it seems that he cannot help at the same time to summon Stevens' sound-play: "He lifted up, among the actuaries,/a grandee crow. Ah ha & he crowed good./That funny money-man./Mutter we all must as well as we can./He mutter spiffy" (*VW* 10).

Just as challenging as it is to chart the elements of Stevens' musical practice, so it is with poets coming after Stevens who extend his musical inheritance. More striking, however, than the effort to classify or tabulate poets' musical practice after Stevens is the degree to which poets gesture to the musical drama that underlies the elements which make up his musicality—that is, the extent to which they seem aware of Stevens' musical narrative in which he works to renew language that carries us from the perception of noise to sound to an intermittent harmony.

Although Stevens memorably writes, in "Two or Three Ideas," that "To see the gods dispelled in mid-air and dissolve like clouds is one of the great human experiences," he also maintains that "we shared likewise this experience of annihilation," which, he goes on to say, "left us feeling dispossessed and alone in a solitude" (*CPP* 842). Stevens' musical narrative traces the rediscovery of language and the poet's effort "to resolve life and the world in his own terms" (*CPP* 843). This narrative often begins with the poet's encounter with random noise in the world—the "clattering" bucks of "Earthy Anecdote" (*CPP* 3); "the sound of the wind" in "The Snow Man" (*CPP* 8); the "noise the motion of the waves/Made on the sea-weeds and the covered stones" in "Hibiscus on the Sleeping Shores" (*CPP* 18)—and sounds from which the poet draws to recreate "the world in his own terms" (*CPP* 843): "the immense dew of Florida" that "Brings forth hymn and hymn/From the beholder" (*CPP* 77) or the wind that seems to ache for a "syllable … In the distances of sleep" (*CPP* 77).

Fifty years after Stevens penned "Two or Three Ideas," American poets touched by him often gesture toward or evoke a similar Stevensian tale in their verse. Doug Anderson writes a moving poem in the form of a letter to his forebear, entitled "Dear Wallace":

> I begin where you leave off, that palm
> beyond which the real has not yet formed
> that place/time always raw, just grasping
> what is not quite there, the demon
> trembling in the hedge, the far thought
> running just out of range, pink foot visible
> at the entrance to the maze.
>
> (*VW* 3)

While these first lines of "Dear Wallace" take Stevens' late poem "Of Mere Being" as the starting point ("The palm at the end of the mind,/Beyond the last thought" [*CPP* 476]), his poem simultaneously evokes the starting point of Stevens' musical narrative, the point at which the speaker encounters "that place/time always raw." Anderson even uses the word "raw" twice, in fact, framing his poem with it—"time always raw" in the third line and "the raw elixir" toward its close. He may not explicitly refer to Stevens' musical vocabulary or structures, yet he evokes the bare moment when the speaker must "resolve life and the world in his own terms" (*CPP* 843) and when we feel at once the bareness of the world and the richness of its possibilities—what we might call an anticipatory musical moment (a rest before the speaker meets with the sound of the world in all its motion), the precise moment before, in Stevens' poem, "A gold-feathered bird/ Sings in the palm ... a foreign song" (*CPP* 476).

Paul Auster, in his beautiful poem "Quarry," also seems to inhabit the solitude that Stevens discusses in "Two or Three Ideas," though, at the same time, his title suggests that "this place" to which the speaker returns and from which he begins his song is a "quarry," a bountiful source out of which we build the world in our own terms. Auster, too, employs sound and musical images that carry on Stevens' musical legacy, echoing Stevens' language in "The Snow Man" (the "Nothing that is not there and the nothing that is" [*CPP* 8]): "We have been here, and we have never been here," he writes in stanza two (*VW* 5). For Auster, as for Stevens, the journey in this place is a journey in sound for sound: "For the crumbling of the earth/underfoot/is a music in itself, and to walk among these stones/is to hear nothing/but ourselves" (*VW* 5).

If Anderson's and Auster's poems seem to evoke the starting points of Stevens' musical narrative—those moments when the poet encounters the external world and seeks to find words to match the sounds of "the crumbling of the earth," expressive of ourselves and our human predicament—Peter Gizzi evokes the ways that external sound, in Stevens' work, both breaks down our notion of belonging to the physical world and opens up harmonic possibility. In "Saturday and Its Festooned Potential," Gizzi probes the familiar theme of our human relationship to the natural world, and he does so, as does Stevens, through sound. At one moment, "the notions of myth/or collective anything/is undone by wind chimes/by a gentle tink tink" (*VW* 42). And in the stanza immediately following, he evokes the moment "When the mind is opened forth/by gentle tink tink/or light speckled/and whooping in the periphery" (*VW* 42).

Gizzi's expression of such harmonic possibility—the wind chimes that at once gather and disperse our perceptions of the world—seems to emerge from or respond to Stevens' contention that whatever understanding we achieve ("the notions of myth/or collective anything"), we reach by variation; that is, we move toward a "supreme fiction" by variation, for, as Stevens writes in his letters, "the essence of poetry is change and the essence of change is that it gives pleasure" (*L* 430). Stevens composes some of his most distinctive poems in the form of musical-poetic variations, in which he sets forth a theme, or set of themes, and repeats it many times as the poem unfolds, each time in a slightly different manner. So it is in some of Stevens' most characteristic poems, both early and late: "Thirteen Ways of Looking at a Blackbird" and "Six Significant Landscapes"

(*Harmonium*); "Like Decorations" (*Ideas of Order*); "The Man with the Blue Guitar" (*The Man with the Blue Guitar*); "Variations on a Summer Day" (*Parts of a World*); "Credences of Summer" and "Notes Toward a Supreme Fiction" (*Transport to Summer*); "The Auroras of Autumn" (*The Auroras of Autumn*)—and we could name many more. Stevens' variational mode occurs both structurally, as in the outer form of the titles just mentioned, and within the workings of individual poems—that is, in the way Stevens varies particular themes, images, and words within poems.

It is not surprising, then, that subsequent poets attuned to his musical aesthetic compose poems in variation forms reminiscent of those of Stevens. Of the variation poems collected in *Visiting Wallace*, it is James Longenbach's that stands out most poignantly, thematically and formally. Longenbach takes up Stevens' question of human life after the dispelling of the gods (and the spirit of annihilation that we share) in his poem "In a World without Heaven," the title of which he borrows from Stevens' "Waving Adieu, Adieu, Adieu." Stevens begins stanza two as follows: "In a world without heaven to follow, the stops/ Would be endings, more poignant than partings, profounder,/And that would be saying farewell" (*CPP* 104). He ponders finality in a variety of ways in his poem, testing out what happens to our human consciousness after the gods have been dispelled—whether gesturally ("waving," "in the eyes," "the stops," "just to lie there still") or in terms of speech ("saying farewell," "repeating farewell," "never to say a word" [*CPP* 104]). As if he were taking inspiration from Stevens' assertion in the last stanza that "One likes to practice the thing" (*CPP* 104), Longenbach composes a poem of six cantos, in which he, too, imagines "a world without heaven to follow." In doing so, he sets forth a narrative that unfolds in the shape of a myth about the youngest of three sisters who outlives, and has been abandoned by, her mother and sisters.

"In a World without Heaven" is a complex poem, within which the speaker presents one aspect or moment in the narrative in each successive canto. Longenbach frames the tale in the present. In the first canto, we learn what the youngest sister feels, alone in the present: she "feels the winter stars receding/ As willows raise their skirts and wave good-bye" (*VW* 75); and, later, in the penultimate canto, he returns to the present to elaborate: "The youngest feels days accumulate/Like objects in the room" (*VW* 76). In the intervening cantos (2, 3, and 4), Longenbach gives us the stuff of myth (what Stevens calls "the mythology of modern death" [*CPP* 374]); "Time was," he writes in canto 2 (*VW* 75), when the youngest would hear stories that would explain finality or death.

Yet, the speaker tells us in a later canto (4): "The sisters/Didn't believe the story./ Nor did she" (*VW* 76).

More important, however, for the question of Stevens' musical legacy than Longenbach's particular narrative is the musical texture of the poem. Not only is the poem composed of variations (cantos), which disclose a back-and-forth movement between present and past reminiscent of Stevens, but the speaker advances the tale with a distinctly musical vocabulary. To express her feeling at "the winter stars receding" in canto 1, the youngest "sings herself a lullaby, mimicking/Her sisters' voices" (*VW* 75). In canto 2, when the speaker recounts the past, it is again in auditory terms: we hear that "When the youngest cried at night," she "cried harder/Than [the sisters had] cried themselves." "One night," the speaker continues in canto 3, the youngest heard "one voice/Gathering from their bodies as they wept"; "No one could listen," the speaker tells us, "For the youngest who, once they were gone,/Would have to live alone the longest time" (*VW* 76). And, in the fifth canto, to emphasize the quiet of the world without the sisters, "a world without heaven," Longenbach contrasts the "lullaby," "cries," and "voices" with a characteristic Stevensian quietness, a sound soft as "feathers":

> The youngest feels days accumulate
> Like objects in the room. Days cut and stacked
> Like wood waiting to be burnt to ash
> And swept away, ashes soft as feathers
> On the floor.
>
> (*VW* 76)

I cannot help but feel that behind Longenbach's three female figures stand Stevens' secular muses in "To the One of Fictive Music"—"Sister and mother and diviner love" (*CPP* 70), stripped of the ornaments that used to adorn the gods ("no thread/Of cloudy silver sprinkles in your gown" and "No crown is simpler than the simple hair")—a poem that calls to the poet/musician to "give back to us" the sense of our own origins (*CPP* 71). While Longenbach writes his own beautiful and moving poem, in his overall variation structure and in the musical vocabulary with which he punctuates "In a World without Heaven," even in the elaborate tale he folds into the poem to explain that this night is "only a night like any night, one more/Good-bye" (*VW* 77), he pays tribute to the elder poet, once again giving back to us, years after Stevens, "The imagination that we spurned and [still] crave" (*CPP* 71).

III

Susan Howe is a poet whom we tend to associate with the Language school, and certainly with those poets who represent a poetic lineage and experimentalism that derives more from H. D., Gertrude Stein, and William Carlos Williams than from Stevens. In a recent *Paris Review* interview, Howe confirms this lineage and identifies poets who have been important in her development, including "Stein, Williams, Spicer, Riding, Mac Low, Zukofsky, and other Objectivists" (165). She mentions T. S. Eliot and H. D. as well. However, she also says, "I'm not a hard-core Language poet," and continues, "I should insert here that my favorite twentieth-century poet is Wallace Stevens" (166). Though Stevens (like Ashbery, also important to her) "doesn't really fit into" the company of poets such as Stein, Williams, and so forth, he stands out as crucial to her development and practice (166). Howe explains further that she has a very difficult time speaking about Stevens or locating exactly what it is that continuously draws her to his poems. Of her recent lecture "Spontaneous Particulars of Sound" (the Trilling Seminar at Columbia University), Howe concedes, "I set out to give a lecture on Stevens's late work in *The Rock*, but I am so much in awe of his power—he is the father figure, if you like—that Williams and the library section of *Paterson* seemed more humanly possible to discuss, because the work is both fallible and fabulous" (167).

Again, as with Rohrer and Roethke, we meet Stevens as father figure, though this time we find Howe trying to push beyond the acknowledgment of his importance and attempting to explain. Although she says that Stevens (like Ashbery) is a poet without a huge "governing project" (in the sense of Olson or Williams), she then qualifies her statement by adding, "apart from the most important one—nobly riding the sound of words" (166). It is Stevens' understanding and practice of sound, and, more deeply, the musical narrative that underlies his work that constitutes the "governing project" ultimately kindling Howe's far more experimental sound and musical practice.

It is striking, and perhaps not altogether surprising, that Howe would have initially revisited Stevens' *The Rock* as she pondered composing her Trilling lecture, for it is in his late work that Stevens addresses the "sound of words" in ways that seem to resonate in her poetics and in her own poetry. That Stevens continues to use sound—and the ear—as a basic measure for our relation to the physical world is clear in late poems, and certainly sound-play persists in his late verse. In "The Hermitage at the Center," it is sound that unleashes the poetic meditation. Sounds awaken the poet's own compositional process and memory and give rise to a creative effort parallel to the one he finds in nature or the exterior world: "The leaves on the macadam make a noise—/ ... /Like tales that were told the day before yesterday"—and it is the "intelligible twittering" of birds which the poet hears and with which he wrestles that gives him the material for poetic thought (*CPP* 430). The "wind," too, sounds variously in late poems, and often mirrors the poet's own breath: in "Two Illustrations That the World Is What You Make of It," the wind "Seemed large and loud and high and strong" (*CPP* 436), while in "Looking Across the Fields and Watching the Birds Fly," "The same wind, rising and rising, makes a sound/Like the last muting of winter as it ends" (*CPP* 440). Yet, Stevens' sounds and musical references in late verse increasingly point to a music much less tangible than in earlier work, and most often do not culminate in the "huge, high harmony" (*CPP* 378) that the poet often seeks in the earlier verse. Stevens' musical narrative culminates in the more abstract or muted music of his late verse, a music that originates in sound and reaches toward a more irrational kind of knowledge—"unintelligible thought," as Stevens calls it in "The Hermitage at the Center" (*CPP* 430). It is this more abstract music that spurs and inspires Howe's poetic practice. Behind her more experimental poetic music, we can discern the doubleness Stevens evokes in his late poems (e.g., "To an Old Philosopher in Rome"). We can feel the figure "lured on by a syllable without any meaning" from "Prologues To What Is Possible" (*CPP* 438), we can hear "A sacred syllable rising from sacked speech" in "St. Armorer's Church from the Outside" (*CPP* 448) and grasp Howe's attempts to reach in language what Stevens calls, in "The Noble Rider and the Sound of Words," "things that do not exist without the words" (*CPP* 663), things that we wish to utter in "these—escent—issant pre-personae" (*CPP* 443).

Certainly, a first reading of Howe's poems does not readily bring Stevens' work to mind: her long poems straddle and blur the lines between poetry and prose and seem far from Stevens' tighter forms, for even his longer sequences appear in often symmetrical cantos with numbered sections (such as "Things of August"). Still, however different Howe's more open-ended forms are from Stevens' structures, her auditory and musical approach to lyric ("phonic measure is everything in poetry," she says in the *Paris Review* interview [159]) recalls Stevens in striking ways. "Poetry," she proclaims in "That This," "false in the tricks of its music, draws harmony from necessity and random play" (*That This* 24). As if she were gesturing to or describing Stevens' abstract and quiet late verse, she explains further what she seeks to reveal in poems and the solace we might find there: "sound-colored secrets, unperceivable in themselves, can act as proof against our fear of emptiness" (24–25). It is exactly these "sound-colored secrets, unperceivable in themselves," that Howe unearths in "118 Westerly Terrace," the poem she wrote in tribute to Stevens. In "118 Westerly Terrace," Howe imagines herself entering Stevens' Connecticut house, and into the "sound-colored secrets" she finds there.

Even a brief look at the opening of this poem demonstrates Howe's evocation of Stevens' late and abstract music. In the language that she uses to describe Stevens' "The Course of a Particular," in her epigraph to "118 Westerly Terrace," she evokes in this poem "what is secret, wild, double, and various in the near-at-hand" (*Souls* 74). Consider the words with which Howe invites the reader to enter the house: "In the house the house is all/house and each of its authors/passing from room to room" (77). Howe firmly positions us in place and time: we are "In the house the house is all." The spare and monosyllabic language echoes Stevens' own lean language in the late poems and approximates the gentle inaudible movement that will guide speaker and reader through the house/poem. She embeds the subject of the poem—"authors/passing"—in the only two-syllable words in the opening tercet, as if to ask us to join her as she journeys through the interior spaces of the house, as she imagines one poetic spirit encountering another. Her repetitions, much as Stevens' own—she repeats "house" three times and "room" twice—create a "doubleness," which prompts us to feel that we are doing what others have done before, that we join "each of its authors," all who have lived here, including Stevens, to feel the "sound-colored secrets, unperceivable in themselves," that are hidden there (*That This* 24–25). In the next two lines, Howe guides us as to how to read the poem, as Stevens can, too, in poems like "Credences of Summer" or "Variations on a Summer Day." What follows, she suggests, are "Short eclogues as one might/say on tiptoe" (*Souls* 77).

The poems—vignettes, variations—that comprise "118 Westerly Terrace" resemble Stevens' late great poems of variation—"Things of August," with its irregular stanza forms, comes to mind—poems that allow Stevens to "[pierce] the physical fix of things" (*CPP* 317) and, inasmuch as possible in language, to render what is impalpable, invisible, and quiet in the sounds of words. As eclogues, the stanzas in Howe's poem are short poetic vignettes, each of which expresses one aspect of her subject. Howe is careful to remind us not only of form itself ("Short eclogues") but of how we should speak, quietly—"as one might/ say on tiptoe" (*Souls* 77). Such descriptions of how to read and speak the poem punctuate the verses, as if Howe were offering us guidance as to how to move from stanza to stanza—and, analogously, from room to room (*stanza* meaning room in Italian)—along the way: it is at once a string of "eclogues," it is a "draft ode," and toward the end, the "tallest racketty poem" (77, 84, 94).

Those accustomed to Stevens' variation poems may initially find "118 Westerly Terrace" structurally rambling, without a tight design; there are no numbered sections, nor can one easily discern neat divisions as we can in Stevens' work. However, Howe's poem has an architecture that mimics its subject of the house. The stanzas range in length from two and three lines in the first half of the poem, and, in the second half, as if we were mounting the staircase onto a different floor, the stanzas are of seven, or sometimes eight, lines. Howe varies the voicing of the poem so that as we move through the stanzas/rooms, we alternately hear an omniscient speaker, the dialogue that ensues between the author who moves through the house/poem and the one who lives there, and the internal dialogue of the speaker herself. Much as Stevens guides his reader from one canto of "Variations on a Summer Day" to the next, "As a boat feels when it cuts blue water" (*CPP* 214), Howe guides hers in time and space, from twilight to sunset (*Souls* 80, 86), "Back to the doorway" (84) or "at stairhead" (109). The tone intensifies, too, in the second half of the poem, as if Howe were approximating in her voicing the meeting place of these two poetic spirits:

> Who's down there with you
> One and the selfsame giant
> Sometimes bereft in quietness
> he makes me as I meet him
> grasp his arm—Going about
> the house we enter the shade
> of a careworn masterpiece
>
> (93)

It is as if Howe, in the above lines, were calling to another poetic spirit from the top of the staircase. Her sounds render their imaginary meeting a physical one as the speaker reaches to "grasp his arm."

Most important to our musical subject in this chapter, Howe, like Stevens, integrates all manner of sound into her poem, and in great tribute to the earlier poet all sound images—random and sustained, grating and harmonious— together make up its musical texture. It is, in large part, these sound images that bring the house to life: "the/scales the dogs the boots," the "scraps of tunes/ and the scraping of chairs," and the intermittent harmonies that, at times, occur: from the "implicit/melody" early in the poem to "The tone of an oldest voice/

Still one of great multitude" to be heard in the later stanzas (*Souls* 81, 82, 81, 92). Howe's music, like that of Stevens, incorporates the random cry and the "implicit/melody" into the fabric of the poem. All sounds, for both poets, reach toward an intangible knowledge—in Howe's words, the moment in which we can feel simultaneously "Sound and stillness astir" (104).

Stevens' poems express a "disaffected intensity," Al Filreis writes, that is "a marvel, since it prevents a definitive legacy" that leaves us "everywhere and nowhere" at once (xi). Filreis maintains that this quality of being "everywhere and nowhere" (omnipresent and absent) is true of Stevens' stylistic legacy as well. One can certainly say the same about his musical legacy, because his practice is so wide-ranging and pervasive that it is nearly impossible to locate a definitive legacy. However, it is, in large part, his hard-to-pin-down virtuosity, his playfulness, his experimentation with musical images and structures and the way he incorporates every aspect of noise and sound (external, internal, inherited, nonsensical, rational, irrational)—from the most spontaneous and unexpected to the most exquisitely ordered—that constitutes his most distinctive musical influence. Stevens' sheer delight in sound—his contention in "The Noble Rider and the Sound of Words" that "above everything else, poetry is words; and that words, above everything else, are, in poetry, sounds" (*CPP* 663)—is perhaps the feature of his verse that most unifies the poems composed after him. There may be as many "Stevenses" as there are poets touched by him, yet however different they may be, they all respond and gesture to the new life that Stevens breathes into the musical-poetic analogy, a vibrancy that is palpable in the work of so many contemporary poets.

Notes

1   All poems quoted from *Visiting Wallace* will be referenced by means of the abbreviation *VW*. Theodore Roethke's poem "A Rouse for Stevens" was originally published in *The Collected Poems of Theodore Roethke* (Doubleday, 1966). I list the following poems from *Visiting Wallace* in the order in which I discuss them in this chapter to note their original publishers: Dick Allen, "Memo from the Desk of Wallace Stevens," *The Day Before: New Poems* (Sarabande, 2003); Kurt Brown, "The Hierophant of Hartford," *Redivider* (Emerson Coll., 2008); James Merrill, "The Green Eye," *Collected Poems* (Knopf, 2001); John Berryman, "Dream Song 219," *The Dream Songs* (Farrar, 1969); Paul Auster, "Quarry," *Collected Poems* (Overlook, 2004); Peter Gizzi, "Saturday and Its Festooned Potential," *The Outernationale* (Wesleyan University Press, 2007); James Longenbach, "In a World without Heaven," *Threshold* (University of Chicago Press, 1998).

Works Cited

Allen, Dick. *The Day Before: New Poems*. Louisville: Sarabande, 2003. Print.

Auster, Paul. *Collected Poems*. New York: Overlook, 2004. Print.

Barone, Dennis, and James Finnegan, eds. *Visiting Wallace: Poems Inspired by the Life and Work of Wallace Stevens*. Iowa City: University of Iowa Press, 2009. Print.

Berryman, John. *The Dream Songs*. New York: Farrar, 1969. Print.

Brown, Kurt. *Redivider*. Boston: Emerson Coll., 2008. Print.

Filreis, Alan. "Descriptions without Places." Barone and Finnegan xi–xii.

Gizzi, Peter. *The Outernationale*. Connecticut: Wesleyan University Press, 2007. Print.

Grennan, Eamon. "My Stevens: The Romantic Spiked with the Commonplace." *Wallace Stevens Journal* 35.1 (2011): 108–10. Print.

Hollander, John. "The Sound of the Music of Music and Sound." *Wallace Stevens: A Celebration*. Ed. Frank Doggett and Robert Buttel. Princeton: Princeton University Press, 1980. 235–55. Print.

Howe, Susan. *Souls of the Labadie Tract*. New York: New Directions, 2007. Print.

Howe, Susan. *Spontaneous Particulars: The Telepathy of Archives*. New York: New Directions, 2014. Print.

Howe, Susan. *That This*. New York: New Directions, 2010. Print.

Howe, Susan, and Maureen N. McLane. "The Art of Poetry No. 97." *Paris Review* 203 (2012): 144–269. Print.

Longenbach, James. *Threshold*. Chicago: University of Chicago Press, 1998. Print.

McLane, Maureen N. "My Stevens: Thinking Songs." *Wallace Stevens Journal* 35.1 (2011): 116–23. Print.

Merrill, James. *Collected Poems*. New York: Knopf, 2001. Print.

Roethke, Theodore. *The Collected Poems of Theodore Roethke*. New York: Random House, 1966. Print.

Rohrer, Matthew. "My Stevens: Father to Our Calling." *Wallace Stevens Journal* 35.1 (2011): 126–27. Print.

Rosu, Anca. *The Metaphysics of Sound in Wallace Stevens*. Tuscaloosa: University of Alabama Press, 1995. Print.

Stevens, Wallace. *Letters of Wallace Stevens*. Ed. Holly Stevens. Berkeley: University of California Press, 1996. Print.

Stevens, Wallace. *Wallace Stevens: Collected Poetry and Prose*. Ed. Frank Kermode and Joan Richardson. New York: Library of America, 1997. Print.

Willis, Elizabeth. "My Stevens: Habits and Habitations." *Wallace Stevens Journal* 35.1 (2011): 137–40. Print.

12

"Ghostlier Demarcations, Keener Sounds": Stevens, Susan Howe, and the Souls of the Labadie Tract

Joan Richardson

A "poet with faith to fling election loose across the incandescent shadows of futurity": this is how Susan Howe in her groundbreaking study, *My Emily Dickinson*, characterizes the poet, a characterization that fits *her* perhaps even more accurately (49). In *The Great Code: The Bible and Literature*, Northrop Frye describes typology as "a revolutionary form of thought and rhetoric" (101). Typology was the Congregational ministers' practice of reading the Christian Bible as fulfilling the coded promises contained in the Hebrew Scriptures. An inherited but secularized version of this imaginative power to form links across time and history informs, as I hope to demonstrate in these pages, both Wallace Stevens' saying in his "Adagia" that "Poetry is a health" (*CPP* 913) and Howe's attending throughout her work, in the manner of the most astute physician— or, better, *meta*physician—to what she calls, in *Souls of the Labadie Tract*, "the psychic past of America" (130). This aspect and her own haunting by Stevens' studious ghost is nowhere more explicit in Howe's corpus than in *Souls*.

Howe opens her text with two epigraphs. The first is from Jonathan Edwards' *Images or Shadows of Divine Things* and illustrates his noted loosening of typology's method, adapting it to read not only biblical narratives but elements of his own experience as well. The second epigraph is from Stevens' "Adagia" and reveals Howe's own habit of reading typologically—in this case, Stevens forecast by Edwards. (The attributions, with the exception of the page number indication for the "Adagia," are as they appear in Howe's text.)

The silk-worm is a remarkeable type of Christ, which when it dies yields us that of which we make such glorious clothing. Christ became a worm for our sakes,

and by his death kindled that righteousness with which believers are clothed, and thereby procured that we should be clothed with robes of glory. (Vid. Image 46. See II Sam. 5.23, 24; and Ps. 84.6: The valley of mulberry trees.)
                    —Jonathan Edwards, "Images or Shadows of Divine Things" (50)

The poet makes silk dresses out of worms.
                    —Wallace Stevens, "Adagia" (*CPP* 900)

It is to be especially remarked of this habit of reading and writing that within its practice "all mean egotism vanishes"—to adopt a phrase describing transcendence from Ralph Waldo Emerson's *Nature*—since what is being recorded is one's own voice emptied of its "I," made transparent, as it were, inscribing what Emerson elsewhere called an "irresistible dictation," a translation from one timescape into another (10, 943). Or, perhaps more precisely, what is being recorded is a response in an imaginary conversation where the ineffable calls all the shots, where "self"/ego is realized simply as a kind of transcription factor—to borrow a term from cell biology—copying, echoing the invisible, channeling "ghostlier demarcations, keener sounds" (*CPP* 106): *Read me. Copy me.* As Howe writes in *Souls of the Labadie Tract*, "while I like to think I write for the dead, I also take my life as a poet from their lips, their vocalisms, their breath" (16). What I am suggesting in these offerings is an understanding of poetry as an *over-hearing*: the lines set down, *uttered*, revealing in their reverberations and resonances the mere being of the poet as no less a scribe of the sacred, a priest of the invisible, than the prophets and apostles—albeit in the case of our later poets, with the understanding of the sacred transcending any anthropomorphic aspect to include what Stevens was more inclined to evoke as the hissing and spinning of the stars and planets, auroras and shades. This naturalized sense of the sacred is that described by William James in the second chapter of *The Varieties of Religious Experience*: "*the feelings, acts, and experiences of individual men in their solitude, so far as they apprehend themselves to stand in relation to whatever they may consider the divine*" (36; emphasis in original). In the modern instances of typological reading and writing illustrated by Stevens and Howe, the individual becomes "a remarkeable type" of the *universe*—"part or particle of God," in Emerson's phrase (10), "Part of the res itself and not about it," "sky that thinks" in Stevens' (*CPP* 404, 145). "To get at [this kind of knowing]," William James tells us, "you must go behind the foreground of existence and reach down to that curious sense of the whole residual cosmos as an everlasting presence, intimate or alien, terrible or amusing, lovable or odious, which in some degree every one possesses" (39)—though, I would add, we depend on the poets to guide us, help us recognize it, as Virgil led and helped Dante.

When, as in the case of Dante—familiar himself with complex typologies (some readers, like Edward Jabra Jurji in *Illumination in Islamic Mysticism*, even see the Tuscan poet translating into his schema a set of symbols belonging to the early *Ishraqi* school of Sufi mysticism [4–6])—when, then, as in the case of Dante and, in our moment, Stevens and Howe (and, of course, paradigmatically, James Merrill), the poet is self-conscious about the mediating/medium-like nature of poetic practice, the range of reference and/or depth of field captured in the words, lines, stanzas, and images extend their matter into spirit, into infinity. We recall Emerson in "Experience": "Spirit is matter reduced to an extreme thinness: O *so* thin!" (475; emphasis in original). And Howe in the fifth section of *Souls of the Labadie Tract*, titled "118 Westerly Terrace," where she is in most direct conversation with Stevens and renders this experience with intense perspicuity:

> I heard myself as if you
> had heard me utopically
> before reflection I heard
> you outside only inside
> sometimes only a word
> So in a particular world
> as in the spiritual world
> (96)

And William James again, in the third chapter of *Varieties* (significantly titled "The Reality of the Unseen"), describing the effect of this kind of work: "It is as if there were in the human consciousness a *sense of reality, a feeling of objective presence, a perception* of what we may call '*something there*,' more deep and more general than any of the special and particular 'senses' by which the current psychology supposes existent realities to be originally revealed" (59; emphasis in original). Howe would recognize in this account, as much as Stevens would have, what Jonathan Edwards detailed as "the sense of the heart," a sixth sense in touch with what James called the "cosmical *It*" informing "the human ontological imagination" (65, 72; emphasis in original), and composing, like Stevens in the persona of "The Man with the Blue Guitar," "A tune beyond us, yet ourselves" (*CPP* 135).

In a piece published in a 2013 issue of *Raritan*, entitled "Time's Ear: Listening the Lyric," Kenneth Gross—someone fortunate enough, like myself, to have had as mentor John Hollander, who prepared us to attend fiercely to *The Untuning*

of the Sky (the title of one of his early books, adapting a line from Dryden)—
observes in closing his essay on the "primal or elemental" way that "lyric poems
do their work":

> I am thinking of the way that the most compelling lyrics return again and again to
> the question of how a poet's words take up the world, how they translate, reorder,
> and wrench apart the world, which includes how they wrench and wrestle with
> language itself, our sense of its sounds, syntax, and history. Here we may feel the
> poem working at the limit of what can be said in words, even as it will transfigure
> its own failures of speech, its own silences. I am thinking as well of how a poem's
> language grasps those who read the poem, asking us to register impulses and
> rhythms of thought (in ourselves as well as in the poem) that are at once more
> fundamental and more strange, things that indeed may wound us, even as they
> illuminate and enchant. This way of reading helps me to frame the poem's struggle
> to find words that mark our presence in the world, that help us to think, live, and
> survive in time, making of time a gift rather than a prison, a blessing as much as a
> wound. It suggests how a lyric poem can make of what we merely hear, of something
> that comes from outside us, an endowment of our will, mind, and memory, an
> endowment banked on the force of what is merely possible, merely imagined. Such
> a claim in listening becomes a crucial aspect of what Samuel Johnson calls "the
> force of poetry ... that force which calls new powers into being, which embodies
> sentiment, and animates matter." This life of listening in the poem is something
> that may help to free us from more binding and corrosive words, even if only
> temporarily, and even if the poem also marks its own complicity with those words.
>
> (144)

Gross traces the mantic filigree of a number of poets through his essay, Stevens
among them, citing both lines from "The Course of a Particular" and Stevens'
"evocation of the story of 'The Roamer'" in "Certain Phenomena of Sound"—"one
who speaks in 'a voice taller than the redwoods,/Engaged in the most prolific
narrative,/A sound producing the things that are spoken'" (139–40). Gross does
not mention Susan Howe, but what he describes in the passage just above is as
accurate in relation to her work as it is to Stevens'. Indeed, just preceding the
"118 Westerly Terrace" section of *Souls*, Howe writes, "Today while out walking I
experience ways in which Stevens' late poem 'The Course of a Particular' locates,
rescues, and delivers what is secret, wild, double, and various in the near-at-
hand" (74). I shall return further on to elaborate these connections.

For the moment, I suspend that discussion with a *seemingly* personal experience
illustrating how words do their work—"what a great part in magic *words* have

always played," William James astutely observed in "What Pragmatism Means," the second lecture/chapter of his 1907 *Pragmatism* (509; emphasis in original). I will describe how it is that I came to listen with Ken Gross through "Time's Ear."

During the March 2014 meeting of the Renaissance Society of America in New York City, there was a special session devoted to the work of Angus Fletcher, like John Hollander another monumental figure fully attendant to time whispering through the sounds of words, and, again, someone from whom both Ken and I have learned more than we know. (It is worthwhile to note that both Hollander and Fletcher were at different moments students of I. A. Richards.) Ken gave a talk in honor of Angus; I did not, but we and a few others later shared a meal with Angus to complete the celebration. After a few days, I received an email from Ken, installed back at his home in Rochester, expressing how nourishing it had been for him to be once more in Angus' presence, listening to him think; he also sent as an attachment "something I thought you might like to read," as he put it. I wrote back saying that I would look forward to doing so but was for the present overwhelmed with meeting deadlines of one kind or another and did not expect I could get to it before the end of the term. My composing this essay, in its original version delivered as a talk at the symposium set up to prepare the current book in Antwerp in late spring 2014, was one of the items on my deadline agenda, though I had begun writing, had already wrestled down, and was quite happy with the first two pages. I was particularly pleased with having caught somewhat adequately, to my mind, the nature of the poet's voice and of poetry as an *over-hearing*. I was also pleased to claim as title "Ghostlier Demarcations, Keener Sounds," elevating these words from the abstract I had submitted to the symposium's organizers to make my pitch and set the tone.

My habit when writing is to give the best, freshest hours of the day to it, and so I prepared early one morning to return to this piece you are reading now. I opened my laptop and read through the little more than two pages I had already gotten down, thinking, as I read, about how to weave together Emerson's observation of the continuity between spirit and matter with Howe's and James's similar reflections. I located the lines from *Souls of the Labadie Tract* that I would thread through, those offered just earlier, beginning "I heard myself as if you"— feeling how very eerie they are but that I nonetheless recognized as precise in the sense they render. Then, just before adding the cadence that James's exquisite evocation of *"something there"* provides, I got up and walked around a bit before settling onto my sofa with my iPad intending just at least to download "Time's

Ear" into the *iAnnotate* app. But somehow I could not resist going on to read. At the end of Ken's fifth paragraph, I found this:

> Robert Frost writes a Shakespearean sonnet on a Miltonic theme, "Never Again Would Birds' Song Be the Same," that is shaped around the surmise of both a pre- and a postlapsarian hearing, the possibility that we might ourselves still hear surviving what the birds of Eden heard of the soft eloquence of Eve, a supplemental sound, "her tone of meaning but without the words." Wallace Stevens begins "The Course of a Particular" with the words "Today the leaves cry," inviting us to imagine in this sound, in this imagined hearing, "in the final finding of the ear," an idea of voice stripped of the ear's hunger for ghosts of divine or even human meaning, a voice in which one yet "feels the life of that which gives life as it is." It is only one instance of the poet's lifelong fascination with the act of hearing, its gifts and its wounds, his wish to apprehend in words "ghostlier demarcations, keener sounds" by which to speak of "ourselves and of our origins."
>
> (125–26)

Ken and I were writing the same essay! Its subject is, in his words, "how the poem makes a drama of the experience of our taking its words into our ears and minds, and into our mouths; … how the poem gives our hearing a voice." "Such an expanded hearing," Gross goes on to observe, "which makes available things otherwise silent, has an unsettling aspect" (126, 128). Unsettling, no kidding! Talk about *frisson*. Needless to say, I emailed Ken immediately on finishing *his* half of our joint essay, telling him that I had not been able to resist reading … and that I was at work on something called "Ghostlier Demarcations, Keener Sounds" that for all practical purposes was a continuation of "Time's Ear." It is this kind of thing, this kind of *over-hearing*, but at a much higher pitch, that goes on with poets, and most spectacularly with Susan Howe in relation to Stevens in *Souls of the Labadie Tract*. It is nothing less than a variety of secular mystic experience. As Michel de Certeau observes in *The Mystic Fable*:

> The music hoped for and heard, echoes in the body like an inner voice that one cannot specify by name but that transforms one's use of words. Whoever is "seized" or "possessed" by it begins to speak in a haunted tongue. The music, come from an unknown quarter, inaugurates a new rhythm of existence—some would say a new "breath," a new way of walking, a different "style" of life. It simultaneously captivates an attentiveness from within, disturbs the orderly flow of thought, and opens up or frees new spaces. There is no *mystics* without it. The mystic experience therefore often has the guise of a poem that we "hear" the way

we drift into dance. The body is "informed" (gets form) from what befalls it in this way, well before the intellect becomes aware.

The poem's canorous gait, then, traces out a novel path of meaning. It regulates the progress of a train of thought.

(297)

I had known for quite a long time before *Souls* appeared of Howe's particular responsiveness to Stevens' late poems, and of how she had internalized the habit of walking to cadenced revelations. (Her epigraph to "118 Westerly Terrace" is quoted from Henry James's "The Jolly Corner": "His alter ego '*walked*'—" [76].) And I knew, too, that her fascination with Jonathan Edwards equaled my own; indeed, we had spent a long afternoon together at the Beinecke Library in the spring before *Souls* appeared poring over Edwards' manuscripts and even unfolding and gently fingering the white linen bedsheet thought to have been spun by Edwards' mother, Esther Stoddard Edwards, and supposed to date from her marriage to Reverend Timothy Edwards in 1694. We also held in our palms a square fragment of azure blue damask, 1 x $1^{1/8}$ inches, believed to be from the dress worn by Sarah Pierpont on the day she married Jonathan Edwards, July 28, 1727; I could not help hearing Stevens in/as "Peter Quince": "Thinking of your blue-shadowed silk,/Is music" (*CPP* 72)—she was seventeen and he twenty-four; they would rear eleven children. (Jonathan Edwards, born in 1703, was himself one of eleven children, and the only son; his father, the Reverend Timothy, often referred to his "sixty feet of daughters.") I first came to learn about Edwards through Stevens, and he has become, like Stevens, one of my best imaginary friends. Susan Howe believes that "An Ordinary Evening in New Haven" is all about Edwards. We had often talked about and continue to talk about these things. Still, I was not at all prepared for the effect of reading her *Souls*—beginning with the epigraphs I quoted in opening this essay. Having myself stopped so often at the same places, those passages—on my finding them opening *Souls*—pierced me, my body made electric; I felt the charge illuminating—actual. I noted in my copy of *Souls*, just beneath the epigraphs, that it was so, in almost the same words I have used here. It was as though I were being seen by the text, or that the text was reading *my* soul, something that was repeated at various moments as I read through Howe's pages. This experience was of the same kind that is described as the effect of icons for attendant Byzantines and monks—still, chanting their diapasons, *being seen* by the image of Christ or the Virgin to which they pray.

While it is questionable whether Stevens would have read Edwards' *Images or Shadows of Divine Things*, he certainly knew of the theologian's catalyzing effect through the Connecticut Valley during the First Great Awakening. Indeed, the Dutch Reformed Church, with which Stevens' family was affiliated, was deeply structured by Edwards' brand of Calvinism. Susan Howe knows this territory well. Additionally, it is her angelic pointing through *Souls* that sends us back to what Stevens might have learned about Jean de Labadie. As she notes in opening the third movement of her extraordinary, palimpsest-like text—there are six movements in all: *Errand*, "Personal Narrative," "Souls of the Labadie Tract," *Errand*, "118 Westerly Terrace," and "Fragment of the Wedding Dress of Sarah Pierpont Edwards"—as she notes, then:

> I found the term "Labadist" in reference to the genealogical research of Wallace Stevens and his wife Elsie Kachel Moll Stevens during the 1940s.
>
> Jean de Labadie. His reach is through language hints; through notes and maps. In the lapse of time the pressure of others. So it's telepathic though who knows why or in what way ...
>
> (23)

Before finding references to the "Labadists" in his genealogical researches, Stevens might have come across Jean de Labadie and his complex wandering history from reading (Abbé) Henri Brémond's *Literary History of Religious Thought in France* (New York: Macmillan, 1926–36). We recall that the poet draws importantly from Brémond in his 1936 lecture "The Irrational Element in Poetry," noting, among other things, that he "elucidated a mystical motive [in the writing of poetry] and made it clear that, in his opinion, one writes poetry to find God ... [He] proposed the identity of poetry and prayer" (*CPP* 785). I found my way to Brémond's *Literary History* in the notes to Michel de Certeau's *The Mystic Fable* (304n9). Of Labadie's texts, de Certeau writes, "His texts do not make up a system. They are the effects ... of a way of experiencing space" (272). (We think of Stevens composing his poems on scraps of paper he kept in his pockets as he walked to and from his office on Asylum Avenue through Elizabeth Park and of Edwards, as Howe in *Souls* reminds us, "riding through the woods and fields of Massachusetts and Connecticut" stopping to pencil ideas on similar scraps of paper that he then "pinned ... on his clothing, fixing in his mind an association between the location of the paper and the particular insight" [9].) Labadie's writings, de Certeau continues,

> form the strange, fantastic punctuation of a landscape progressively emptied of the real, which they reject as they discover it; they are filled with the extraordinary

they project without ever finding it. Each time, they construct a land of fiction relative to a lacking institution … They are fragments of the framework of an autobiography that has no text proper. Each fragment appears only to say: the "I" is no longer here … This account, proliferating on thresholds, relates events that, in various circumstances, are always falls avoided by miracle. [The poet makes (blue-shadowed damask) silk dresses out of worms.] But each text, fixed at the present moment, like an ec-stasy, forgetful of the preceding ones, unaware of those to come, taken up with an imminent fall and grace, is also a variant of "this cannot last." In this staccato form, all the texts taken together repeat an almost abstract form of the spatial experience …

(272–73)

"Ariel was glad he had written his poems./ … /His self and the sun were one/And his poems, although makings of his self,/Were no less makings of the sun" (*CPP* 450). De Certeau could just as easily have been writing of Stevens, or of Howe in, as she describes early on in *Souls*, "a vocalized wilderness format of slippage and misshapen dream projection" (17–18). (I am convinced that Howe knows de Certeau's text, though we have not discussed it.) In any case, we recall in this context, as well, from James Longenbach's review of Stevens' *Selected Poems* (2009), the following:

Stevens stands simultaneously among the most worldly and the most otherworldly of American poets, and it is paradoxically through his otherworldliness—through poems whose plain-spoken diction feels spooky— that his respect for the actual world is registered … [His] tone … make[s] small means feel magical.

(n. pag.)

The "spooky" feeling of Stevens' diction derives, as it does for Howe, from how profoundly he knew himself, as a poet, to be "Made Out of Words" (*CPP* 309), and knowing/experiencing the role of poet to be amanuensis to *their* life, to them as incarnations of spirit, with all the force of creation shaping them—"And the Word was made flesh."

I close with another personal experience of how lines, phrases, titles from "some saltier well/Within" (*CPP* 10)—these incarnations of spirit—up-pour to lead us by the hand, as it were, back to them. (In this I am reminded, too, of Ludwig Wittgenstein's ambition to lead words back home from their metaphysical to their ordinary use, especially in the context of Stevens' aspiration: "For myself, the inaccessible jewel is the normal and all of life, in poetry, is the difficult pursuit of just that" [letter to Henry Church, January 21, 1946 (*L* 521), and part of Susan Howe's *Errand* (Envoi) to "118 Westerly Terrace" (74)].)

It was the very end of fall, approaching my birthday and the solstice, with the rather extraordinary evening of New York City light in that season into deep violet and cold blue, when I thought or, more, *felt* that this was the light into which I was born, the light remembered from first being, as I got up from my worktable to begin moving around the room to light lamps. I had been working on the Stevens chapter of *A Natural History of Pragmatism* (2007) and so had his *Collected Poetry & Prose* at hand. I picked the volume up. About to light the first lamp, looking out again at the winter sky—not wanting to disturb its severe beauty—I let the book fall open and turning my eyes down, read:

> Light the first light of evening, as in a room
> In which we rest ...
> ....
>
> Out of this same light, out of the central mind,
> We make a dwelling in the evening air,
> In which being there together is enough.
>
> (*CPP* 444)

I read through all the lines of the poem, "Final Soliloquy of the Interior Paramour," of course, but refrain here from transcribing them all to avoid copyright disputes. I trust readers who do not know the poem will take down their Stevens volumes to get a fuller sense of how, through the highest forms of poetry, "We feel the obscurity of an order, a whole,/A knowledge, that which arranged the rendezvous" (*CPP* 444), and perhaps they will feel a *frisson*.

Works Cited

Certeau, Michel de. *The Mystic Fable. Volume One: The Sixteenth and Seventeenth Centuries*. Trans. Michael B. Smith. Chicago: University of Chicago Press, 1992. Print.

Edwards, Jonathan. *Images or Shadows of Divine Things*. Ed. Perry Miller. New Haven: Yale University Press, 1948. Print.

Emerson, Ralph Waldo. *Ralph Waldo Emerson: Essays and Lectures*. Ed. Joel Porte. New York: Library of America, 1983. Print.

Frye, Northrop. *The Great Code: The Bible and Literature*. New York: Harcourt, 1982. Print.

Gross, Kenneth. "Time's Ear: Listening the Lyric." *Raritan: A Quarterly Review* 32.4 (2013): 123–44. Print.

Howe, Susan. *My Emily Dickinson*. 1985. New York: New Directions, 2007. Print.

Howe, Susan. *Souls of the Labadie Tract*. New York: New Directions, 2007. Print.

James, William. *William James: Writings 1902–1910*. Ed. Bruce Kuklick. New York: Library of America, 1987. Print.

Jurji, Edward Jabra. *Illumination in Islamic Mysticism*. Princeton: Princeton University Press, 1938. Print.

Longenbach, James. "A Music of Austerity: The Poetry of Wallace Stevens." *Nation*. August 26, 2009. December 20, 2015. Web.

Stevens, Wallace. *Letters of Wallace Stevens*. Ed. Holly Stevens. Berkeley: University of California Press, 1996. Print.

Stevens, Wallace. *Wallace Stevens: Collected Poetry and Prose*. Ed. Frank Kermode and Joan Richardson. New York: Library of America, 1997. Print.

13

How John Ashbery Modified Stevens' Uses of "As"

Charles Altieri

To launch my contribution, I am going to tell a very condensed and abstract story about the recent history of poetics in the West. There will be many omissions and almost no evidence, since my story is only a prelude to developing what I see as John Ashbery's view of Wallace Stevens' poetic accomplishment. I persist in this enterprise because I think I can carve poetics at its joints, where the greatest pressure is experienced, to suture constitutive concepts capable of providing rationales for large-scale agreements on the roles poetry has to play. And I do so not to develop arguments about these concepts as such but to indicate how some poets can confront the pressures created by the need to believe that their own practices are worth committing to.

Classical, rhetorical poetics had—and should have—a great deal of power. Its primary question was how poetry could both delight and instruct. Its basic answer was that poetry consisted in rhetorical performances that modified public modes of speaking in two ways. Emphasis was on how the maker dealt with somewhat private or domestic emotions rather than on the capacity of the speaker to produce identifications with modes of ethos directly representing the community. The primary source of delight, then, was in how poets deployed their craft. But the stress on making also performed an important public function because it produced a different kind of persuasion: not persuasion by argument but persuasion by invention could render particular situations morally and culturally exemplary. Imaginative writers produced intricate possibilities for identifying with characters and afforded a sense of magnitude for the concrete examples they chose. Poetry was primarily a social relationship between what authors could project as compelling engagements with imaginative worlds and how readers could retain the openness necessary to try out these efforts at persuasion by identification and projection.

This poetics could not provide two values that became especially important during the Enlightenment. A poetics based on rhetorical performance can reinforce religion but it cannot direct experience in such a way as to provide moments charged by a sense of discovery about the abiding order of things. Classical poetry could not make enchantment something that carried metaphysical weight apart from religious contexts. Nor could it produce a sense that reading sustained any kind of freedom—of reader from author (since the focus was on how the reader might bind the self to the author's world) or of the individual reader from bondage to a community (largely because there was no distinctive ontological ground in this art on which individual freedom might be nourished by responding to exemplary authorial performances).

So with the waning of doctrinal religion and the cultivation of individual freedom as a political ideal, poetics had to change. The most influential change took place by means of the cultural path from Immanuel Kant and Friedrich Schiller to Modernist writers and painters, with a few variations along the way. In this dispensation, genius gives the rule to nature, so that genius acquired the power to engage and elaborate the domain of the numinous without the sanction of religion. One could directly experience the sense of value leading one to put the world together in an imagined world. Then, because the reader's task was to compose a world under the guidance of the text, readers could claim that reading afforded distinctive powers of self-consciousness as one observed oneself putting together a world. Readers could see themselves free to encounter nature afresh because the experience of reading managed to embody reflective interests and powers that were not given by or sanctioned through society. Intensity of encounter became the primary vehicle for enchantment. And this intensity transformed the enchantment from depending on social relations between authors and audiences to a dependency on how aspects of an abiding world could be valued within the individual experience. The reader's experience seemed to offer access to an abiding sense of the numinous within the natural world that organized religion could only rhetoricize about. But this difference from any dependence on the doctrinal depended on a sense that objectivity had to be realized at each instant by and for individual self-consciousness.

In short, among the artistic children of the French Revolution was the emergence of a possible new expressive aesthetic capable of realizing the numinous in our experiences and of cultivating dialectical powers for self-consciousness, two affordances that were inextricable from one another.

There are many variants of this expressive aesthetic. But they all seem to work on the following three principles: (1) making art is not representing a situation but making present a force in the world; (2) this force has numinous power because it holds out the promise of unifying the subjective energies that go into discovery and the energies within nature or social scenes that had hitherto been inchoate or not realized with sufficient intensity or clarity; and (3) the effect of this making present is a freeing of the reader to align self-consciousness with the activity of valuing what the world could seem to become in the individual experience of reading. For all three principles, alignment with the author was far less important than alignment with what charged the experience with intensity and so made it a form of enchantment within the real world.

Post-Enlightenment poetics could stress two particular powers that could make these ideals attainable. First, it could stress the act of making as something approaching visionary states of consciousness. Art was not just craft; it was a process of realization objectified by distinctive attitudes toward image and metaphor. Image was no longer the rhetorical manipulation of sensuous material in order to make texts vivid and produce *energeia*. Instead, it became the achievement of showing how writing could realize objective conditions while simultaneously making visible the constructive energies that demonstrated how the subject's emotional drives were inseparable from those objective conditions. And metaphor took on similar powers. It was no longer primarily a rhetorical device to enhance persuasion by encouraging participation in the angle by which authors developed their perspectives. Rather, it became a fusion of passion and perception, opening onto numinous forces captured in the text.

One might elaborate the new theory of the image through Ezra Pound's prose. And one could turn to William Butler Yeats for powerful versions of metaphor as a condition by which the subject transforms an alien world into something habitable and charged with resonance. Just think of the implications of Yeats's figure, "the soul's a bride/That cannot in that trash and tinsel hide" (284). It is as if the soul could sustain its denigration of the body by the power of its rhetorical disdain. So if readers could fully participate in what texts realized as possible worlds, they could take on new powers as spiritual beings not requiring any doctrinal religion.

Nevertheless, while the rhetoric of the image could insist on the fusion of subject and object, it always ran the risk of being too bound to the world, too dependent on attuning to the objective rather than pursuing all the possible implications of the act of making. Realizing the full power of self-consciousness may involve learning to participate in everything possible for the mind as it creates relationships that are capable of locating the numinous within a shared world. So poets and artists also turned to a second model of what could be made present by expressive activity. One could stress relationships rather than objects, since the idea of relationship stresses an equation between making and discovering.

More concretely, there could be a new poetics based on the power to establish correspondences that directly create real, living poetic objects because they are composed entirely of relational forces. The poem could stress how various kinds of objects reveal their participation in analogous forces. Or it could stress what the mind can realize about itself as it manages to bring its own participation in these relationships to self-consciousness. We enter the world of "correspondences" elaborated by Ralph Waldo Emerson and by Charles Baudelaire. And we see the background for this statement by Stéphane Mallarmé that I think is the best realization of what G. W. F. Hegel meant by a Romantic art stressing inner sensuousness:

> We renounce that erroneous esthetic … which would have the poet fill the delicate pages of his book with the actual and palpable wood of trees, rather than with the forest's shuddering or the silent scattering of thunder through the foliage … For what is the magic charm of art, if not this: that … beyond the book itself, beyond the very text, it delivers up that volatile scattering which we call the Spirit, Who cares for nothing save universal musicality.

> (40)

All of these new dispensations, however, were haunted by two basic fears that proved to be a creative source of further elaborations of the expressivist picture. The biggest problem was in generalizing from conditions of experience to something like truth conditions that had implications for our understanding of features of our world for which we could claim objectivity. The theologian and the rhetorician speak for everyone in society; the expressive poet can speak only about individual experience. When a poet tries to claim more authority, the rhetorical or ideological glue risks becoming obvious: claims for truth involving imaginative acts have little or no sanction in any plausible philosophical account relying on reason. And Modernist ideals of expression had to promise significant freedom for self-consciousness shaped by such experiences, even though the vehicle was sheerly imaginary and the freedom without a sense of social obligation. So a similar problem occurred with anchoring self-consciousness as a location for significant freedom. Why would the imaginative life be a source of anything but an escape from the burdens of labor and social obligation? Writers could provide answers to such questions, but I suspect they had to recognize their partial inadequacy. Even the most intense image or metaphor might not be the equivalent of any real object subject to natural laws. And analogy by definition enables the mind only to make comparisons rather than reveal laws and deep structures.

Here I want to discuss one aspect of this presentational aesthetic that may have better claims to endure than its corollaries. This is the aspect of analogical poetry that raises the entire process of presentation to an abstract dimension. Instead of talking about how mind and matter meet, or subject and object fuse together, we can talk about how mind can make itself present in such a way as to implicate directly the activity of other minds. If we pursue this path, we find ourselves necessarily talking about the later poetry of Wallace Stevens. But I want to focus on evidence that this path has in fact survived better than other Modernist alternatives, so I have to concern myself with how John Ashbery redirects what he inherits from Stevens.[1] It took most of my book *Wallace Stevens and the Demands of Modernity* (2013) to characterize how after the Second World War Stevens often explored a mode of imagining I called "aspectual thinking." Now I want to elaborate how Ashbery picked up this aspectual thinking, partially transformed it, and made it central to devising plausible ways of engaging how writing can modify the world by how it makes itself present for a reader as a means of staging self-consciousness.

Such writing directly tests the powers of imagination not by producing a fictive world, or even imagined versions of fusing subject and object, but by calling attention to how one might produce senses of mystery, fluidity, and connectedness within the activity of writing as it engages aspects of the world. So when it is done well, this activity of writing continues Mallarmé's efforts to escape any form of objectivity that gives authority to the static quality of copulative verbs. In *George Oppen and the Fate of Modernism*, Peter Nicholls shows beautifully how the core values in the Modernist cult of the image and the responsive metaphor are likely to lead to Oppen's fascination with the power of the copulative to resist time and establish a sense of presence. Stevens and Ashbery show why and how the imagination thrives more dynamically and evocatively in writing based on "as" than it does in writing based on "is."

Let me give a brief example of how Stevens presents aspectual thinking in poetry before turning to Ashbery's modifications:

> Each person completely touches us
> With what he is and as he is,
> In the stale grandeur of annihilation.
>
> (*CPP* 430)

These lines from "Lebensweisheitspielerei" invite us to reflect upon three contrasts between the copulative sense of "is" and what I will call the analogical force established by the grammar of "as" for assertions about being. The first contrast involves the ability to move from referring to a person to enacting that person's presence as it becomes something that touches us. Even while the sentence acknowledges that the specific person inhabits a quite separate world from the speaker, it also calls attention to the domain of *temporal equivalence* where two different states occur in parallel dimensions of the present tense, within essentially the same imaginative processes. "Being as" is a fundamentally relational state. Faced with "the stale grandeur of annihilation," each person finds the self in the same imaginative situation. In fact, the sounding of the long *a*'s and the magisterial Latinity of that phrase reinforce a sense of presentness that is virtually impossible to avoid.

The second development of analogical imagining offers what I call *modal equivalence*. Each person touches us because the focus can be on how that person actually constructs a world in a way that is virtually shareable with all the other people facing annihilation. "What he is" will require images of discreet identity. But "as he is" focuses on possible affective states that anyone can enter who appreciates what the state involves. "As he is" can completely touch us "as" we become attuned to such states. Being "touched" is not just a metaphor— think again of Mallarmé's analogies for processes that make present relational structures as modes of inner sensuousness.

Finally, Stevens has frequent recourse to what I want to call the *participatory equivalence* established by the grammar of "as." Stevens can feel himself justified in using the first-person plural—"Each person completely touches us"— because the "as" allows a sense that a reader can not only identify with the state the poem addresses but also will that identification as a condition of self-consciousness. The modal equivalence defines the possibility of a shared world; the participatory equivalence actively takes up this possibility by affirming it and testing its parameters. "As he is" becomes an active corollary of "as I am" because it presents the realization of what is involved in sharing the same confrontation with "the stale grandeur of annihilation." Indeed, this line of thinking suggests that some poetry can claim to have the status of exemplar not because of how it represents the real but because of how it stages the possibility for everyone willing to participate in what becomes articulate through the poem's assertions. Attentive reading enables participating in what analogies make irreducibly present. "What he is" is inseparable from "as he is" for every reader attuned to the manner by which he is made to appear: "And there he walks and does as he lives and likes" (*CPP* 449).

From the start of his career as a poet, Ashbery could not have embraced the poetics of the expressive image or the elaboration of single metaphoric modes of self-presentation. These would have seemed far too strenuous and imperious in their confidently making present a compelling sense of the self in the world. But he could be comfortable in reworking and reinterpreting the Stevensian capacity to elaborate the effects of analogy—either playfully, as in "The Instruction Manual," or plaintively, as in "Some Trees." And he came to see that he could turn what began as a fundamentally defensive strategy into a means of exploring aspects of the psyche in relation to a sense of fluid time that seemed fundamental to his way of being in the world. By shifting from an empirical speaking "I" to second-order reflections on ways of staging first-person investments, he could elaborate a world of never-ending analogical chains that enabled him to develop what we might call a poetics of indefinite experience. Every "as" can sponsor another "as," switching the focus of the poem as well as the level on which the poet seems most invested in what language affords—from first-order experiencing the world to second- and third-order reflections on who he becomes during various modes of experiencing.

The insistence on equivalences can elaborate an insistently anti-pictorial poetry resistant to all of the assertions about identity that are basic to the copulative verb. Stressing equivalences allows Ashbery's poetry to explore feelings that are not anchored in the world shaped by perception but in chains of possible feelings, some experienced directly by the speakers and some embedded in the language the poet has to use. In both cases, the primary challenge is to cultivate modes of attention and imaginative valuation that cannot depend on things as they are. They need the constant presence of something like a blue guitar, or multiple guitars playing somewhat at cross-purposes.

So Ashbery clearly does not imitate Stevens. He recognizes how Stevens establishes aspectual thinking, but then puts it to very different purposes. Stevens subordinates the aspectual to the practice of formulating specific experiences in which an overall purposiveness defines the place for most of the poet's syntactic gestures. Ashbery turns against Modernist ideals of formal coherence by showing instead how the constant pressure of "as" gives a home to the enigmatic and the indecipherable while placing such states ineluctably within our social reality.

This cultivation of multiple and divergent possibilities is asked to do a good deal of work even in Ashbery's more stylistically conservative poems, like the opening of "Self-Portrait in a Convex Mirror":

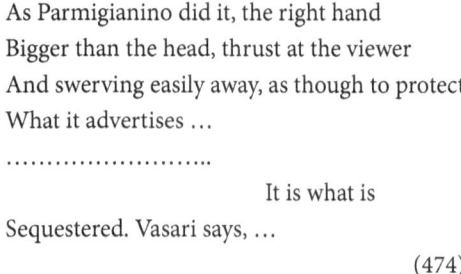

As Parmigianino did it, the right hand
Bigger than the head, thrust at the viewer
And swerving easily away, as though to protect
What it advertises ...
....
                    It is what is
Sequestered. Vasari says, ...

                                    (474)

This poem stages the meeting of two mannerists, and perhaps clarifies the possibilities of producing what Gertrude Stein might call "Everybody's Self-Portrait." So it has to be first and foremost about the manners (in every sense) of composing and attending to what becomes partially free from its anchor in matter. Critics typically do not pay sufficient attention to the labor performed by the opening word "as," especially in its capacity to recast what the impersonal pronoun can refer to in the fourth line.

Notice first how "as" creates a complex temporal space introducing Ashbery's version of a poem that includes history. The first verb is properly in the past tense, referring to Parmigianino's achievement. But "as" allows the poem immediately to equate achievement with response by absorbing the past tense into what appears as present, although painted in the past. There is also a modal equivalence referring to the manner by which Parmigianino composed the work. The poet's entire response is offered as an elaborate set of analogies for what is accomplished by the painter's art. Visual detail gives way to a capacious dramatic sense of the painting that allows the painter's soul to establish itself "in a recurring wave/Of arrival" (474). But then we also have to ask who is really arriving and where in order to develop the other side of the modal equivalence. For the poet's description soon brings out his own need for identifying with what it might mean for his own vulnerable body, with its own defenses and projections, to manage a sense of recurrent arrival in a space where the hand is sufficient to ward off threats to the soul's stability.

Ultimately, Ashbery pushes the third aspect of "as," the opportunity to develop participatory equivalence, considerably further than Stevens does by treating this poem as inviting identification with the careful visual arrangement provided by the painting.[2] This is achieved primarily by refusing to collapse the portrait into a historical gesture or a commodity to be possessed by a contemporary interpretation. The poem emphasizes the present tense of the painting as establishing a continuing dialogue between its own purposive integrity and the poet's needy inquiry into why that work of the past continues to fascinate. Participatory equivalence stages a present liveliness of expressive detail always subject to dissipation and transformation because the details live only in the mind's responsiveness to the record of another mind's manner of acting.

These possibilities for responsiveness are all summarized in the poem's brilliant closing figure of encountering "cold pockets/Of remembrance, whispers out of time" (487). These whispers come from somewhere remote in time but also not quite defeated by the "stale grandeur of annihilation" (*CPP* 430). There is much that time destroys. But in art, at least, there is a strange sense of the malleability of time that itself escapes time, at least partially. We cannot "know" why Parmigianino painted his self-portrait. However, we need not be obsessed by this limitation. We can turn it into a form of liberation by concentrating on the rhythms afforded by shifting analogies as we read with the intention of honoring what remains of the artist's act. There are aspects of intentions, like the curve of the hand, that seem to impose themselves on the present—not to shape meaning so much as to afford the imagination paths for its own reflections on selfhood. Turning from "meaning" demands trust that the proliferation of analogies is not an escape from the real but a distinctive mode of making sense where otherwise the mind would have to sacrifice much of its interest in the particular situation:

> I go on consulting
> This mirror that is no longer mine
> For as much brisk vacancy as is to be
> My portion this time. And the vase is always full
> Because there is only just so much room
> And it accommodates everything. The sample
> One sees is not to be taken as
> Merely that, but as everything as it
> May be imagined outside time—not as a gesture

> But as all, in the refined, assimilable state.
> But what is this universe the porch of
> As it veers in and out, back and forth,
> Refusing to surround us and still the only
> Thing we can see?
>
> (482)

Here the convex mirror proves crucial because it is not just a vehicle for copying the face. It mobilizes the relation between the face and its surroundings—from the details of the room to the question of what the frame can and cannot include, to the way the painting reaches to the life of the city and to other Renaissance artists. (Vasari's interpretive efforts become a prototype for the possibility that the work can create its present at the same time as it risks being absorbed by what its audiences want their present to be.) The imagination produces a "today" that can celebrate the portrait's capacity to preserve its datedness because it also affords a space for analogical identifications in the present. By feeling the pressure of what cannot be recovered across historical time, the reader ironically becomes attuned to the various dimensions of loss that continue to solicit the developing of analogies capable of bringing continued vitality to just what Parmigianino accomplished.

"Self-Portrait in a Convex Mirror" matters for my argument because the poem accomplishes two tasks: it puts to use the full range of Stevensian equivalences established by "as," and, despite the fact that this is conservative Ashbery, the text breaks substantially from Stevens' essentially Modernist sense of the poem as a construct controlling the equivalences within a more comprehensive sense of imaginative purposiveness. Ashbery approaches the possibility that one does not need specific markers of equivalence like "as" because the entire poem offers a continuous process of gathering and dissipating equivalences, without a more comprehensive purposiveness. There is the possibility that reading poetry can be simply entering a site where participation gravitates toward observation and back to identification, where sympathy modulates into self-regard and then back toward compassion for all that needs protecting by the artist's hand, and where the sense of destruction through change and decay is modified continually by what emerges as whispers through time.

"Self-Portrait in a Convex Mirror" is not quite that poem. Ashbery seems here to reign in his more radical gestures in order to let appreciation of Parmigianino's work provide a firm grounding that is visible as structural control over the poem's fluid textures. So, we should turn briefly to two much more emphatic versions of what equivalence becomes in Ashbery's basic style from at least 1966 to 1984. All three modes of equivalence in Stevens still play central roles, even if they are not always marked by grammatical operators. Ashbery is even more insistent than Stevens on resisting copulative forms of identity in favor of provisional and process-based analogies between kinds of movement for the mind. That insistence, in fact, calls for what we might consider a fourth, more pervasive mode of equivalence treating these analogical processes as fundamental ontological principles. In much of this poetry, there need not be any grammatical operator like "as" because analogies are basic to how any kind of identity is established. There is simply no identification or act of naming that does not have to be aware of the incompleteness of any positive distinction because the phenomenon will also be haunted by its opposite or its negation—at least in matters of the psyche and of how language works in the world. Contrast and comparison pervade efforts at definitive assertion.

In these domains, there are no simple positive states; nor are there simple negative states. Poetry is the effort to find gradients that acknowledge the constant co-presence of opposites in continual flux, present in different degrees perhaps, but always constantly modifying each other. Ashbery is oddly the practicing poet who most calls upon models like the inverted cones in Yeats's *A Vision* as means of engaging states defined by multiple shifting coordinates. Nothing is quite private without a public dimension built in from the start—including how we manifest affective lives. Conversely, nothing is quite public because all of us have distinctive histories that compose individual features in how we take up public phenomena (like language). Similarly, almost nothing is quite in focus, or out of focus; nothing is quite pronounced in the foreground or entirely lost in the background; no speech is quite direct, no indirection without hints of clear investments; nothing is stable, but nothing is so much in flux as not to suggest repetition and obsession. This is why we have to talk of indeterminacy in his poetry, yet also have to recognize this as not at all the result of anything like postmodern irony.[3] For Ashbery, to be indeterminate is to give a mostly positive and mostly accurate account of how experience turns out to be constituted, and how it changes as we try to observe ourselves carefully.

Let me illustrate these claims by turning to two poems—the first as an instance of how Ashbery imagines the dynamics of responding to experience, and the second as an indication of what kind of affective power such dynamics can possess as one turns toward self-reflection. This is the concluding section of "And *Ut Pictura Poesis* Is Her Name":

> Something
> Ought to be written about how this affects
> You when you write poetry:
> The extreme austerity of an almost empty mind
> Colliding with the lush, Rousseau-like foliage of its desire to
>   communicate
> Something between breaths, if only for the sake
> Of others and their desire to understand you and desert you
> For other centers of communication, so that understanding
> May begin, and in doing so be undone.
>
> (519–20)

Here there should be almost no need for commentary: the language is clear, although what it refers to is quite complex. Yet what the language does is worth noticing because it manages to enact what the poem asserts, and so to take advantage of the modal analogy between assertion and demonstration.

The primary material feature of these lines is their persistent enjambment, as if no single line could quite stabilize the sense as it flows into supplemental statements. The flow generates a state that stretches the possibility of communication by offering an increasingly elliptical concentration (or condensation) of meaning in the concluding four lines. In effect, the poem concludes that there has to be the undoing of any general model allowing understanding in order to take seriously what other centers of communication can present as meaningful. The meaningful tends toward what individuals display rather than what they assert. Or, we can make the stronger statement that the very possibility of individuality involves something breaking out of the conceptual structures that constitute understanding.

But this way of reading is not quite satisfying because it does not offer the best way to understand what the poem is performing. For the poem is less interested in providing a conclusion than in enacting the very union of the austere, and hence the wary, with the lush rhetoric generated by the desire to communicate. The poem ultimately proposes its own activity as an alternative to the goals posited by traditional models of understanding. Rather than fix a present moment, as if the present could be a secure space in time, the poem labors to remind us that there is another sense of present that involves the constant flow of time and the constant proliferation of linguistic modifiers.

My second example is the conclusion of the poem "As We Know," because it fleshes out how for Ashbery indeterminate equivalences in the space of meaning may be the best means for separating the space of meaning provided by understanding from the experience of meaning that depends on the unfolding of time. In order to elaborate this contrast, the poem invites us to modify our sense of how subjects establish values—or at least the kind of values that alter their senses of identity. Here the force of subjectivity consists primarily in the capacity to negotiate this world of opposing forces while holding off the demands for believing in an inner self. For that belief establishes an alternative locus for one's concern rather than locating value concretely in how experience takes form.

The title "As We Know" evokes first a sense that knowing is a present-tense activity that goes along with other mental processes, like caring or worrying or celebrating. "As" correlates these activities temporally and modally because knowing in this poem ultimately depends on our always adjusting for perspective and occasion. Knowing is less a relation to fixed matter than to the vagaries of manner that occupy consciousness while it is aware of the relations it is negotiating in the present tense. And in the participatory mode of equivalence, reading emphasizes the "we" that becomes possible in correlating how people come to share what knowing can contain.

But the irony in the title's hint of jaded conventionality requires us to be careful in positing who or what this "we" involves. In one sense of the term, "we" is utterly bound by convention. If we stress the knowing, we find ourselves risking any flexibility to adapt to the vagaries of the present tense. Yet there is also a consoling dimension to "as we know" that stresses the idea of coming to know in a manner that allows for the use of the first-person plural. On this level, knowledge seems to depend only on the work that writing performs in the present tense, without any overarching plan for readers to realize or, more important, to fear that they have failed to realize what the other is thinking and feeling.

The more imaginative dimensions of the title depend on our becoming involved in what I am calling the "ontological dimension of equivalence" established by this poem.

Consider the opening stanza:

> All that we see is penetrated by it—
> The distant treetops with their steeple (so
> Innocent), the stair, the windows' fixed flashing—
> Pierced full of holes by the evil that is not evil,
> The romance that is not mysterious, the life that is not life,
> A present that is elsewhere.
>
> (661)

"We" refers primarily to the lovers. But because of the lack of concrete identification, "we" also becomes anyone capable of fleshing out this penetrating "it." That process turns out to involve a series of oxymora involving "the evil that is not evil" and "the life that is not life."

As with "And *Ut Pictura Poesis* …," it is not too difficult to assign meanings to these intricate abstractions. The basic contrast seems to play off what can be elaborated in the imagination (like erotic desire) against what are typical terms for characterizing disturbing transitions. But the more important consideration is how one can enter the space characterized by such oxymora. Here the poem suggests that flexibility about how the self is constituted becomes a crucial virtue. The repeated "you" in the second and third stanzas offers a marvelous parallel to the oxymoronic, since we have to identify it as an address to a romantic partner but cannot stop with this specific reference. In one direction, "you" vacillates into addressing the self; in another, it invites the reader to share the range of intensities that anchor the details of the speaking. Then bringing life to these details produces in itself all the alternative we need to more abstract versions of "I" that are armored against how imagination can complicate its existence.

All this ambiguity ultimately functions to sustain a somewhat new vision of the kind of satisfaction lyric can produce. We need to reflect only on how this poem, in its final stanza, renders the shift from background context to the capacity for fully invested speech in the present:

> The light that was shadowed then
> Was seen to be our lives,
> Everything about us that love might wish to examine,
> Then put away for a certain length of time, until
> The whole is to be reviewed, and we turned
> Toward each other, to each other.

The way we had come was all we could see
And it crept up on us, embarrassed
That there is so much to tell now, really now.

(661)

This poem stages a fusion of opposites that is quite different from the organicist ideals shaping much of twentieth-century poetry. For when the speaking reviews the whole, the particular synthetic shape taken by this whole simply does not matter. What does matter is how the speaking develops an appreciation of all that can be gathered into the present tense.

This appreciation occurs as the proliferation of pronouns settles into forming a "we." And "we" takes on power as it learns to identify with the transition from "now" to "really now." Here romantic plenitude arises not from anything heroic the individual agents might perform. Rather, it arises because the speaking can find a new relation to time, which had been seen in the poem only as the enemy of any possible bliss deriving from treating home as a place "to get to, one of these days" (661). By the end of the poem, "we" dissolves into an affirmation of the difference between ordinary time and the kind of time that can warrant the adverb "really." It is not important what details allow for that new sense of reality, so long as the agents feel the difference from the kind of time that simply passes. We have to see only that "really now" can be asserted without reference to any specific images. For it affirms a relation between people in the present, not a relation to specific aspects of memory. "Really now" affirms the possibility of a charged sense of the present tense to emerge in which "telling" can replace "reviewing" and the moment of being replace any need for meaning beyond all that it takes for the telling to constitute a sense of plenitude. If that "now" could be represented in terms of images, we would destroy the sense of reality that matters most for romance.

Notes

1   Stevens saw that poetry seeking this kind of presentation of thinking had to pass the first test of any art that relies on abstraction: it has to make literally present that which can embody the powers to which it refers. Think of Mondrian on dynamic balance and Malevich on non-objective feeling. Such work shows how there can be an art that does not concern itself with any kind of picturing of what might be real.

There is no mysterious evocation of the real, only a redirection of how we imagine our relationship to the act of writing. And Ashbery shows just how much this Stevensian redirection can accomplish.

2   We might say that the first kind of "as" dominates paragraphs one and four in the poem, the second paragraphs two and five, and the third paragraphs three and six, although we have to make room for Ashbery's refusal to let any structure dictate too tightly the metamorphic aspects of imaginative life. In effect, the first "as" records the trap of the subject attempting to capture itself as object while trying to retain sufficient control as subject to combat the objectification of the soul into an image. The second use of "as" introduces the contemporary subject's entering empathetically into Parmigianino's imaginative situation while also wanting to elicit the full pathos of Parmigianino's effort to create a specific face to which he can attribute the energies of the doing. So while the first "as" introduces the role of pathos, the doing that composed the self-image, the second renders Ashbery's awareness of that pathos and his reflections on its consequences for his own historical situation. Finally, the third "as" stages the resources by which the painting itself enters time and stands over against the efforts by the painter and the responding poet to bind the work to specific historical circumstances. This "as" calling attention to the work of the work beautifully complements the great closing figure of "whispers out of time" that combines the ideas of whispers from within time and whispers that suggest bindings beyond time (Ashbery 487).

3   I want to say a little more about different versions of indeterminacy. Most critical contemporaries who posit indeterminacy as a value do so in accord with Marjorie Perloff's celebration of its negative force. Indeterminacy encourages the freedom of readers to become co-creators of the poem rather than slavish interpreters of a master structure. But this stance traps poetry into a version of negative freedom that fails to address what seems to me a central need for contemporary culture. We need to have our expressive lives align with the rejection of established authority and the hope that values can be determined by objective conditions; but we also have to have a positive sense that agents can be fulfilled within such indeterminacy because it gives them power to establish themselves as capable of fostering alternative modes of meaningfulness where mutual understanding and cooperation are still possible—hence Ashbery's indefinite "we" and "you." These pronouns are certainly indeterminate. But rather than permitting agents to make of the reference what they can, these pronouns can be seen as invitations to take on more of the language of the poem than might be allowed were we to act in accord with the boundaries we establish for what we think are our personal identities. Indeterminacy in Ashbery—perhaps in most poets who stress analogical thinking—is less a mode of negative freedom than a kind of inexhaustible

plenitude of imaginative possibilities and tonal variations. Readers share the awareness that as they read they enter a process of determining possible paths among pleasures and implications that for each reader promises a provisional completeness just because there is no place for failure to capture the intentions of the master. There emerge only paths of possibility opened by a fourth dimension of the grammar of "as"—its capacity to dwell in the provisional and temporary that makes it capable of attuning and re-attuning to what happens in the present tense.

Works Cited

Altieri, Charles. *Wallace Stevens and the Demands of Modernity: Toward a Phenomenology of Value*. Ithaca: Cornell University Press, 2013. Print.

Ashbery, John. *John Ashbery: Collected Poems, 1956–1987*. Ed. Mark Ford. New York: Library of America, 2008. Print.

Mallarmé, Stéphane. *Selected Prose Poems, Essays and Letters*. Trans. Bradford Cook. Baltimore: Johns Hopkins University Press, 1956. Print.

Nicholls, Peter. *George Oppen and the Fate of Modernism*. Oxford: Oxford University Press, 2007. Print.

Stevens, Wallace. *Wallace Stevens: Collected Poetry and Prose*. Ed. Frank Kermode and Joan Richardson. New York: Library of America, 1997. Print.

Yeats, William Butler. *The Collected Poems of W. B. Yeats*. Ed. Lisa M. Finneran. New York: Macmillan, 1973. Print.

14

Silly to Be Serious: Lateness and the Question of Late Style in Stevens and A. R. Ammons

Juliette Utard

snow came before frost this year,

hard frost I mean: so over by the
hill next to the bridge, snow bent

leaves over the road as for an arcade:
the traffic had to one-line

and slow as through a tunnel: it was
most remarkable, like reading a poem

by Stevens ...
(Ammons, Glare 105)

In these lines, taken from A. R. Ammons' late collection *Glare* (1997), Wallace Stevens is named in passing, in a kind of textual byway, to describe the effect of early snow on traffic. While most of us would agree with Ammons that reading Stevens often involves a great deal of slowing down, of taking one line at a time or "one-lining," the fact that these words should appear in a poem that maintains couplets, or double-lining, from cover to cover tends to make the reference to Stevens more ambivalent than it first appears. The stanzaic break and resulting enjambment ("to one-line/and slow") both postpone and dramatize Stevens' unexpected entrance into the fabric of the poem, so that we need to backtrack a little to ask ourselves: what exactly is "reading a poem/by Stevens" like, according to Ammons?

The tension between one-lining and two-lining, between moving alongside or merging, aptly describes the ambivalent connection between Ammons and

Stevens. In his introduction to *A. R. Ammons*, a *Modern Critical Views* volume published in 1986, Harold Bloom remarks that the beginning of Ammons' poetry coincided with the end of Stevens' career: "In the lengthening perspective of American poetry, the year 1955 will be remembered as the end of Wallace Stevens's career, and the beginning of Ammons's, himself not Stevens's heir but like Stevens a descendant of the great originals of [the] American Romantic tradition, Emerson and Whitman" (1). Both a friend of Ammons' and one of his early champions, Bloom was of course referring to 1955 as the year when Ammons published his first book and Stevens died. But he was also implying that Ammons was belated, not simply late—a fact that Ammons' persona "Ezra," in the poet's first book, already conceded: "yes I am late" (*Ommateum* 31). Though Bloom was careful not to present Ammons as "Stevens's heir," he did however trace a literary line from Stevens to Ammons, opening a path that a number of critics have since fruitfully explored.[1] Ammons himself was well aware of the connection, and much of his verse self-consciously acknowledges, or at times challenges, his debt to Stevens, as when he apostrophized the older poet in *The Snow Poems* ("Stevens, you should be here/now") in a poem fittingly, though ironically, entitled "You Can't Imitate" (199).

Drawing on textual parallels between Ammons' *Glare* (1997) and Stevens' *The Rock* (1954), this chapter moves beyond Bloom's notion of cultural belatedness and the construction of *post* as merely a coming after, to show how Ammons used Stevens' late poems to seek and perfect his own late style. Indeed, Ammons did not simply come after Stevens, he also took after him, quoting his poems, using Stevens' name provocatively to question the older poet's status in American academia, eventually shaping his own late style against Stevens' to the point where *Glare* partly reads as a book directed against Stevens—or, to use Ammons' titular metaphor, *glaring* at Stevens. Yet, despite these attacks, Ammons also relied on Stevens—and, to a lesser extent, Walt Whitman, W. B. Yeats, and Robert Frost— to challenge the codes and conventions of "late writing."

The first section of my chapter will try to reveal the extensiveness of Ammons' textual borrowings, ultimately to show Stevens' key role in Ammons' search for a late style. The second section argues that *Glare* only partly fulfills the aesthetic expectations of a late style as delineated by Frank Kermode in *The Sense of an Ending*, and instead appears closer to Edward Said's definition in *On Late Style: Music and Literature against the Grain*. While Said makes way for an agonistic definition of lateness—one that claims discord over concord as its preferred mode, which will help us look at *Glare* as an agonistic response to Stevens—

Gordon McMullan, in his landmark study *Shakespeare and the Idea of Late Writing*, moves beyond both Kermode and Said by calling late writing one of the last Romantic myths, a construct that needs to be historicized. The third and last section of this chapter, entitled "How Serious Should Late Poetry Be?," will specifically examine the ways in which Ammons in *Glare* plays with the conventions of late style as implying a sternness of tone that much of late Stevens exemplifies. Neither the wise old poet of Whitman's late verse nor the Yeatsian figure of the silly old man, Ammons invented a third way by exploring the histrionics of lateness ("I try to/hide the old fool playing the fool" [293]) so that *Glare* ultimately reads as an attempt to perform a post-Stevensian lateness that turns out to be a collage of his own poetic voices and those of his predecessors.

The Rock and *Glare*: Last Looks, Last Books, and the Search for a Late Style

Both *The Rock* and *Glare* were written in old age by poets whose first book had been published several decades earlier. Like *The Rock*, which appeared in 1954 at the end of *The Collected Poems* shortly before Stevens died, *Glare* was the last book to be published in its author's lifetime. (One other book did come out under the title *Bosh and Flapdoodle*, but it was published posthumously.) And like Stevens' last collection, it is filled with intimations of mortality. "*Glare* shiver[s] under the tocsin of warning," Helen Vendler notes in her review of the book ("Last" 157), and indeed, inscribed within are recurring references to Ammons' near-lethal heart attack a few years earlier ("lawsey-dawsey, it's the sixth/anniversary of my first death," he records in poem 23). Moreover, both books bear titles that are made to resonate within the poems as powerful reminders of death: the carefully timed occurrence of "glare" in poem 33 of Ammons' volume—"but the/boulder over and over is revealed,/its grainy size and weight a glare" (94–95)—reads as an allusion to the glaring reality of a death, the baby brother's, whose memory can no longer be averred, and which now merges with the speaker's sense of his own frailty at the beginning of the same poem: "I feel more *ex*/than *dis* (tinguished, I mean)" (93). Like the boulder in Ammons' poem 33, Stevens' rock image reads both as a stepping stone and a tombstone: "the gray particular of man's life,/The stone from which he rises, up—and—ho,/The step to the bleaker depths of his descents" (*CPP* 447).

However, what ties these two books together is probably less the theme of old age and fear of death than the search for, and questioning of, a late style.

Glare's opening line addresses the matter without delay: "wdn't it be silly to be serious, now," it asks (3). As often with Ammons, the book opens with a lowercase letter, as if to flaunt any expectation of a fresh start: the poems that make up the collection, it suggests, should be read as a sequel, as was Ammons' first book *Ommateum*, whose opening line, "So I said I am Ezra," also began *in medias res* (25). In this case, however, the abbreviated "wdn't" adds a sense of urgency, presenting the unfolding poem as a series of annotations hurriedly typed and seemingly unrevised. The importance of time and timeliness in *Glare* is made clear thanks to the adverb "now," poised at the end of its opening line, uncomfortably caught between a comma and a colon. "Now" becomes the time from which to contemplate things past and search for an appropriate ending.

But where do we draw the line between timely and late or, for that matter, between "serious" and "silly," which are semantically opposed yet acoustically joined? If "now" is too late to be serious, or write serious poetry, then when is it timely to do so? In other words, how late should late poetry be? That there is no easy answer to these questions is confirmed by the ensuing exegesis, introduced by "I mean" in Ammons' second line. My argument, then, is that *Glare* should perhaps be read as a book-length answer, however tentative, to the question of lateness and late style.

The *topos* of a life-review and recapitulation, which Ammons resorts to at the beginning of *Glare*, is at the core of Vendler's recent study of last works by five American poets, *Last Looks, Last Books: Stevens, Plath, Lowell, Bishop, Merrill*. "In many lyrics," Vendler begins, "poets have taken, if not a last look, a very late look at the interface at which death meets life." She describes her topic as "the strange binocular style [those poets] must invent to render the reality contemplated in that last look" (1). *Glare* and *The Rock* both fit Vendler's definition of a late style as exploring the "interface" of life and death—in fact, Vendler even mentions Ammons as a poet who "could equally well have been chosen" for her study, and both of them strove to invent "modern and disturbing styles of farewell, both structural and stylistic," as she writes of Stevens (2, 46). Both Ammons and Stevens did, "with death approaching," "tak[e] the last look" and "make the rounds of [their] territory" (1). I wish for my part to reconsider this "last look," which Vendler in her introduction links to an Irish custom, as partaking fully of a search for a late style that is to be viewed, not as the natural development of old age and old-age writing, but as a historically determined genre in constant conversation with prior literary models.

Glare's poem 43, for instance, eerily echoes *The Rock* in its staging of a "last look": "sometimes I get the feeling I've never/lived here at all, and 31 years seem/ no more than nothing," Ammons writes, before describing how a wave "slices through,/canceling everything, and the space/with nothing to fill it shrinks and/time collapses, so that nothing happened,/and I didn't exist, and existence/ itself seems like a wayward temporizing,/an illusion nonexistence sometimes/ stumbles into" (121). Readers familiar with Stevens' final collection will perceive in these lines an echo of its titular poem "The Rock," whose first section, entitled "Seventy Years Later," begins with a similarly negative affirmation: "It is an illusion that we were ever alive,/Lived in the houses of mothers, arranged ourselves/By our own motions in a freedom of air" (*CPP* 445).

Beyond the lexical borrowings ("lived," "never," "years," and "illusion" appear in both poems), the choice of a continuous stanzaic pattern (Stevens' growing preference for triplets in his late poetry is paralleled by Ammons' late taste for couplets),[2] and the way both poems keep count of years gone by—"seventy years" in Stevens is taken up by "here/at nearly 70" in another of Ammons' poems (*CPP* 445; *Glare* 88)—what is even more striking is the way both speakers pose as old poets surveying the terrain they have heretofore explored, as Vendler rightly underlines, ultimately to declare, however, that all is vanity. Cancellation, rather than completion, awaits them at the end of their journey: "Even our shadows, their shadows, no longer remain./The lives these lived in the mind are at an end./ They never were," Stevens writes in "The Rock" (*CPP* 445). *Ecclesiastes* is one of the underlying sources here ("What profit hath a man of all his labour which he taketh under the sun?" [Eccles. 1:3]), a powerful subtext that informs both poets' choice of imagery and point of view (take, for instance, Stevens' "River of Rivers" that "flows nowhere, like a sea" [*CPP* 451], an image derived from rivers that "run into the sea, yet the sea is not full" [Eccles. 1:7]).

These, then, are deeply self-conscious (and often self-critical) poems, constantly "edging … toward the/closure that is our temporary but/essential solution" (*Glare* 108). When Stevens writes that "The sounds of the guitar/Were not and are not. Absurd. The words spoken/Were not and are not" (*CPP* 445), he seems to be belatedly reappraising his own poetry, and more specifically his early poetry, as the sounds of *the* (presumably blue) guitar suggest. Having arrived at the end of their poetic journeys, the speakers of these late poems wonder whether it is still possible to make a difference and thus distinguish themselves, not just extinguish themselves, to paraphrase Ammons: "it's not/the verse that counts but the difference," Ammons writes, for "there really was nothing for me to amount to/except the nothing I am" (*Glare* 204). Likewise, in "Long and Sluggish Lines," Stevens writes, "It makes so little difference, at so much more/Than seventy, where one looks, one has been there before" (*CPP* 442). The speaker's avowed purpose is to search for "the outlook that would be right,/Where he would be complete in an unexplained completion:/The exact rock where his inexactnesses/Would discover, at last, the view toward which they had edged,/Where he could lie and, gazing down at the sea,/Recognize his unique and solitary home" (*CPP* 435). This retrospective, all-encompassing point of view from the "edge" of things ("edging" is a recurrent word in both Stevens and Ammons) may indeed be considered one of the defining features of both Stevens' and Ammons' late styles.

Vendler's readings of last books by Stevens and others, although they draw our attention to this liminal time and space that late poems repeatedly explore, seem nevertheless to fall short of explicitly questioning late style as a critical category, which is what this investigation eventually hopes to do. "Last books," a chronologically stable category, turn out to be more problematic when it comes to ascribing them a number of common thematic, stylistic, or aesthetic features. Unlike last poems, "last books" can, in most cases, readily be identified after their author's death. But why would last books share any common features at all? What is there to compare between, say, last books by young poets without any prior achievements and last books by poets who have decades of poetry to account for? Moreover, last books as a group exist only through the retrospective point of view of critics whose judgment will naturally embrace a poet's entire production, studying them against the grid of their ability to crown an entire oeuvre, which in turn changes their individual scope and meaning.

Like Stevens, Ammons was interested in finding "the outlook that would be right" and played with the idea of providing an appropriate ending for his lifelong work. *Glare*'s inaugural poem bluntly asks, "how am I sagely to depart from/all being (universe and all … / …) without calling out—just a/minute, am I not to know at last/what lies over the hill: over the/ridge there, over the laps of the/ocean, and out beyond" (5). The tension rises (from "how am I to" to "am I not to know at last") and the voice becomes shrill, before it is momentarily undercut and abruptly defused by the return to daily duties—"no, no: I must/get peanut butter and soda crackers/and the right shoe soles (for ice)" (6)—only to reach dangerous ground again (why else bother to find the "right shoe soles"?) as the poem ends with the mounting anxiety over the task of preparing one's legacy ("and leave something for my son and/leave these lines, poor things, to/you, if you will have them," the poem continues) until it culminates in a final invitation: "come, let's/

celebrate: it will all be over" (6). As the opening poem ends, its last word—"over"—is left hanging in midair, without punctuation, skillfully shifting its meaning from the spatial preposition ("over the hill: over the/ridge there, over the laps of the/ ocean," as found in the previous lines, where it is repeated, in a way, *over and over*) to the temporal adverb ("it will all be over," or finished), as if deliberately pointing to the poem's hereafter. This, however, is not merely Ammons pondering over his own legacy; it is also one late-twentieth-century American poet taking his cue from Walt Whitman, and merging his last lines with the final section of "Song of Myself": "I depart as air, I shake my white locks at the runaway sun,/ ... /If you want me again look for me under your boot-soles" (247).

Another striking example of this ongoing dialogue between Ammons and Whitman can be found in poem 65: "do I contradict myself, you/say: well, I get interested in both/sides of the argument" (*Glare* 178). *The Rock* appeared in 1954 just as the centennial of *Leaves of Grass* was about to be celebrated and in his correspondence Stevens commented on the fact. Arguably, both Stevens and Ammons looked back to Whitman as their main model to fashion their late style. Like Whitman at the end of the 1891 edition of *Leaves of Grass*, both Ammons and Stevens sought, "in the early candle-light of old age," to cast "backward glances over [their] travel'd road[s]" (656), and comparing past and present led them to adopt the "binocular style" that Vendler so deftly describes. Beyond the mere portrayal of old age and fear of death, there was also the literary question of how to give shape to a late style: how to find a style that would be both recognizably different from and at the same time consistent with what came before? Only within a literary tradition would that be possible, and to look at Ammons' *Glare* as coming after Stevens' *The Rock* and Whitman's *Leaves of Grass* is to delineate a tradition, perhaps even a genre, whose implicit expectations they both fulfilled and flaunted. *Glare* and *The Rock* were self-consciously composed as last books, which means they both obeyed and resisted the literary imperative of providing an appropriate ending for their author's lifelong output.

Glaring at Stevens: Ammons, Late Style, and the Agon

While Ammons often quoted Stevens' verse in his poems—in *Garbage*, for instance, he typically creates his own version of a "supreme fiction" that is "not supreme (how tedious)/and not a fiction (how clever)" (39)[3]—it was not until *Glare* came out that he repeatedly mentioned him by name, initiating a different kind of "paper conversation" altogether from the one he had carried on so far (Ammons, *Tape* 47). As Stephen Burt once remarked, *Glare* "brings 'Mr. Stevens' in, by name, over and over" (115). Burt goes on to quote Vendler's appraisal of August Kleinzahler's poetics as issuing "from the unlikely combination of Ammons and Stevens" (qtd. on 118). If the combination of Ammons and Stevens is indeed unlikely, why then did Ammons choose to name "Mr. Stevens" repeatedly in that particular book? Why him rather than Whitman—a hovering presence from *Ommateum* onwards, as we have seen—or, for that matter, William Carlos Williams, who is summoned in the opening page of *Garbage*: "someone somewhere may be at this very moment/dying for the lack of what W. C. Williams says/you could (or somebody could) be giving" (13)? And, most important, why so late in his career? What was it that made Stevens such a key figure in Ammons' late phase, a choice that would durably connect him with lateness in Ammons' oeuvre?

Not only did *The Rock* constitute a subtext for *Glare*, Stevens' name itself also became instrumental to Ammons' fashioning of a late style, as I now hope to show. It appears no less than eight times in the volume (four times in poem 8, once in poems 12, 38, 42, and 48), just a few times less than in all of Ammons' poetry, and each time in ambivalent praise, if not downright mockery: "who could/warp the obvious into half an hour/of tangled nothingness," Ammons asks, "like Mr./Stevens: but Mr. Stevens's lines!/laid like a railbed, tie after tie" (*Glare* 25). The name reappears most provocatively in poem 42, in one of *Glare*'s most vulgar lines, presumably to underline the older poet's avoidance of any lapse in taste: "smegma/afloat in the round of a bauble of/pussy piss: that is vulgar: that/is so vulgar: Wallace Stevens wd/never say anything like that" (116).

Repeatedly in *Glare*, Ammons launches his attacks against Stevens, to the point where Roger Gilbert felt he should "mount a defense of [Stevens'] style" (191). Gilbert quotes interviews in which Ammons voiced his criticism, for instance: "I think [Stevens] is a great poet who sometimes writes below the level of a high-school freshman" (qtd. in Gilbert 191). Interestingly, fragments from these interviews tend to resurface in the poems themselves, as in *Glare*'s poem 12: "I've heard that the greatest novelists/in all languages were not good writers," Ammons starts, before asking, "is that what guarantees Stevens's/greatness: freshpersons confused by/so heavenly a daze would be dismissed/from my classroom: but great persons/need not apply the rules of rubes" (36). The poem, which pits the adjective "great" (together with its derivatives, "greatest novelists," "Stevens's greatness") against "good," suggests that Stevens' reputation is inflated (as the superlative and hyperboles make clear) and artificially maintained: "Stevens's/greatness," an association that the line break undermines, does not guarantee that he is actually good. However, staging Stevens against a vivid backdrop of campus life ("freshpersons," "dismissed/from my classroom") makes us wonder whether it was Stevens' verse that so irked Ammons or the Stevens that had been canonized by academia.

Ammons clearly enjoyed tampering with Stevens' good name, nowhere more so than in poem 8, where the criticism is directed against Stevens' style (not just his reputation) and more specifically against his use of both passive and static verbs. Gilbert explains how "Ammons loved to complain about what he saw as [Stevens'] stylistic shortcomings, chief among them his heavy reliance on the verb 'to be.' The poet John Brehm recalls that Ammons would 'read a passage from Stevens and point out all the weak verbs, "is, is, is, was, was, was, like a bunch of fuckin' bees buzzin' around in there"'" (191). In poem 8, situated near the beginning of *Glare*, "Mr. Stevens" is summoned for the first time but without a first name, as if to signify from the start that Ammons and he are not on a first-name basis. The line break between "Mr." and "Stevens" additionally suggests a pause or hesitation before actually "nodding" Stevens in, so that the last name is deferred (though not deferred *to*). The poem's first lines ("if Homer can nod, I can have/narcolepsy"), derived from Horace's *Ars Poetica* ("even good old Homer nods"), allow the later poet to look down upon his predecessor who, he says, "was a poet when he/was scarcely himself" and whose head "buzzed/ wuz, wuz, wuz, wuz, although,/nodding, he sometimes slipped an active/verb through" (25).

The dynamic at the core of the poem is playful, yet agonistic—"my outrage, my anger is/oceanic: it is free as/my verse: lovingly I empty/myself of it: lovingly I write/out my loathing" (*Snow* 251). Dragging Stevens onto a poetic battlefield, Ammons challenges his status, debunking him as a false idol among creative-writing students. Perhaps he was experimenting with a new form of epic poetry, as the inaugural reference to Homer prepares us for and the plea in favor of action verbs tends to confirm. But he was also mocking old poets in general, Homer, Stevens, himself, and probably Yeats as well, picturing them all side by side, equally "old and grey and full of sleep"—or worse, narcoleptic—"And nodding by the fire" (Yeats 41), in "millennia of evenings around/the fires" (*Glare* 3).

How Serious Should Late Poetry Be? Stevens, Ammons, and the Histrionics of Late Style

Ammons' late poetry, in general, and *Glare*, in particular, seem intent on antagonizing their readers, as both Vendler and Justin Quinn have noted. Quinn, for instance, writes that

> Ammons can also bore for long stretches, nowhere more so than in *Glare* ... Clearly, the Elizabeth Bishop-model of poetic production is not applicable (a slim volume every ten years or so), but it is a widespread standard of poetry reading and Ammons, to some readers' minds, cannot stand comparison to the less-productive and more polished poets. But for other readers, and I count myself among them, the boredom is a small price to pay for Ammons at his best.
>
> (n. pag.)

Like Quinn, who singles out *Glare* as a collection that shows Ammons both at his most tedious and his best, Vendler, in a 1973 review of Ammons' *Collected Poems, 1951–1971*, exposes the poet's increasing reliance on "annoying" verbal tics:

> Ammons has developed an annoying tic of turning clichés mechanically around ("being there is the next best/thing to long distance") and a somewhat distracting habit of doodling on the typewriter ("overwhelm whelm helm elm"). All poets do those things in the margins, but they usually leave them behind when the poem reaches the printed page ...
>
> ("Ammons" 78)

But what if Ammons' "annoying tics" were to be understood as a defining feature, not just a failing, of his late style? What if they were an integral part of his stylistic explorations? "I don't write to trim/my way into your approval," he explains in *Glare* (203). And again: "I was not thought/likely, never likable" (204). Are not the book's final words, "FLAWS AND DRAWBACKS" (294), printed in uppercase letters obviously set to catch our attention, a statement of purpose, designed to disappoint any expectation of a memorable ending? Surely, the title for his very last book, *Bosh and Flapdoodle*, would indicate he had no intention of gratifying our expectations of a serious, stern ending?

Edward Said's "Thoughts on Late Style" throw a revealing light on Ammons' late works and, more specifically, his agonistic connection with Stevens. In this 2004 essay from the *London Review of Books*, later adapted and included in his posthumously assembled book *On Late Style: Music and Literature against the Grain* (2006), Said proposes to

> look at the way in which the work of some great artists and writers acquires a new idiom towards the end of their lives—what I've come to think of as a late style. The accepted notion is that age confers a spirit of reconciliation and serenity on late works ... Each of us can supply evidence of late works which crown a lifetime of aesthetic endeavour. Rembrandt and Matisse, Bach and Wagner. But what of artistic lateness not as harmony and resolution, but as intransigence, difficulty and contradiction?
>
> ("Thoughts" 3)

Against Frank Kermode's "fictions of concord"—"We need, and provide, fictions of concord," Kermode writes in *The Sense of an Ending*, "For concord or consonance really is the root of the matter, even in a world which thinks it can only be a fiction" (59, 58)[4]—Said sets out to define lateness not as concord but as discord, not as conciliation but as confrontation. "It is this second type of lateness that I find deeply interesting," he writes, "it is a sort of deliberately unproductive productiveness, a going against" ("Thoughts" 7). Said's definition makes way for a lateness that refuses to "go gentle into that good night," to use Dylan Thomas' words (128). Starting with a reading of Theodor Adorno's remarks on Beethoven's late style, he builds his argument upon the example of Ibsen's late plays, which to him "suggest an angry and disturbed artist who uses drama as an occasion to stir up more anxiety, tamper irrevocably with the possibility of closure, leave the audience more perplexed and unsettled than before" ("Thoughts" 7).

By redefining lateness as a form of exile, Said was of course incorporating it into his own discourse on dissidence, and serving his personal and political agendas. But he was also teaching us to distrust our own assumptions about late style as a form of homecoming or newfound peace. That version of late style, he suggested, was a myth that begged to be challenged. Gordon McMullan, in his study published shortly after Said's book, *Shakespeare and the Idea of Late Writing*, went even further in his critique of late style (a term that, incidentally, he is careful to avoid in his title): the very notion is a myth, McMullan argues, whose origin can be traced back to Romanticism, and it is time we recognized it as stemming from one particular moment in cultural history. "Late style is perhaps the last of the great overarching critical ideas to be brought before the jury of theoretical or posttheoretical scepticism, as a sub-category of, but nonetheless distinct from, the Romantic concept of Genius," he writes. In other words, we have all been essentializing late style, either as a form of reconciliation

(Kermode) or as a form of rebellion (Said),[5] while in fact lateness is "a construct, not a given": "My argument, simply, is that while artists of the highest ability frequently (though by no means invariably) develop a new and striking style in their latter years, lateness as a critical category is a construct, not a given, and it is this construct, not the varied reality of late creativity, that has shaped the general understanding of late works" (16).

Working from the example of Shakespeare, his original field of expertise, McMullan then embraces a wide range of examples from Shakespeare to the present in order to argue, eventually, that lateness has become a self-conscious performance, with *The Tempest* as one of its prevailing literary models to this very day. Subsequent artists, he says, have become "self-conscious about their own lateness and have expressed this self-consciousness by way of an engagement, explicit or implicit, with the late phases of their predecessors." Henry James, for instance, "agonised over Shakespeare's inexplicable decision abruptly to stop writing at the height of his powers, in his middle years, addressing it repeatedly in his stories"; Pablo Picasso "began suddenly, in the last six or so years of his life, to identify with the late Rembrandt" (169). Like them, Ammons suddenly found in Stevens' late poems both a model and a counter-model for his own last books—a "manipulable paradigm" in McMullan's phrase (61)—and both he and Stevens arguably looked back to Whitman, rather than Shakespeare (though *The Tempest* did provide a useful paradigm for *The Rock*), to fashion their late style.

"I'm sick of good poems, all those little rondures/splendidly brought off, painted gourds on a shelf," Ammons writes in *Sphere*; "give me/the dumb, debilitated, nasty, and massive, if that's the/alternative" (72). Rather than accepting to choose his last words carefully to gratify his readers with memorable quotes that might guide them in their approach of old age, Ammons took the risk of antagonizing his readers by deliberately feeding them "bosh and flapdoodle" at the end—a dangerous strategy indeed, and one that must have lost a number of them along the way. (After all, Ammons' last book did *not* make it into Vendler's *Last Looks, Last Books*, even though she has written some of the most perceptive articles ever published on Ammons.) In this context, Stevens provided an outlet for Ammons' "rage against the dying of the light" (Thomas 128)—with glaring one of the more obvious antidotes—as well as a foil for his own late style. But more importantly perhaps, it helped him perfect his own literary version of a late style, one that refused to travel just one road, as his brilliant parody of "Mr. Frost" (*Glare* 135)—another companion on this much-traveled road—

underlines: "I don't care what becomes of me now, I'm/already become of: the end is clear (and/clearly dark) but getting there can be a rugged/road." Poem 101 continues, "I/suppose I would prefer one road to another,/though they go to the same place, but way leads/on to way and you can't tell which road you're/on at first, they look about the same: ages/and ages from now, if there's any story left/ to tell there'll be no telling what the story/is"—before exclaiming, in yet another bout of self-parody, "this is so/philosophical! but I better look out: I/might miss the road" (261).

Late style, then, does not need to be serious. But neither does it need to be entirely silly. What if, in the end, it were to be both? Ammons' purpose in *Glare* may have been to forgo any attempt "sagely to depart" (5), to relinquish the obsolete archetype of the wise old man and "let wisdom out the door": "I affirm nothing except/that I affirm nothing: just give me/breezes in the treezes and let wisdom/out the door" (17). But neither did Ammons refrain from the more serious strain, for in the end "'twere foolish to be foolish/and wise to be wise" (291). Perhaps one of his greatest stylistic achievements lies precisely in his ability to combine different strains, exploring the whole gamut from pathos to bathos, from comic to tragic, as in the following lines from poem 45:

> will I will the will to go on—what?—
> from here, where does going go, except
>
> to gone? oh, I dream in this wise,
> now, yes, yes, yes—images—the
>
> body bent to the cane ...
>   (*Glare* 127)

In *Glare*—and in *Bosh and Flapdoodle*, for that matter—Ammons managed to resist perpetuating any constraining representation of old age and old-age writing, thus challenging long-inherited constructions of old age in a culture that tends to set aging people apart in comfortable categories. Ammons instead offers us a compound of voices that successfully explodes these inherited models, resulting in the puzzling style that many critics have noted—a "sort of deliberately unproductive productiveness, a going against," as Said puts it ("Thoughts" 7). As *Glare*'s final poem suggests, the histrionics of lateness participate in a self-conscious self-fashioning that is to be heard as the belated answer to the volume's first line: "I try to/hide the old fool playing the fool, but you/hear, don't you, the young man, still young,/still under there saying yes yes to the new/days darkened howsomever." Of course, "it is a sad song but/it sings and wants to sing on and on and … /bring relief and the future singers in … /FLAWS AND DRAWBACKS" (293–94; final ellipsis in original). Eventually, Ammons' lateness is one that revels in a newly acquired freedom, as poem 56 suggests: "one good thing about being too late/is like too late to worry" (151).

Late style is "a construct, not a given," as McMullan's pivotal work shows. One might even say it has become a poetic subgenre, one that remains to be recognized as such, with its codes and conventions and subsequent post-Romantic transformations—"grecian urns not forever fair," as Ammons writes on the opening page of *Glare* (3). If "Two roads diverged in a yellow wood" (Frost 105), I would argue that Ammons, contrary to most of his predecessors, has tried to travel them both. "I feel it is so necessary to get/ahead of somebody and so unkind to/do so (and humiliating not to)," he explains in poem 33 (*Glare* 93). Ammons in *Glare* wrote against the grain of Stevensian lateness, not to overtake him, but to liberate himself of predetermined models of late styles by bringing together the late voices of his predecessors.

Notes

1   I am thinking here of Helen Vendler, Bonnie Costello, Roger Gilbert, John Adames, Justin Quinn, and Gyorgyi Voros, all of whom have written about Ammons in connection with Stevens. In fact, Ammons has often been read through the lens of Stevens' work, one reason for this being that a number of critics who have been writing about him were Stevens scholars to begin with, or at least critics sufficiently engaged in Stevensian studies to nurture the connection.

2   Simon Critchley, for instance, remarks that "As his work developed, Stevens created a unique meditative form, most often in the late verse, the blank verse triplet, often grouped into units of six or seven stanzas" (15–16).

3   John Adames' article offers "a reading of *Sphere* as Ammons's own notes toward a supreme fiction" (41) and Bonnie Costello calls Ammons' poem "For Harold Bloom," a "sublime reworking of Stevens's 'Anecdote of the Jar'" (422).

4   For Kermode's response to Said, see "Going Against."

5   As McMullan points out, "Said's work on the subject is characteristically engaging and polemical, but it is not a critique of the idea of lateness: on the contrary, it is a celebration of a certain manifestation of lateness—lateness as difficult, irascible, resistant, unreconciled" (13).

Works Cited

Adames, John. "A. R. Ammons's Stevensian Search for a Supreme Fiction in *Sphere*." *Twentieth Century Literature* 43.1 (1997): 41–56. Print.

Ammons, A. R. *Bosh and Flapdoodle*. New York: Norton, 2005. Print.

Ammons, A. R. *Garbage*. New York: Norton, 1993. Print.

Ammons, A. R. *Glare*. New York: Norton, 1997. Print.

Ammons, A. R. *Ommateum: With Doxology*. 1955. New York: Norton, 2008. Print.

Ammons, A. R. *The Snow Poems*. New York: Norton, 1977. Print.

Ammons, A. R. *Sphere: The Form of a Motion*. New York: Norton, 1974. Print.

Ammons, A. R. *Tape for the Turn of the Year*. 1965. New York: Norton, 1993. Print.

Bloom, Harold. Introduction. Bloom 1–31.

Bloom, Harold, ed. *A. R. Ammons*. Modern Critical Views. New York: Chelsea House, 1986. Print.

Burt, Stephen. "Charles Baxter, August Kleinzahler, Adrienne Rich: Contemporary Stevensians and the Problem of 'Other Lives.'" *Wallace Stevens Journal* 24.2 (2000): 115–34. Print.

Costello, Bonnie. "The Soil and Man's Intelligence: Three Contemporary Landscape Poets." *Contemporary Literature* 30.3 (1989): 412–33. Print.

Critchley, Simon. *Things Merely Are: Philosophy in the Poetry of Wallace Stevens*. London: Routledge, 2005. Print.

Frost, Robert. *The Poetry of Robert Frost*. Ed. Connery Lathem. New York: Holt, 1979. Print.

Gilbert, Roger. "Verbs of Mere Being: A Defense of Stevens' Style." *Wallace Stevens Journal* 28.2 (2004): 191–202. Print.

Kermode, Frank. "Going Against." *London Review of Books* 28.19 (2006): 7–8. Print.

Kermode, Frank. *The Sense of an Ending: Studies in the Theory of Fiction*. New York: Oxford University Press, 1968. Print.

McMullan, Gordon. *Shakespeare and the Idea of Late Writing: Authorship in the Proximity of Death*. Cambridge: Cambridge University Press, 2007. Print.

Quinn, Justin. "A. R. Ammons' Cookie-Cutter." *Contemporary Poetry Review*. July 19, 2003. February 7, 2016. Web.

Said, Edward. *On Late Style: Music and Literature against the Grain*. New York: Pantheon, 2006. Print.

Said, Edward. "Thoughts on Late Style." *London Review of Books* 26.15 (2004): 3–7. Print.

Stevens, Wallace. *Wallace Stevens: Collected Poetry and Prose*. Ed. Frank Kermode and Joan Richardson. New York: Library of America, 1997. Print.

Thomas, Dylan. *The Collected Poems of Dylan Thomas, 1934–1952*. New York: New Directions, 1971. Print.

Vendler, Helen. "Ammons." Bloom 73–80.

Vendler, Helen. "A. R. Ammons's Last." *Yale Review* 90.1 (2002): 157–75. Print.

Vendler, Helen. *Last Looks, Last Books: Stevens, Plath, Lowell, Bishop, Merrill.* Princeton: Princeton University Press, 2010. Print.

Voros, Gyorgyi. "Wallace Stevens and A. R. Ammons as Men on the Dump." *Wallace Stevens Journal* 24.2 (2000): 161–75. Print.

Whitman, Walt. *Walt Whitman: Poetry and Prose.* Ed. Justin Kaplan. New York: Library of America, 1982. Print.

Yeats, William Butler. *The Poems.* Ed. Richard J. Finneran. New York: Macmillan, 1983. Print.

15

Unanticipated Readers

Lisa M. Steinman

I have for some time been considering how to talk about Stevens and race. Although I would not claim yet to have sorted out what I ultimately want to say on the topic, the focus of this volume—*Poetry and Poetics* after *Wallace Stevens*— has offered me a new angle from which to approach the question, or at least a related question about how a series of later African American poets have been reading his work. On the question of Stevens and race, there have been some (if relatively few) things written. Aldon Lynn Nielsen's work in *Reading Race: White American Poets and the Racial Discourse in the Twentieth Century* may be best known. Nielsen cites Stevens' letters, including Stevens' remarks on those who are not white (and also those who are economically disadvantaged), concluding that Stevens viewed such others as "brutish" or lacking "finer" feeling; then turning to the poems, he notes a "generalized exoticism of the black subject" in particular, seeing Stevens' images of African America as "local color" in a way that places African Americans outside of the cultural traditions within which, Nielsen argues, Stevens saw himself operating, while placing himself as an instructor of those he thought of as outside of culture (61–62).[1] Nielsen mentions but says less about judgments like Randall Jarrell's on how Stevens "treats with especial sympathy Negroes, Mexican Indians, and anybody else he can consider wild" (60, citing Jarrell 138), a perspective Lisa DuRose examines further while discussing the power dynamics involved in Stevens' use of blackface as a bid for freedom imagined as the prerogative of outsiders, which DuRose concludes ultimately, if unwittingly, widens the disparity between black and white.[2] Jacqueline Brogan has also entered the debate, noting that critics often ignore the way Stevens' views on and use of images of racial others altered during and after the Second World War, challenging those like Adrienne Rich, Rachel Blau DuPlessis, and Mark Halliday who simply dismiss Stevens (Brogan ch. 8).

Critical investigations to date of Stevens' biographical, historical, or poetic relationship to racial issues and images leave room for further elaboration, but that is not my project here. What interests me is the surprising number of contemporary African American writers who look back at Stevens' poetry in more mixed tones, which has led me to ask what it is that poets such as Thylias Moss, Reginald Shepherd, Carl Phillips, Terrance Hayes, and C. S. Giscombe— in different ways—say they hear in Stevens' poetry.[3] Not all of these writers take Stevens as a primary influence. Even so, how poets such as these characterize their relationships with Stevens' work is interesting. Hayes's 2009 poem "Snow for Wallace Stevens," for instance, suggests a kind of love/hate relationship when he writes of his "capacity for love without/forgiveness," having earlier asked, "How, with pipes of winter/lining his cognition, does someone learn/ to bring a sentence to its knees?" (57).[4] Hayes's image of how winter has lined Stevens' "cognition" refigures a "mind of winter" (*CPP* 8) not only as white but also as entailing an unfeeling distance from or unexcused ignorance of the everyday realities of the lives of actual African Americans. Moreover, Hayes's figure of "love without/forgiveness" is not a bad way to describe Thylias Moss's relationship to Stevens' poetry in her earlier "A Reconsideration of the Blackbird," a poem in dialogue with popular culture (film, educational pieties, and nursery rhymes) as well as with Stevens; Moss opens with the line: "Let's call him *Jim Crow*" (*Pyramid* 10).[5] Throughout *Pyramid of Bone*, the 1989 volume in which "A Reconsideration of the Blackbird" first appeared, Moss explores how cultural icons and languages are understood differently from different cultural positions. And yet even in *Pyramid of Bone*—written before what Moss describes in a 1992 interview as her reevaluation of the influence of Ai's [Florence Howe's] "bleakness"—Moss's poems call Stevens on his racialized language but at the same time display a decidedly Stevensian sense of language, that is, of Stevens' linguistic playfulness, as well as his thematization of turning to poetry for comforts comparable to those once offered by religion (Moss, "Interview" 299; Moss, *Tale* 207, 235).

Before turning to some other African American poets' responses to Stevens, I want to underline Hayes's attention to Stevens' style, his ability "to bring a sentence to its knees," because I want to focus less on echoes of particular poems by Stevens and more on what in Stevens' style and poetics speaks to several African American poets, allowing a retrospective dialogue that Stevens might not have quite anticipated, or at least allowing questions to be—to quote from a poet, C. S. Giscombe, to whose work I will return—"fielded" (*Prairie* 22, 31).

Hayes writes that Stevens could "bring a sentence to its knees." Sentences—
the use of ellipses, repetition, enjambment, and especially longer sentences, or,
more precisely, the one long sentence in "Crude Foyer"—are what Carl Phillips
singled out at the 2014 Association of Writers and Writing Programs' convention
in Seattle as marking Stevens as a "poet of the lack of closure," able to "enact"
the "restlessness of thought."[6] Phillips, finally, focused on the linguistic features
and on the suppleness of Stevens' poem to suggest how Stevens' language enacts
what might be called a poetry of inconclusion, which is not quite a poetry
of inclusion but is perhaps a poetry *of*—not just poetry that calls forth—the
ambivalence I just noted in Hayes's and Moss's responses to Stevens, a style that
(to quote Phillips) "catalyzes figure." Similarly, if in a slightly different vein,
Major Jackson's widely read 2008 post—titled "Wallace Stevens after 'Lunch'"—
on the Poetry Foundation blog *Harriet* begins by recounting Jackson's interest
in how people viewed Gwendolyn Brooks's receipt of the Pulitzer Prize in 1950,
and then uses Joan Richardson's account of Stevens' racially charged remark
about Brooks (388) before moving on to considerations of mid-century cross-
cultural and especially interracial literary friendships. It is the comments posted
on the blog over the following two weeks that I find most interesting.[7] For
instance, Reginald Shepherd concludes that "the matter of race, in Stevens' case
… is complicated and ambiguous, and doesn't lend itself to easy condemnations
(or easy exonerations)." Not all the voices in the conversation agree—although
Jackson does, and Vivek Narayanan, a writer of color (though not African
American), notes both his own and Brooks's admiration for Stevens' work,
and says he feels like "an unintended reader, an interloper," reading Stevens'
poems with "a certain minor distance, a watchfulness," a stance he concludes is
"productive and even enabling."

"Ambiguity"—Shepherd's term—and ambivalence—a word that might
characterize most of the comments on the blog—are, of course, not quite the
same; the first presumably marks the obliquity of Stevens' language as well as the
shifting perspectives that such language makes available; the second marks how
the readers I am citing feel about the perspectives thus opened. Still, it seems to
be in part the complexity of Stevens' style that allows or even requires ambivalent
responses. Moreover, both ambiguity and ambivalence have a place in African
American literary traditions—as detailed, for instance, in Henry Louis Gates, Jr.'s
description of "signifying" in *The Signifying Monkey* (1988) or by Ralph Ellison
in *Invisible Man* (1947)—a fact that may cast light on the tone of many of the
responses to Stevens' poetry that I have mentioned, namely Moss's, Hayes's,

Phillips, and those on the blog *Harriet*. This helps suggest, too, how many of these readers, while dismayed by Stevens' racist language, admire how his use of language (seen as enacting "lack of closure," "complication," or productive watchfulness) allows African American poets to position themselves (not, or not only, as Nielsen or DuRose have it, to feel themselves unwillingly positioned) as "unintended readers." In another essay, written for *Contemporary Authors* and quoted on the Poetry Foundation website, Shepherd describes being formed by a tradition and language that was not his (given that he was a gay black man who grew up in Bronx housing projects), but he specifically mentions Stevens as a predecessor whose work made him "possible as a writer"; he also notes, "I wrestle with this necessary angel and rise renamed, blessed but also lamed."[8] This, writes Shepherd, foregrounded for him "the problem of language," and in a formulation not unlike that used by Phillips he ends by saying he has "been oppressed by many things in [his] life, but not by literature, which for [him] has always represented potential and *not closure*" (emphasis added).

In the remainder of this chapter, I want to consider how a similar sense of Stevensian language works in the poetry and essays of another African American poet: C. S. Giscombe. In 2004, at an MLA convention in Philadelphia, Pennsylvania, as a member of a panel on "Poetry and the Oblique," Giscombe responded to a question from the audience about whether he considered himself more as an African American poet or as an experimental poet by saying he had a "resistance to being placed," concluding: "You can be black and still have ambivalence, which *is* imagination." This comment can be aligned with Shepherd's remarks on the difficulties of seeing one's black self in the literary canon even while seeing the appeal of linguistic complexity and open-endedness, or what Giscombe (in an essay on Africadia first published under the title "Our Variousness") calls "the trope of an inassimilable open-endedness" (*Back* 133).[9] There is what might well be called ambivalence in Giscombe's choice of the adjective "inassimilable." In particular, the trope to which he refers is that of the ocean, which is obviously a historically charged image for African Americans, although the ocean in Giscombe's essay is not just a reference to the slave trade but to Nova Scotia as a staging area from which "Black Loyalists" during the Revolutionary War might have returned to Africa, a story Giscombe says is as inassimilable as the ocean.

There is no sense that Giscombe has Stevens' "The Idea of Order at Key West" in mind; indeed, most of his quotations from Stevens are from the collected aphorisms in "Adagia" (*Back* 6, 137; see also *Back* 8 and *Prairie* xi–xii, 79–80 for additional references to Stevens). Still, his ocean's "inassimilable open-endedness" can help show how Stevens' differently inassimilable sea might be reread by what Giscombe calls "unanticipated" writers (*Back* 94),[10] a phrase that he takes from Harryette Mullen and that is echoed in Narayanan's image of being an "unintended reader." The rereadings of Stevens' tropes, which Giscombe's comments invite, may make me an unintended reader of Giscombe, although my association of Stevens' sea with Giscombe's ocean is not, I think, out of line. Bodies of water and human bodies are, for Giscombe, consistently figured as vexed, or, one might say, ambiguous, given how black bodies and voices are typically figured in natural landscapes; that is, Giscombe frequently points out that it is not only literary canons but nature in which black bodies have difficulty defining themselves, although he also says that he tends "to 'read' ... locations as though they were poems—ambiguous, contradictory, riddled with echoes of other poems and other places" (*Back* 149).[11] Nonetheless, he writes in an essay originally titled "Natural Abilities & Natural Writing," "Our words don't mean—it's our bodies that mean, that's where our nature is. And because of this we have no particular agency there, in the depiction of nature ... we are not other enough from the natural world to be able to find metaphors of ourselves there." The paragraph ends: "Instead, we *are* the natural world, we're ripe: upon us can be projected metaphors by nature writers or writers about human nature" (*Back* 36).[12]

Thus, as Giscombe traces the relationship between black bodies and images of nature, one might expect him to focus on what Jarrell, Nielsen, and DuRose argue is Stevens' attitude toward and uses of the wildness of "others," and perhaps to share the love/hate relationship—that is, the sometimes enabling ambivalence—found in Phillips' comments or Hayes's poem. But that is not quite what one finds.

Giscombe recently cited Stevens in the introduction to the third issue of *Mixed Blood*—a journal associated with a reading project he helped to found—saying he wanted the project to foster

> talk about the relationship ... between "difficult" work and race ... [by including in the journal pieces that] track some edges of the conversation. (Stevens wrote, "When the blackbird flew out of sight,/It marked the edge/Of one of many circles.") Race informs all categories (including the work of Wallace Stevens). The question here might be ... What are the edges here? What borders are crossed and, more interestingly, how are they crossed?
>
> (3; ellipses added)[13]

How borders and categories are crossed interests me, too. In the passage just quoted, it seems Giscombe does read his body as being figured by Stevens' blackbird, but he then claims that identification more positively, if obliquely, in a way that suggests his interest is in the contradictions (or ambivalence) and ambiguities in Stevens. In Giscombe's own writings, edges are most clearly racial as well as poetic—but also, I am suggesting, Stevensian (even when they involve unanticipated readings of Stevens).

For those who know Giscombe's poetry, it is clear that edges (meaning peripheries, borders, and—to some extent—edginess) have long preoccupied him. As he noted in an interview with Mark Nowak about his most recent full-length book of poetry, *Prairie Style*, talking about listening to a Jamaican lecturer (in 1980) whom he had previously and erroneously assumed was black, edges and borders are "flexible—national ones as well as racial ones … [T]he flexibility and interesting uncertainty that I'd always understood about race was even bigger than I'd [previously] imagined" ("Prairie" n. pag.). In short, the way Giscombe suggests he is marking the edge of one of many circles himself is not surprising. By 2012, when he quoted "Thirteen Ways of Looking at a Blackbird" in the introduction to *Mixed Blood*, Giscombe would certainly have been aware of Moss's and Hayes's poetic responses to Stevens' work, even if his conversation with Stevens is not quite theirs. He also had probably read the exchanges on Jackson's *Harriet* post, so that his may be at least a four-way conversation. I should add that the unanticipated reading of Stevensian edges also gestures toward and mixes the "many circles" or reading communities in which Giscombe's work circulates: his writing has appeared in collections of Canadian poetry (although he is not Canadian), nature poetry, black nature poetry, and experimental poetics, not to mention his writings on railroads, disability studies, and popular culture.

I have so far focused on Giscombe's essays. To end, though, I would like briefly to trace how his poetry also enacts the ambivalent and contradictory exchanges (or border crossings) using language that may be called Stevensian (even if not exclusively so) as well as tracing a poetics that similarly is and is not Stevensian. Or is unanticipatedly Stevensian. *Prairie Style* includes a prose poem entitled "Palaver," which means "chit-chat" but also carries the connotation of chatting someone up. The word shows up, too, in Giscombe's previous poetry collection, *Giscome Road*, where it is suggested he knows the word's etymology: "palaver" comes from the Portuguese by way of early West African Pidgin as a trader's term for negotiations with West Africans (in the slave trade) and is more distantly related to the Latin *parabola*, meaning "comparison" (23, 33). Not least, the word appears in chapter eleven of Ellison's *Invisible Man*, where the second definition ("chatting someone up") is most salient. This is a long preamble to the poem itself, but—to use Giscombe's version of Stevens—language that moves in or marks the edges of "many circles" requires lengthy preambles. Here is "Palaver":

> Neighborhood? Proximities change on you sooner or later. There's a level of artlessness; my luck has changed more than one time. Love could be an embankment, even an esker, or Customs; or a sailing ship, noisy at the horizon.
>
> The idea was that the wind could *carry* your voice from here to there, from one side of the field to the other. I was always leaving a place at the point where I'd begun to care for it. This was the gain of singing; the devil's hungry (in a song), the devil is sweet. How do I look? Neighborhood's a little fishtail in the substances.
>
> (8)

I am not arguing that there is a reference here to Stevens' "The World as Meditation"—despite the ship on the horizon—but his poem (its tropes, its use of free indirect discourse, its syntax) opens shifting subject positions for readers throughout in part because by the time he wrote "The World as Meditation," Stevens was specifically imagining his poems, including his earlier poetry, as read and internalized by later reader-poets (cf. Steinman). Giscombe's poem thus draws on the open-endedness he sees in Stevens (making Giscombe a not entirely unanticipated reader) and also redeploys, if in a somewhat different neighborhood (to use Giscombe's image), Stevens' use of language to open multiple subject positions.

To start, "Palaver" makes words, as well as voices, carry a good deal of weight. Another poem in *Prairie Style*, titled "Lazy Man's Load," tropes on racial stereotypes and on the use of the idiomatic expression "a lazy man's load" to refer to how lazy men, not wanting to make many trips, carry heavy loads. In this vein, in "Palaver," "fishtail" may echo the hunger attributed to the devil; or it may refer to fishtail braids, figuring how images, ways of speaking, and ideas are braided together in the poem; as well as resonating with the definition of the word that means sliding in an uncontrolled way—artlessly—as when the end of a car slides from side to side, here with erotic overtones ("fishtail" being also a dance move in blues dancing).[14] Neighborhoods—like circles, like word usage or idioms—thus slide, perhaps with a bit of *sprezzatura*, changing over time and in relationship to one another. Even the song to which the poem refers crosses genres and carries across fields: the lyrics are from "Gibsom Street," from Laura Nyro's 1969 album, *New York Tendaberry*; moreover, as Giscombe has noted, the song title resonates, if only at the edges, with the title of his book of poetry *Giscome Road* ("Re: A Small" n. pag.).

"Palaver" is a meditation on love, on intersubjective and cross-cultural exchange, on race and geography, on borders that may be natural or policed by Customs (in both senses of the word, that is, with or without the capital *C*), but above all on how perspectives shift. "How do I look?" is a question not only about appearances and bodies but also about how one looks at the world as things are placed further from or in closer proximity to one another. We as readers then move from what at first blush seems an abstract meditation on community and "proximity"—the Latinate, polysyllabic word in itself indicates formality—to a more personalized address, sliding between second and first person, from blues dancing to Nyro's song as "covered" by Giscombe's book, and, ultimately, to the instability and energy—a "fishtail"—of changing alliances (neighborhoods, fields, lovers) that make "substances" (by which I take it we are invited to think of essences, in a more abstract sense, as well as of materiality) flexible and interestingly uncertain—to return to Giscombe's comment on recognizing racialized voices. In other words, the poem "fields" the question (as noted earlier, the pun is Giscombe's) of how edges, borders, and categories are defined and crossed.

All this is to sketch how unfolding thought is enacted in "Palaver"; one could also underline how Giscombe's language insists on a lack of *closure*, to use the formulation both Phillips and Giscombe associate with Stevens. To quote from another poem in *Prairie Style*, for Giscombe "transition *is* happiness" (76), a Stevensian proposition the poems enact or perform. What we hear may be framed as a form of signifying, as well, although it is also an echo of Stevens on the need for poetry to change and give pleasure. Further, while Giscombe's syntax is not exactly Stevens', both poets might indeed be said to be able to use syntax, point of view, diction, and tone to "bring a sentence to its knees."

"Cry Me a River," the poem that precedes "Palaver" in *Prairie Style*, cites Kenneth Burke's *A Grammar of Motives* on metaphor (although Burke is explicitly mentioned only in the Acknowledgments) as indicating that "value exists in relation to opportunities for exchange—seeing something in terms of something else" (7); Burke adds that metaphor is "the 'carrying-over' of a term from one realm into another, a process that necessarily involves varying degrees of incongruity" (504). This Burkean view of metaphor also links Giscombe's and Stevens' poetics. Giscombe admittedly is interested in placing everything (including places) not only in more than one light but also in more than one culturally specific language, among other things placing in relationship the various ways in which different readers or reading communities read poems and places in different registers. Moreover, the poems invite more than just literary exchange in a way that is not as clearly a *thematic* focus of especially Stevens' earlier work. Nonetheless, I am suggesting that this form of exchange (perhaps, as Burke says, with some incongruity) is in part what allows and motivates Giscombe's, Phillips', Shepherd's, Hayes's, and Moss's conversations with Stevens and his poems.

My conclusions are tentative. I have lightly suggested that Stevens' poems (especially after the Second World War) self-consciously look forward to "unanticipated" readers, if not specifically those I discuss here. This is to say the African American poets responding to Stevens teach us something about reading Stevens; one could say I have been tracing not just responses to Stevens, but a kind of call and response between Stevens and later African American poets. Less lightly, I hope to suggest something about what it means for poets like Hayes, Moss, Phillips, Shepherd, and Giscombe to associate Stevens with ambiguity, open-endedness, and (above all) ambivalence, namely how being even a completely unanticipated reader might be unsettlingly *productive*. Certainly in Giscombe's work, we find an invitation not only to read African American poetry through Stevens but to read Stevens' poems to find what is "ambiguous, contradictory, riddled with echoes," including clearly unintended echoes. I might reiterate that the ambiguity and ambivalence Giscombe is not alone in associating with Stevens' language are themselves also recognizable—historically and rhetorically—as African American tropes. In light of this, I would like to conclude by returning to Giscombe's metaphorical equation of ambivalence with imagination—and his self-conscious echo of the end of *Invisible Man*: "I condemn and affirm, say no and say yes, say yes and say no" (566). This is not so ambiguous, but it is surely productive ambivalence. Thus, Giscombe places Ellison and Stevens in relation to one another, beginning another conversation after the fact.

Notes

1   Nielsen mentions "The News and the Weather" (*CPP* 238), section five of "The Auroras of Autumn" (*CPP* 358), "Owl's Clover" (*CPP* 159–60), "Exposition of the Contents of a Cab" (*CPP* 52), "In the South" (*CPP* 535–36), "Two at Norfolk" (*CPP*

92), and "The Man with the Blue Guitar" (*CPP* 998–99), among other poems. He also links poems like "The Greenest Continent" section of "Owl's Clover" to Vachel Lindsay's association between Africa and fatality in "The Congo" (Nielsen 32–33) and contrasts Stevens' "Like Decorations in a Nigger Cemetery" with Howard Nemerov's "A Negro Cemetery Next to a White One" (131, citing Nemerov 372).

2   Nielsen also mentions how Stevens sometimes signed his letters "Sambo" (60, see Holly Stevens 199). At least in their readings of—for instance—"Owl's Clover," DuRose develops a more nuanced interpretation of the poems (16–18), although Nielsen first raised the question of how to talk critically about Stevens and race.

3   The list here might also have looked back in time, for instance to Raymond Patterson's *26 Ways of Looking at a Blackman and Other Poems* (1969), especially section XXVI of the title poem.

4   "Snow for Wallace Stevens"—one strophe of twenty-two lines—was first published in the *Harvard Review* 36 (2009), before it appeared in the poet's 2010 volume *Lighthead*.

5   Moss's understanding of blackbirds as racialized draws on cultural commonplace; in Cincinnati in 1947, on May 13, for instance, the Crosley field organist played "Bye, Bye Blackbird" when Jackie Robinson came on the field (Norwood and Brackman 133). See also Nielsen's argument that Carl Rakosi's "The Black Crow" reads and parodies Stevens' "Domination of Black" as a racial reference (91–92).

6   The panelists were Linda Gregerson, Stanley Plumly, David Baker, and Carl Phillips; the program specifically noted the panelists would address how Stevens "proposes … complex methods of inquiry."

7   Shepherd's comments were posted on February 5; Jackson's reply on the same day; the comments here quoted from Narayanan are dated February 6.

8   Shepherd adds that at the same time Stevens set an "unattainable goal" for Shepherd.

9   "Our Variousness" first appeared in *Race, Romanticism, and the Atlantic*, ed. Paul Youngquist (Farnham: Ashgate, 2013); all essays are quoted here with the permission of C. S. Giscombe from the revised versions found in a typescript manuscript titled *Back Burner*, forthcoming from Dalkey Archive Press under the new title *Border Towns*.

10   First published in "Miscegenation Studies," *Tripwire* 5 (2001).

11   First published in "Boll Weevils, Coyotes, and the Color of Nuisance," the introductory essay in *Black Nature*, ed. Camille Dungy (Athens: University of Georgia Press, 2009).

12   "Natural Abilities & Natural Writing" first appeared in *Chain* 7 (2000), ed. Jena Osman and Juliana Spahr, and published in Oakland, California from 1994–2005.

13   Quoted with permission from C. S. Giscombe.

14   The dance move was common by 1913, further popularized in Rome Nelson's 1929 "Head Rag Hop," and is still popular today. In urban slang, "fishtail" can also mean a purposeful sliding of a car.

Works Cited

Brogan, Jacqueline Vaught. *The Violence Within/The Violence Without: Wallace Stevens and the Emergence of a Revolutionary Poetics*. Athens: University of Georgia Press, 2003. Print.

Burke, Kenneth. *A Grammar of Motives*. 1945. Berkeley: University of California Press, 1969. Print.

DuRose, Lisa. "Racial Domain and the Imagination of Wallace Stevens." *Wallace Stevens Journal* 22.1 (1998): 3–22. Print.

Ellison, Ralph. *Invisible Man*. New York: Vintage, 1972. Print.

Gates, Henry Louis, Jr. *The Signifying Monkey*. New York: Oxford University Press, 1988. Print.

Giscombe, C. S. *Back Burner*. 2013. TS.

Giscombe, C. S. *Giscome Road*. Champaign: Dalkey Archive, 1998. Print.

Giscombe, C. S. "Introduction." *Mixed Blood* 3 (2012): 3–4. Print.

Giscombe, C. S. "Poetry and the Oblique." MLA Annual Convention. Philadelphia. December 2004. Panel.

Giscombe, C. S. *Prairie Style*. Champaign: Dalkey Archive, 2008. Print.

Giscombe, C. S. "Prairie Style: An Interview with C. S. Giscombe." Interview by Mark Nowak. *Harriet*. Poetry Foundation. August 28, 2008. March 10, 2014. Web.

Giscombe, C. S. "Re: A Small Perhaps Silly Question." Message to the author. March 26, 2014. E-mail.

Hayes, Terrance. *Lighthead*. New York: Penguin, 2010. Print.

Jackson, Major, Reginald Shepherd, and Vivek Narayanan. "Wallace Stevens after 'Lunch.'" *Harriet*. Poetry Foundation. February 4–16, 2008. March 10, 2015. Web.

Jarrell, Randall. *Poetry and the Age*. New York: Knopf, 1953. Print.

Moss, Thylias. "Interview: Thylias Moss." Interview by Sean Thomas Dougherty. *Onthebus* 4–5.2 (1992): 296–301. Print.

Moss, Thylias. *Pyramid of Bone*. Charlottesville: University of Virginia Press, 1989. Print.

Moss, Thylias. *The Tale of a Sky-Blue Dress*. New York: Avon, 1998. Print.

Nemerov, Howard. *The Collected Poems of Howard Nemerov*. Chicago: University of Chicago Press, 1977. Print.

Nielsen, Aldon Lynn. *Reading Race: White American Poets and the Racial Discourse in the Twentieth Century*. Athens: University of Georgia Press, 1988. Print.

Norwood, Stephen, and Harold Brackman. "Going to Bat for Jackie Robinson: The Jewish Role in Breaking Baseball's Color Line." *Journal of Sport History* 26.1 (1999): 115–41. March 10, 2014. Web.

Patterson, Raymond. *26 Ways of Looking at a Blackman and Other Poems*. New York: Award, 1969. Print.

Phillips, Carl. "Reading Stevens for Writers: The Mind at the End of the Palm." AWP Annual Convention. Seattle. March 1, 2014. Panel.

Richardson, Joan. *Wallace Stevens: The Later Years, 1923–1955*. New York: Beech Tree, 1988. Print.

Shepherd, Reginald. "Reginald Shepherd." Poetry Foundation. N.d. March 10, 2014. Web.

Steinman, Lisa M. "Cross-Dressing as Stevens Cross-Dressing." *Wallace Stevens Journal* 28.2 (2004): 166–74. Print.

Stevens, Holly, ed. *Souvenirs and Prophecies: The Young Wallace Stevens*. New York: Knopf, 1977. Print.

Stevens, Wallace. *Wallace Stevens: Collected Poetry and Prose*. Ed. Frank Kermode and Joan Richardson. New York: Library of America, 1997. Print.

16

"This Song Is for My Foe": Olive Senior and Terrance Hayes Rewrite Stevens

Rachel Galvin

Wallace Stevens announced in a 1948 letter to José Rodríguez Feo that he did not actually read poetry, as "a way of defeating people who look only for echoes and influences" (*L* 575). And in 1954, he famously wrote to Richard Eberhart,

> I am not conscious of having been influenced by anybody and have purposely held off from reading highly mannered people like Eliot and Pound so that I should not absorb anything, even unconsciously. But there is a kind of critic who spends his time dissecting what he reads for echoes, imitations, influences, as if no one was ever simply himself but is always compounded of a lot of other people.
>
> (*L* 813)

Stevens wished to claim that he was a unique and self-identical writer and that his poems sprang forth through a kind of parthenogenesis. But of course the opposite is precisely the case: all writing is composed of other writing, as critics from Julia Kristeva to Haroldo de Campos have shown. Despite Stevens' "deeply rooted originality neurosis," as Bart Eeckhout calls it, his poetry is the product of a conscious or unconscious recycling of literature and philosophy—and it has, in turn, actively invited "extraction and grafting" by poets and critics alike (53, 50).[1]

There is a fundamental problem, however, with the terms of Stevens' claim and the critical reception of it. Harold Bloom's model of influence is too limited and the vocabulary used to describe it in US poetry criticism insufficient. It is inadequate for conceptualizing the relationship between contemporary black poets and a canonical white poet, for example, given that the terms for literary relationality that get bandied about (influence, imitation, mimicry, pastiche, parody, plagiarism), in their understanding of authorship and authority, are born from ideologies of race, empire, and patriarchy. How can we discuss these relationships without remaining mired in the colonial logic of mimesis? In this chapter, I suggest neither accepting nor rejecting the Bloomian model, but instead turning to other models entirely. My method is prompted by poems written by two black poets working within different national literary traditions, Olive Senior and Terrance Hayes. As a postcolonial subject educated in the aftermath of Jamaica's liberation and currently residing in Canada, Senior is part of several traditions; Hayes is an African American poet living in the United States. Their disparate contexts show that Stevens' poetry resonates throughout the Americas as a generative and problematic exemplum. In rewriting and responding to Stevens, Senior and Hayes engage with a tradition of resistance to the colonial logic of mimicry. The hemispheric priorities I uncover in their strategies offer an alternative to Bloom's model, and they indicate that there are political concerns and literary connections that link black aesthetic practices with a broader, postcolonial, hemispheric frame.[2] Senior's and Hayes's work opens the potential for alternative methodologies and a reconsideration of the critical language used to discuss intertextual relations more broadly. As I will show, crucial optics for analyzing literary relations—a vocabulary and a theoretical framing—are found in black diasporic and postcolonial responses to discourses of mimicry as well as in Latin American theories (of consumption, cannibalism, and retrospective influence) that understand literary generational relationships as non-teleological.

My goal is to contribute to the development of a hemispheric poetics that considers poetry across languages, in translation and in the original, and not only examines poetry's "cross-cultural knotting" and "translocal stretch," as Jahan Ramazani writes (12, 14), but also draws on multilingual theory and criticism from across the Americas.[3] By assembling an archive of poems and drawing on a set of hemispheric critical theories that grapple with displacement, diaspora, power, and authority, I aim to develop a mode of analyzing literary relations that is attentive to colonialism and power. The poetry I examine in this chapter requires an expansive model for understanding influence, imitation, and inheritance in the Americas. Such a model will also reveal the ideology underpinning Stevens' own articulation of his practice, even as he rejects the suggestion that he has been influenced.

There is a difference in the vocabulary that US poetry critics use to describe the relationship between white writers and between white writers and people of color. The "influence" of white writers upon each other may be described with a range of tropes. At the symposium organized in preparation for this volume, for example, Stevens' work was characterized as a "spur" (Eeckhout) and an "infectious example" (Bonnie Costello). Responses to his poetry were called a "reprise" (Eeckhout) and poets were said to "extend Stevens' inheritance" (Lisa Goldfarb). Charles Altieri spoke of "reappropriation" and Angus Cleghorn of "channeling." Joan Richardson employed the terminology of "overhearing" and "haunting." These vivid terms are all relatively value-neutral.

John Ashbery, for one, is often said to "channel" or "borrow from" Stevens. It would be surprising for a critic to describe Ashbery as "mimicking" the older poet. And yet, in a laudatory review of Terrance Hayes's work in *Poetry* magazine, Abigail Deutsch describes Hayes precisely as a "gifted mimic" of his predecessors (475). She stresses that Hayes "looks—and sometimes talks—back to ancestors both poetical and political" (473). He "holds in his ear … the tones of African-American discourse—that exploration of hyphenation … When he spots self-seriousness in such conversation, he parrots and parodies" (473–74). Deutsch describes Hayes as an accomplished imitator with an "interest in impersonation," who plays a "game of dress-up" in *Lighthead*, giving the collection "the feel of a variety show" (475).

Deutsch's focus on imitation conditions her discussion of Hayes's poems to the occlusion of other significant elements. She cites the following lines from Hayes's poem "Arbor for Butch," a long *pecha kucha* poem about a father–son relationship:

> In the far south where history shades everything,
> there are people who fear trees. I once heard an old man say
> *I may be black as a crow, but I'm white inside.*
> Nowhere else does the sky do what the sky does there,
> where the graves are filled with dirt the color of fire.
>
> (qtd. on 475)

Deutsch calls the poem "lovely, elusive," an example of Hayes's "mysteriousness." She passes over in silence Hayes's allusion to the history of lynching, his exploration of intergenerational dialogue, and the complications of racial self-identification, instead emphasizing what she views as Hayes's imitative capacities: "Tuned in to the sounds that precede and surround him, Hayes is a gifted mimic: his poems offer imitations of ad campaigns, CD copy, job applications" (475). Describing African American artists as "gifted mimics" has been a dismissive if not derogatory gesture for centuries, in a cultural economy in which "originality" is prized above all. Racially determined power dynamics undergird conventional notions of literary relationality and the vocabulary used to describe them, designating the link between canonical white male writers as one of influence, heritage, and patrimony, while relationships between white male writers and women or people of color are often coded as derivative, secondary, or imitative. Deutsch is not wrong—Hayes does have a great ear—but her essay is freighted with a historical problem that it does not acknowledge. It is not necessarily a testament to the reviewer's bad faith, but to the paucity of critical vocabulary in US poetry criticism.

Henry Louis Gates Jr., in his seminal work of African American literary criticism *The Signifying Monkey*, analyzed and historicized the terminology of imitation and the racist assumptions that underpin it. He developed a notion of "textual revision" as a way to designate how black writers have employed reference and revision to propose negative critiques and declare filiation simultaneously. Gates describes such a text as a "double-voiced utterance" when it "Signifies upon another text, by tropological revision or repetition and difference" (88). In this vein, Hayes's "Snow for Wallace Stevens," for example, fuses homage with critique, expressing "love without/forgiveness" (57). Hayes cites a few lines by Stevens, weaving them into his own poem, so that his poem carries Stevens' lines within it and preserves them, even as the speaker announces that Stevens is his "foe." This double articulation is an instance of "mimicry" in Homi Bhabha's sense: "a complex strategy of reform, regulation and discipline, which 'appropriates' the Other as it visualizes power," posing "an immanent threat to both 'normalized' knowledges and disciplinary powers" (122, 123). Both Hayes and Senior revise Stevens by claiming filiation with his work at the same time as they criticize it and the socio-political system that facilitated its production and dissemination. Such critiques lay bare the racism of the cozy transmission of literary inheritance among homogenous groups or between writers of equal social positions.

Further, with their poems, Senior and Hayes have rewritten Stevens and transformed his work through retrospective influence, an idea developed by the Argentine writer Jorge Luis Borges.[4] They have changed the way that the canonical work of the high Modernist Stevens can be read, so that when a reader encounters Stevens now, he or she may hear the echoes of Senior's and Hayes's poems responding to him. Senior's and Hayes's work insists on the blanks in Stevens' poetry—the socio-historical contingencies left unmentioned—and makes them stand out starkly. These poets record an alternative narrative of the oppression and violence integral to the development of what kind of art is considered poetry, what kinds of experiences poems can record, the kind of language that is deemed acceptable, and the institutions that have been fashioned to create and legislate those values. Their poetry performs this political critique at the same time as it explores the resources of poetic form; the aesthetic and political charges of their poems are inextricable.

To be more specific, after reading Senior's work, one may now perceive the elements of Stevens' poetry that would not exist without the benefit of Senior's vision. Her work modifies our conception of the past, even as it modifies the future, to paraphrase Borges. This modification occurs in the same way that Kafka's work changes how Browning is read, as Borges asserted in "Kafka and His Precursors," an essay on the nonlinear relationship between works of literature:

> In each of these texts we find Kafka's idiosyncrasy to a greater or lesser degree, but if Kafka had never written a line, we would not perceive this quality; in other words, it would not exist. The poem "Fears and Scruples" by Browning foretells Kafka's work, but our reading of Kafka perceptibly sharpens and deflects our reading of the poem.
>
> (201)

In formulating this theory, Borges himself is carrying out a critical adaptation: he is drawing from T. S. Eliot's "Tradition and the Individual Talent" while departing from it in a key way.[5] He reverses Eliot's map of the flow of cultural capital, and indeed temporality, identifying elements of current works in those past (Castro 57). Borges' ideas about authorship, originality, and (the impossibility of) plagiarism have proven fruitful for many writers and critics in elaborating new theories of literary history, and I draw on them here as one way to begin rethinking the conventional direction of influence and, more broadly, literary relationality or non-dynastic "adjacency," as Edward Said called it, between texts (10).[6]

In "Thirteen Ways of Looking at Blackbird (after Wallace Stevens)," Olive Senior recasts the blackbird as an African slave who has recently arrived at a sugarcane plantation. The article "a" is missing in Senior's title, transforming "Blackbird" into a proper name. Where Stevens meditates on non-dualism in his poem (IV, *CPP* 75), in Senior's corresponding section IV, she insists that unity is not possible and identity is difficult to ascertain. Abased and enslaved, a "Survivor of the crossing," Blackbird is "the lucky one in three" (II), and "no longer knows/if he is man or woman or bird or simply is" (IV) (47). In this way, Senior writes into the historical blanks of Stevens' poem and shows that culturally constructed concepts of what is legible and meaningful are inextricable from the violent history of racism in the Americas. Her poem "problematizes the signs of racial and cultural priority, so that the 'national' is no longer naturalizable," as Bhabha writes. "What emerges between mimesis and mimicry is a *writing*, a mode of representation, that marginalizes the monumentality of history, quite simply mocks its power to be a model, that power which supposedly makes it imitable" (125). In the closing section, Senior's Blackbird is found at a second remove, in the shadows and among the traces of dead slaves: "In the dark/out of the sun/Blackbird sits/among the shavings/from the cedar coffins" (49). This scene is at once a form of mourning and a testament to the persistent situation of black writers throughout the Americas who must "negotiate gaps or conflicts between their artistic goals and the operation of race in the production, dissemination, and reception of their writing," as Evie Shockley writes in her discussion of black aesthetics in *Renegade Poetics: Black Aesthetics and Formal Innovation in African American Poetry* (9). Blackbird is seated among the "shavings" or splinters of the wood that had housed the bodies of the dead. The slivers of wood are akin to shredded paper or the slender sections of the poems. Senior's poem rewrites Stevens' tranquil vision by insisting that the history of slavery is inseparable from the history of the development of ideas about self, personhood, and the nature of the literary. The work of mourning, commemoration, and the construction of literary lineage converge in her poem.

Senior's rewriting has the potential to change how readers encounter Stevens. When we reread section III of Stevens' poem, the words "whirled" and "pantomime" leap out from "The blackbird whirled in the autumn winds./It was a small part of the pantomime" (*CPP* 75). They now recall a man named Blackbird who was "bought and sold and bought/again" (Senior 47), and the white-painted faces of mimes who tell a story by using their bodily gestures instead of speech, indicating that the physical displacements of Blackbird articulate his history. Reflecting on the phrase "the bawds of euphony" in section X (*CPP* 76), Stevens now seems to echo Senior's assertion "No euphony," which implies a cacophonous cry of suffering at "Even the sight of the whip" (48). Stevens' line in section VIII, "the blackbird is involved/In what I know" (*CPP* 76), suddenly stands out starkly as a historical statement: the history of slavery is integral to what poems know. Senior insists with the entirety of her poem that the poetic speaker's knowledge of aesthetics and the creative patterning of speech in "noble accents/And lucid, inescapable rhythms" are inextricable from Blackbird's enslavement (*CPP* 75). By implication, the history of racism is enmeshed with the history of what is considered honorable and "lucid," which is to say, what is intelligible and what can be commemorated. Black diasporic experience presents an occluded history rendered illegible: "Blackbird traces in the shadow not cast/ the indecipherable past" (Senior 48). Senior's inscription of the history of slavery into the structure of Stevens' abstract, thirteen-part structure is at once a restitution and an appropriative incorporation. It is a way of stressing that what is left out of poetry, within the "Complacencies of the peignoir" (*CPP* 53), is also the ugliness of history.

The next poem in Senior's collection, "Misreading Wallace Stevens," is included along with "Thirteen Ways of Looking at Blackbird" in a section titled "Islanded." Although they might seem topically related, the poems are specifically not grouped together with the other bird poems of the preceding section ("The Pull of Birds"), indicating that Senior viewed the two poems' political critiques as part of her reflection on outsiders' views of the Antilles (such as "Rejected Text for a Tourist Brochure") and the difficult position of the diasporic writer who can never fully return home. "That world no longer exists," she writes in "Blue Foot Traveller" (72). In "Misreading Wallace Stevens," Senior critiques Stevens' portrayal of the Caribbean for its "blue/denial" and "the world arranged just so/for the viewers." The poem alludes to elements from Stevens' favorite lexical field: "the yellow of tropical, the pale green/palms upturned" (50). It critiques the tourist's exoticizing gaze ("How exotic! the travel writers thrill./How perfectly chic!") as well as Caribbean self-presentation-for-export ("the vivid birds preening") (51, 50). The tourists' perception is partial, flawed, and they cannot comprehend what they see or hear: "Understanding/not a word, they immediately/arrange for translation and/publication" (51). These lines refer to the uneven cultural translation that occurs between tourists and inhabitants, as well as the commodification and dissemination of Caribbean culture. The poem objects that in the exoticization and conspicuous consumption of Caribbean culture that occurs through neocolonial tourism, the graves of "black souls/now dressed/in white" go "Unseen" (52)—a word that appears three times in the poem, always capitalized.

Senior's critique may well be applied to a swathe of Stevens' Caribbean imagery throughout his oeuvre, but she has in mind one particular poem that employs a racial slur, "Like Decorations in a Nigger Cemetery." Stevens' title is intended to refer to an excess of ornament, or "the litter that one usually finds in a nigger cemetery," as his friend Judge Arthur Powell wrote to him in a 1934 letter (*L* 272).[7] At the time Stevens composed the poem, the commonly accepted term of respect was "Negro," which Stevens frequently employed, as Eleanor Cook notes.[8] In this poem, however, Stevens conspicuously employs the racist slur. Senior aims her critique not only at Stevens' use of the derogatory term, but also at the racial ideologies that fuel such terminology.

"Misreading Wallace Stevens" pivots on Senior's purposeful misprision of the word "patios" in Stevens' "Like Decorations in a Nigger Cemetery." She reverses the final vowels, recasting the word as "patois" in her poem. The line from Stevens that she places as an epigraph, "The birds are singing in the yellow patios" (*CPP* 123), becomes "a choir of birds singing/in the yellow patois" and, finally, "black souls/now dressed/in white/singing in the yellow patois" (Senior 51, 52). These lines affirm as they mourn, remembering the silenced dead and describing their voices as possessing a local accent, just as the birds have. It re-envisions birdcall, which has been used derisively as a trope for the imitative expressions of New World artists, as Derek Walcott has noted (7), so that it becomes a "choir" that sings in its own tongue. Senior inscribes in the poem a manner of speaking proper to her own culture. Birdsong—which in Stevens' work, and indeed throughout the history of literature, functions as a venerable trope for lyric poetry—has been translated into Jamaican speech. This is one way Senior responds to Stevens' racial slur, which she reproduces in the epigraph to her own poem—reproduces and critiques through double articulation. In response to the poem's racist language, Senior changes the terms to invigorate another, racially coded and specifically local language (one that may be difficult for the tourist to comprehend), casting patois as the language of lyric and the language of lament. "Misreading Wallace Stevens" concludes like so:

> Unseen the black souls
> now dressed
> in white
>
> singing in the yellow patois
> accenting
> towards light
>
> (52)

Senior's choice of "accenting" causes the reader to hear "ascending" within a term for inflected language. This is an instance of denominalization: Senior has taken a noun that may potentially be used to indicate difference and turned it into an active verb. These final two stanzas sum up the examination of black speech and concern with visibility begun in the previous poem, "Thirteen Ways of Looking at Blackbird." But this poem ends with an affirmation. Just as the vowels in "patios" have been juggled and claimed as "patois," and "accenting" one's lyrics is a way of emphasizing and elevating them, so Senior sings her song within and without the landscape of Stevens' poetry. She has absorbed Stevens' lexicon and topology within her own, as a way to potentially transform them. Just as Borges asserted regarding Kafka's relation to his precursors, when readers look back from Senior's to Stevens' poem, her presence and her deliberate "misreading" can suddenly become visible and audible. Words oscillate and letters become anagrams. The reader may at first think her eyes have deceived her, but in fact the words are not quite what was expected. *Patios* is also a *patois*, hiding complex histories within its morphemes, and the canonical Modernist poem containing a racist slur is shown to be what it was and still is, a text urgently in need of revision, of strategic misreading.

Terrance Hayes also writes back to "Like Decorations in a Nigger Cemetery" in his poem "Snow for Wallace Stevens." It is a complex, dialogic response that announces it is both for and against a "foe":

> No one living a snowed-in life
> can sleep without a blindfold.
> ....
> This song is for *the wise man who avenges*
> *by building his city in snow.*
> For his decorations in a nigger cemetery.
> How, with pipes of winter
> lining his cognition, does someone learn
> to bring a sentence to its knees?
> Who is not more than his limitations?
> (57)

Just a slight turn to the preposition matters: in Hayes's rewriting, instead of Stevens offering poetic ornaments *like* cemetery decorations, indicating self-disparagement about his ephemeral lyric flourishes, Hayes has Stevens writing his poetry *in* an African American cemetery, that is, within and on top of a gravesite—a fact to which he is perhaps blindfolded. The citation from section L of Stevens' poem ("But the wise man avenges by building his city in snow" [*CPP* 128]) indicates that Hayes has chosen to "avenge" that history within poetry by building *his* city in snow, which is to say, to construct his own literary edifice in relation to Stevens' work: thus a poem titled "Snow for Wallace Stevens." Hayes's quotations from Stevens are bound up with questions of authority, as citations always are. Citation at once links two disparate elements and reminds the reader of its own displaced status, as Edward Said has noted.[9]

Like Stevens' "A High-Toned Old Christian Woman," which Hayes quotes, "Snow for Wallace Stevens" is a discursive apostrophe mixed with philosophical reflections. Stevens' statement "We agree in principle. That's clear" (*CPP* 47) plays in the background of Hayes's admission that he is compelled by the idea of poetry as the supreme fiction. The supreme fiction is in fact the condition of possibility for the present address to Stevens: "I too, having lost faith/in language have placed my faith in language./Thus, I have a capacity for love without/forgiveness" (Hayes 57). The poem combines references to at least three immediately recognizable Stevens poems: "A High-Toned Old Christian Woman," "The Glass of Water," and "Like Decorations in a Nigger Cemetery." Hayes weaves in phrases from each of these, providing his own humorous rhyme:

> *Light is the lion that comes down to drink.*
> I know *tink and tank and tunk-a-tunk-tunk*
> holds nearly the same sound as a bottle.
> *Drink and drank and drunk-a-drunk-drunk,*
> light is the lion that comes down.
>
> (57)

Bonnie Costello has noted that "the lion in Stevens is always a metaphor for natural energy that makes objects visible, and for poetic will, that 'destructive force' which transforms objects, the light of the mind" (36). Here, Hayes's own poetic volition is a light that comes down like a lion, amidst Stevens' snow, surveying, praising, and criticizing. The poetic speaker makes two deictic statements referring to the textual nature of the utterance and his strategy of intertwining Stevens' lines with his own—"This song is for *the wise man*" and "This song is for my foe" (Hayes 57). These help gloss the title: snow is a figure for a song or a lyric poem. Hayes's version of Stevens is a poet whose cognition is lined "with pipes of winter" and, living a "snowed-in life," must sleep blindfolded—all of which implies a certain coldness and restricted scope of vision caused by immersion in a white world. The poem concludes:

> This song is for my foe,
> the clean-shaven, gray-suited, gray patron
> of Hartford, the emperor of whiteness
> blue as a body made of snow.
>
> (57)

The compound epithet "the clean-shaven, gray-suited, gray patron/of Hartford" (recalling Stevens' public image of isolation and withdrawal, the "snowed-in life") is exceeded in "the emperor of whiteness," a phrase that at once lauds Stevens' great achievement in poetry and points out his canonical status as a white poet. The poem frames its relation to the poet from Hartford and his "supreme fiction," dilating into a statement about the poetic speaker's relation to the wounds of racial oppression in the United States.

The poems by Senior and Hayes I have discussed are reminders that when Stevens claimed his poetry was free of influence, he was articulating a supreme fiction—a fiction articulated by someone holding a position of privilege, who can indulge in mythologizing his or her own writing process and imagine that he or she is an originator. It is not a supreme fiction because Stevens was representing his practice inaccurately, but because it ties into ideological interpretations of imitation and inheritance. My larger point in this chapter is that alternative models of literary relationality are needed to avoid perpetuating such mythologizing. A more expansive way of conceiving literary relationality that is attentive to power is possible when we understand intertextuality as something other than an economy in which original property is bequeathed from one unified subject to another. Borges' idea of "retrospective influence" insists that poems are unstable, shifting, growing organisms, which respond to the touch of writers and readers alike, in a vast web of interaction that has no fixed beginning or end. Contemporary poetry continues to modify our conception of the literature of the past, as Borges wrote, and the culturally resistant "textual revisions" of Senior and Hayes enact a correction, reinserting the history of institutionalized racism and its pernicious cultural manifestations into what would otherwise remain empty spaces in literature. But revision and recycling also stem from the impulse to play, to tangle with, to preserve and commemorate, and to accrete—to graft a slim stem from a long-lived plant such as Stevens' poetry and place it in water to watch new shoots emerge.

The strategies deployed in Senior's and Hayes's poetry share important characteristics with other twentieth-century poetry written throughout the American hemisphere in English, Spanish, French, and Portuguese. A similar convergence of politics and play with form is found in poetry concerned with displacement (of people, language, ideas, property) and the bundle of myths surrounding the concept of origin in the Americas—the imperial, capitalist imaginary that Argentine scholar Walter Mignolo has termed "Occidentalism."[10] Given the shared history of empire, all writers throughout the American hemisphere can be understood as "Americans," as Walcott suggests, and are subject to similar accusations of secondariness. Walcott writes in an essay titled "The Caribbean: Culture or Mimicry?" that in the Americas "language itself is condemned as mimicry … the condition is hopeless and men are no more than jackdaws, parrots, myna birds, apes" (7). Walcott recuperates the term "mimic" from its usual "pejorative, if contradictory, connotations of imitation, servility, and mockery" (Terada 1). His usage resembles how postcolonial writers across the Americas have recuperated the servile character of Caliban, and how Brazilian writers have appropriated the figure of the New World cannibal as a sign for cultural resistance and producing new art by devouring preexisting forms.

Ironically, despite Walcott's careful analysis of literary imitation in the Americas and the ideology of empire that clusters around the idea of imitation, his own work has been infamously disparaged as "mimicry" by critics ranging from Helen Vendler to Cal Bedient. Defenders, too, such as J. A. Ramsaran, write that Walcott "assimilate[s] and transform[s]" the English language, as Rei Terada notes in her study *Derek Walcott's Poetry: American Mimicry*. Terada rightly points out that whichever side critics fall on, they all "begin by assuming that the goal of one text is to *consume* and *digest* previous texts" (46; emphasis added). Terada's observation uncovers the cannibalistic logic of these analyses, even though she does not explicitly mention the Brazilian Modernist notion of cultural cannibalism. Oswald de Andrade's *antropofagia* and the later iterations of his idea, most prominently formulated by Haroldo de Campos, suggest that new texts are made by devouring or radically reauthoring earlier works in a spirit of resistance or usurpation.[11] Unknowingly, then, critics of Walcott—and Hayes, too, such as Deutsch in her *Poetry* review—are viewing his work through the logic of cultural cannibalism.

Pursuing this line of analysis could uncover a productive convergence between literary theories of the American hemisphere. The poetics of *antropofagia* dovetails with how Borges' idea of retrospective influence shifts the conventional teleology of literary history. It is a more politically attuned model than Bloom's concept of influence and the anxiety thereof. These Brazilian and Argentine theories of cultural production within the colonial matrix of power understand aesthetic incorporation, correction, and usurpation as canny, subversive political gestures, rather than disparagingly casting them as secondary. In this light, Olive Senior's and Terrance Hayes's poems that strategically rewrite Wallace Stevens are lyric cousins to playfully subversive poems from throughout the Americas that insist upon a cannibalistic logic of poetic displacement—the works of writers as varied as M. NourbeSe Philip, Mónica de la Torre, Urayoán Noel, and Aimé Césaire. This heterogeneous group of poets shares an impulse to revise race-based, capitalist notions of property and subjecthood; and even as their poems perform that revision, they provide an alternative vision of how poetry itself comes to be.

Notes

1   Harold Bloom's *The Anxiety of Influence* draws heavily from Stevens' poetics and, as Eeckhout notes, is itself "shot through with unmarked, subcutaneous quotations from Stevens." Eeckhout terms this a "critical appropriation" of Stevens (47, 53).

2   I am drawing on Evie Shockley's definition of "black aesthetics":

> it describes the subjectivity of the African American writer—that is, the subjectivity produced by the experience of identifying or being interpolated as "black" in the U.S.—actively working out a poetics in the context of a racist society. Black aesthetics are a function of the writing process, are contingent, and must be historicized and contextualized with regard to period and place, and with regard to the various other factors that shape the writer's identity, particularly including gender, sexuality, and class as well.
>
> (9)

Although Shockley specifically focuses on writers in the United States, her theory is also useful for thinking about the poetry of black Canadian writers such as Olive Senior.

3   Ramazani calls this a "transhemispheric (North/South) … approach" (121), citing Andreas Huyssen's suggestion, in *Geographies of Modernism*, that "rather than privilege the radically new in Western avant-gardist fashion, we may want to focus on the complexity of repetition and rewriting, *bricolage* and translation, thus expanding our understanding of innovation" (qtd. on 119).

4   "Retrospective influence" is my translation of Pierre Bayard's *influence rétrospective*, which is his useful term for Borges' idea. See Bayard 61–69.

5   For a discussion of Borges' treatment of Eliot, see Castro 52–55. Through free translation and loose appropriation of Eliot's texts, Borges "created the Eliot he needed," Castro writes (54).

6   I have examined Borges' ideas and those of Oswald de Andrade and Haroldo de Campos in relation to contemporary US poetry, including Hayes and Senior, in Galvin, "Poetry Is Theft."

7   For further discussion, see Galvin, "Wallace Stevens and Race."

8   "'Negro,'" notes Cook, "is Stevens's more usual, though hardly invariable, term in his letters. The poetry uses both, depending on context" (105).

9   Said writes that a quoted passage "symbolizes other writing as encroachment … As a rhetorical device, quotation can serve to accommodate, to incorporate, to falsify … to defend, or to conquer—but always, even when in the form of a passing allusion, it is a reminder that other writing serves to displace present writing" (22).

10   Occidentalism is a geopolitical figure that links the modern and colonial world systems, according to Mignolo. He describes the colonial imaginary of Latin America—a counterpart to Edward Said's Orientalism—that considers the Indias Occidentales, or America, as a place and a people without history (51). It is the "overarching metaphor around which colonial differences have been articulated and rearticulated through the changing hands in the history of capitalism … and the changing ideologies motivated by imperial conflicts" (13).

11   Cf. Andrade 38 and Campos 177.

Works Cited

Andrade, Oswald de. "Cannibalist Manifesto." Trans. Leslie Bary. *Latin American Literary Review* 19.38 (1991): 38–47. Print.

Bayard, Pierre. *Le Plagiat par anticipation*. Paris: Minuit, 2009. Print.

Bhabha, Homi K. "Of Mimicry and Man: The Ambivalence of Colonial Discourse." *The Location of Culture*. London: Routledge, 1994. 121–31. Print.

Bloom, Harold. *The Anxiety of Influence: A Theory of Poetry*. Oxford: Oxford University Press, 1997. Print.

Borges, Jorge Luis. "Kafka and His Precursors." *Labyrinths: Selected Stories and Other Writings*. Ed. Donald A. Yates and James E. Irby. Trans. Irby. New York: New Directions, 1964. 199–201. Print.

Campos, Haroldo de. *Novas: Selected Writings*. Trans. Odile Cisneros and Antonio Sergio Bessa. Evanston: Northwestern University Press, 2007. Print.

Castro, Juan E. De. *The Spaces of Latin American Literature: Tradition, Globalization, and Cultural Production.* New York: Palgrave, 2008. Print.

Cook, Eleanor. *A Reader's Guide to Wallace Stevens.* Princeton: Princeton University Press, 2007. Print.

Costello, Bonnie. *Planets on Tables: Poetry, Still Life, and the Turning World.* Ithaca: Cornell University Press, 2008. Print.

Deutsch, Abigail. "The Bee's News: Four Books." *Poetry* 196.5 (2010): 471–79. Print.

Eeckhout, Bart. *Wallace Stevens and the Limits of Reading and Writing.* Columbia: University of Missouri Press, 2002. Print.

Galvin, Rachel. "Poetry Is Theft." *Comparative Literature Studies* 51.1 (2014): 18–54. Print.

Galvin, Rachel. "Wallace Stevens and Race." *Wallace Stevens in Context.* Ed. Glen MacLeod. Cambridge: Cambridge University Press, 2016. Forthcoming. Print.

Gates, Henry Louis, Jr. *The Signifying Monkey: A Theory of African-American Literary Criticism.* New York: Oxford University Press, 1988. Print.

Hayes, Terrance. *Lighthead.* New York: Penguin, 2010. Print.

Mignolo, Walter D. *Local Histories/Global Designs: Coloniality, Subaltern Knowledges, and Border Thinking.* Princeton: Princeton University Press, 2012. Print.

Ramazani, Jahan. *A Transnational Poetics.* Chicago: University of Chicago Press, 2009. Print.

Said, Edward. *Beginnings: Intention and Method.* New York: Columbia University Press, 1985. Print.

Senior, Olive. *Over the Roofs of the World.* Toronto: Insomniac, 2005. Print.

Shockley, Evie. *Renegade Poetics: Black Aesthetics and Formal Innovation in African American Poetry.* Iowa City: University of Iowa Press, 2011. Print.

Stevens, Wallace. *Letters of Wallace Stevens.* Ed. Holly Stevens. Berkeley: University of California Press, 1996. Print.

Stevens, Wallace. *Wallace Stevens: Collected Poetry and Prose.* Ed. Frank Kermode and Joan Richardson. New York: Library of America, 1997. Print.

Terada, Rei. *Derek Walcott's Poetry: American Mimicry.* Boston: Northeastern University Press, 1992. Print.

Walcott, Derek. "The Caribbean: Culture or Mimicry?" *Journal of Interamerican Studies and World Affairs* 16.1 (1974): 3–13. Print.

17

"The California Fruit of the Ideal": Stevens and Robert Hass

Rachel Malkin

At the close of Wallace Stevens' "Sunday Morning," a poem Robert Hass singles out for its importance to him, we are offered the consolation that "Sweet berries ripen in the wilderness" (*CPP* 56). Berries matter for Hass, too, but here sweetness is closer at hand. Fruit is one of the motifs by means of which Hass links personal eros both to more communal kinds of experience and to the natural world. In "Maps," from his first collection, *Field Guide* (1973), the line "red berries darken the hawthorns" is shortly followed by a juxtaposition of a lover's outline with the landscape: "your body and the undulant/sharp edges of the hills" (9). These lines link Hass's sources of inspiration in personal experience, including erotic love and family, to California—its landscape, flora and fauna, politics, and history. Landscape in Hass anchors experience in particularity: person and place are mutually imbricated. His choosing to write about California in this way reflects Hass's significant inheritance from poets other than Stevens—he names Kenneth Rexroth, Robert Duncan, Gary Snyder, and Robinson Jeffers in this connection, among others. Yet an intimacy with Stevens remains important throughout his work.

Hass's perhaps most famous poem, "Meditation at Lagunitas," from his next collection, *Praise* (1974), closes with the lines: "There are moments when the body is as numinous/as words, days that are the good flesh continuing./Such tenderness, those afternoons and evenings,/saying *blackberry, blackberry, blackberry*" (5). This ending attests to the closeness between language and the world of sensuality and affective relations. However, as Hass points out, awareness of "framing" has become inescapable, even if "we've returned to some fundamental ground of romantic poetry, having passed through the modernist crucible that led to the denial of the personal project" (qtd. in Gardner 166). This is to say that his is not an unreflexive aesthetic, despite its apparent immediacies. In "Picking Blackberries with a Friend Who Has Been Reading Jacques Lacan," in the same collection, "Charlie,/laughing wonderfully,/beard stained purple/by the word *juice,*/goes to get a bigger pot" (*Praise* 36). Although the prominent reference to Lacan in that poem locates the collection in its 1970s moment, the evolution of a form of self-consciousness about language (it is the words that are "mouth-filling" here) that does not entail dispensing with the ability to revel in its *jouissance* is an aspect of Modernism's legacy that remains of great significance to Hass (Gardner 165).

A further crucial element of Modernism's example is his effort to respond to the demise of what Stevens called the "*triste* contraption" of paradise as a place elsewhere (*CPP* 907). In both poets, fruit sometimes stands as emblematic of the sufficiency of the world, the fact that, as Stevens puts it, the "brilliance of earth is the brilliance of every paradise" (*CPP* 690). Paradise originates as a term for earthly garden or orchard, and as critics have noted, this is a key respect in which Hass's project mirrors Stevens': a view of poetry as endorsing full inhabitation of the life that is near to us, and the rejection of the idea of another. This is one definition of an immanent poetics: that value is to be found in the world at hand, if anywhere. We can understand the impetus to praise in Hass as a willingness to engage with the pleasure the world gives, despite the substantial counterforce of what might be set against it. As is often acknowledged, for Stevens, too, the poet's role is fundamentally that of celebrant in this sense.

Hass shares with Stevens an endeavor to create in verse a space in which "being there together is enough" (*CPP* 444), since the issue of value identified by Modernism has not been resolved, as he explains in an interview with Thomas Gardner: "It's hard to deny that poetry stands in the middle of a wasteland still, a wreckage of all previous metaphysics that made us feel at home in the world or promised us a home elsewhere. If anything, the problem of what the individual can say about the meaning of human experience is more urgent" (167). Poetry thus plays an important role as the medium for this expression. Hass also sounds very much like Stevens when he says, "It seems to me that we all live our lives in the light of primary acts of imagination, images or sets of images that get us up in the morning and move us about our days. I do not think anybody can live without one, for very long, without suffering intensely from deadness and futility" (*Twentieth* 303). Such images are "necessary" despite their inherent limitations. And for both poets, art "refreshes our sense of ordinary life" (*Light* 92). The phrasing belongs to Hass, but it could easily be Stevens, who suggests that "To give a sense of the freshness or vividness of life is a valid purpose for poetry" (*CPP* 900).

Hass has also stated that "the task of art is to over and over again make images of a livable common life" ("Informal" 138), and this, too, resembles the terms in which Stevens casts poetry. Hass may, then, seem to place a high degree of faith in the aesthetic and its powers. However, he cites the Japanese poet Basho's definition of pure aestheticism as "a tree that bears blossoms but no fruit" and argues that art should be, by contrast, "fruit-bearing" ("Common" n. pag.). What he means by this is that art can be generative, since "imagination makes communities" (Cavalieri and Hass 41). Although wary of the usefulness of an explicitly or exclusively political poetry, beyond commonality Hass also has in mind the issue of polity. For Hass, literature can be, specifically, the imagination of a community alternative to the one created by the model we live under, which casts relations as the atomized results of "economic rationalities" (41). Part of Hass's response to this is another sort of immanent poetics, meaning here one that is located and begins from the web of lived life.

The word "fruit" reveals senses helpful for considering Hass's profound but ambivalent relation to Stevens. The Latin "fructus" comprises enjoyment, delight, and satisfaction, as well as the idea of outcome, consequence, or result—the notion of "yield." Thinking about Stevens and Hass involves dynamics of pleasure and solace, and of doubt and guilt. Liesl Olson is attuned to this issue, titling her astute essay on their relationship "Robert Hass's Guilt, or the Weight of Wallace Stevens"—a play on the idea of the weight of Stevens' lines, alongside the heavy imprint of his example, as well as the guilt associated with taking pleasure in his verse (or in the kind of verse that he is seen to represent). I would further suggest that their relation raises questions about what sorts of satisfaction we as critics want from poetry now. Although Hass recognizes there is no direct path between what one of his interviewers calls "the personal world, the political world, and the world of knowledge" ("Informal" 142), both his verse and prose at times acknowledge, and thematize, this absence as a source of sorrow. In this, he is in sympathy with one of the critical moods of our own moment. By contrast, Stevens did not explicitly dramatize regret about the distance between these worlds. Like Hass, he was concerned with the relation between the sensuous and intellectual, and he, too, dismissed pure aestheticism. The issue was not politically framed for him, though he knew the relation between aesthetic pleasure and politics to be a question. However, this is certainly something that can be felt more strongly at some times in his work than others. This may be one reason, alongside Stevens' more clear-cut political failings, that he occasions critical discomfort. Stevens is a poet still important for us, but intractable, not assimilable to the present.

Another link between current critical sensibilities and Hass's own is the desire to connect insight into immanent or phenomenological value with our everyday lives in a more direct way than Stevens often offered, and an important idiom in this context is that of the plain or ordinary. One of the ways Stevens and Hass have been linked by critics is through the idea of common experience, expressed not only in terms of both daily and seasonal rhythms but also, importantly, in terms of the plainness of Stevens' late style. I began thinking about this topic before I had read Olson's piece, but it eloquently lays out the key areas of similarity between them that had seemed apparent to me. On her reading, "Stevens is diffused *everywhere* into Hass's work" (38). She draws attention to this-worldliness, epicureanism, and their shared focus on desire and its transitory fulfillments, as well as the poets' differing aesthetic choices, and the significance of the West Coast to Hass. Olson also suggests that the light Hass retrospectively throws back onto Stevens renders the latter—to his credit—"less abstract," the late collection *The Rock* providing the key example in this connection. This is a Stevens who, as Olson puts it, "fiercely engages with the material world" (37). In recent times, Stevens has been found praiseworthy in terms of this strain of plainness and materiality. Charles Altieri has pointed out that Simon Critchley's well-received analysis of Stevens' late poems along these lines in *Things Merely Are* (2005), for example, is founded on a "model of value" based on "the ideal of 'letting be' and a corresponding eagerness to celebrate what manages to resist the ego's demands and the rhetorician's skills" (70). Altieri, by contrast, has of course tirelessly made the case for Stevens' abstraction and what is enabled by it.

I hope this final chapter will open some additional questions inspired by the collection's interest in "poetry and poetics after Stevens." If we find value in Stevens in terms of his plainness, as outlined by Olson and others, can those aspects of Stevens that are less congenial to such an aesthetic also be defended— his abstraction, willfully luxurious language, and more fanciful or hypothetical subjects? What work do we trust that a more "ordinary" poetics can do that an abstract poetics does not? If we can be aware of the pitfalls of caring about Stevens' work, can we also think through the investments and informing contexts of more personal poetry, such as Hass's? The ethical model of his verse, where a stress on personal perception is linked with broader political concerns, also reflects a time and place. An element of what is in play in a consideration of Hass and Stevens together is the differences between successive phases of American poetic Modernism, both of which Hass inherits.

Hass has in many respects clearly espoused an aesthetic of the ordinary, and while he loves other kinds of poetry, he claims to be "always most amazed by great plainness in language" ("Informal" 128). He has also experimented with prose poems. He seems poised between the Williams and Stevens lines of Modernist descent. He repeatedly alludes to William Carlos Williams' precept "no ideas but in things," but his sensibility is also fundamentally reflexive, as I have mentioned. "It's sort of a blessing, in Vermeer's paintings and much of the art that I admire ... to encounter ordinary people going about ordinary things; it seems an enormous gift" ("Eight" n. pag.). Yet he goes on: "And the height and intensity of this gift demands a separation from it." Hass's sense of the blessing of the encounter with ordinary things, the apprehension of value in the simplest realities, is aligned with Stevens' claim that "The actual is a deft beneficence" (*CPP* 125). What strikes Hass in haiku is "the almost silly preciousness of the most ordinary experiences and ... the fact that we are all going to die someday" (*Light* 82). The deliberate line Hass treads between ordinariness and reflexivity is part of his affinity with Stevens. And despite the divergent influences that come to bear on his work, he consistently attests to the virtues of Stevens' abstractions: "Poetry certainly needs body, but it can get it from the music of its rhythms; it doesn't always have to be sticking to a picture language to stay tactile. Examples are better than arguments. My arguments would be in the general direction of some poems of George Oppen and Wallace Stevens" ("Q&A" n. pag.). Form is meaningful, as Hass argues elsewhere.

In the tradition of haiku, of which Hass is an admirer and translator, images of plainness and ordinariness do not revert to, or hint at, the exceptional or ecstatic. They are dispassionate or "neutral"—one source of Hass's admiration for them. But as Hass is aware, in American verse from Walt Whitman onwards, there is a kind of rapture of locatedness to which plain speaking, precise naming, and specificity are not inimical. In this vein, Hass has complained of the reception of "Meditation at Lagunitas," with its final incantatory repetition of "*blackberry*," that the poem was read as "reopening the mindless door into the American sublime" (qtd. in Gardner 166). Hass does not want to fall into the Whitmanian praise not only of earth but of exceptional American earth. This is to say that in the American literary context, the interplay between the ordinary and the aesthetic is something particular. Hass's poetry is precisely located in a way that Stevens' is not. Perhaps rather than this located alternative to abstraction representing only simplicity or transparency, there are things to be negotiated in each of these approaches.

Hass's oeuvre is to an extent a romance of Californian landscape. Its definitive separateness from him is one of its virtues, an idea he explores in relation to Jeffers. What he likes in Jeffers is the idea of the intransigent world that resists our interpretations. Indeed, he suggests that recognizing the sheer physicality of the world is Jeffers' solution to the problem of a Symbolist impasse experienced by Stevens and others. But he is also distinctly wooed by it, as in an essay where he imagines Jeffers' Carmel bay to be "as beautiful as any place on earth. A rocky coast, ridges of cypress and pine, ghostly in the fog. On clear days the Carmel River glittered past the ruin of an old Franciscan mission, and the surf was an intense sapphire, foaming to turquoise as it crested" (*Light* 129). This is California as a "glittering," "sapphire" jewel, the object of a quest. While Hass uses the language of entrancement to describe the effect of Stevens' verse on him, this landscape, too, presents a kind of aesthetic and sensory seduction, alongside the corrective role it plays in his oeuvre. The speaker of Hass's poems sometimes seems to want "the blissful liaison,/Between himself and his environment" (*CPP* 28). While Stevens' Florida is clearly (and problematically) an exoticized artifact as much as any real place, Hass's more documentary West Coast has its overdeterminations, and Hass his own version of what Stevens calls "banyans and frangipani" (*CPP* 778), especially in the earlier work: "We bought great ornamental oranges,/Mexican cookies, a fragrant yellow tea./Browsed the bookstores" (*Field* 16). The Stevens aphorism from which my chapter takes its title—"The full flower of the actual, not the California fruit of the ideal" (*CPP* 910)—suggests the idea of "California fruit" standing for the ideal, as a sort of impossible plenitude or culmination. California here is a conceit, as well as an instance of the concrete world. Its fruit conjures beauty and sweetness. Some of these connotations seem present in Hass, too, although the bounty in his verse is also local, historical, qualified, and implicated.

The "California fruit of the ideal" is not counterposed with plain actuality as an alternative in Stevens, but rather with another metaphor, the "full flower of the actual." Importantly, the actual remains metaphorical, since there is no end to the process of flowering. The "actual" is not a resting place, but constantly comes into being, the actual and metaphorical being bound together. Even the eponymous stone in *The Rock*, far from presenting an implacable and alien minerality, is a scene of plenty: "the poem makes meanings of the rock,/Of such mixed motion and such imagery/That its barrenness becomes a thousand things/And so exists no more" (*CPP* 447). The poetic actual is shown as a choice of idiom in Stevens: "For so retentive of themselves are men/That music is intensest which proclaims/The near, the clear, and vaunts the clearest bloom" (*CPP* 71). Stevens knew that the aesthetic choice of the near was available as a valence of American Modernism, and he did not choose it, at least not explicitly in the form associated with Williams and those following after him. However, as Alan Filreis has noted, Stevens felt there to be a correspondence between the objectivist project and his own search for a "new romantic" (143), and caused offense to Williams by approvingly describing the latter's work as romantic in a preface of 1934: "The anti-poetic is his spirit's cure" (*CPP* 769). Stevens saw the ordinary aesthetic as a romance, in addition to the other things it may be. This is, I think, a romance we still feel.

If Stevens and Hass are both poets of praise, Hass is more explicitly a politically conscious poet than Stevens, and a less insular one. He engages with the poetic traditions of cultures outside the United States, and directly references political and historical subjects in his verse. As poet laureate, he was an activist and advocate for literacy programs and environmentalism. Both Hass himself and his readers have connected these commitments with his deliberate embrace of an aesthetic that espouses and elucidates the near, the recognizable, and the local. If Hass's approach might occasionally tip into banality or the almost parodic—"Berkeley seemed more innocent/in those flush days/when we skipped lunch/to have the price of *Les Enfants de Paradis*" (*Field* 11)—its intentions are understood as honorable in this wider ethical frame. Like Stevens', Hass's aesthetic was forged in the crucible of a heightened sense of liberal·responsibility, and critics have appraised both poets in the light of these contexts. For Stevens, this was the period of the 1930s and 1940s; for Hass, the crucial moment is the 1960s and 1970s in the United States.

Our own times, at least since around 2000, present another moment of American liberal reappraisal. This mood informed the largely positive response to Hass's 2007 collection *Time and Materials*, which registers overtly the difficulty of a deliberate stance or orientation of praise against the backdrop of, for example, the wars that are committed in one's name. In an op-ed piece of 2011 in the *New York Times*, Hass drew a connection between activism on the Berkeley campus in 1964 and the later activism of Occupy: his particular sense of place specifically includes the legacy of Berkeley as a fulcrum of liberal feeling. Further, the sense that there may be an ethical or even social potential in poetic acts of attention to perception (and to the everyday) is associated not only

with high Modernism but also with the second-wave Modernism for which the
Bay Area was an important center of gravity. While his decision to write about
California is an aesthetic choice for Hass, it also, through his inheritance of local
poets, connotes a politics associated with the view that the intensely personal
remains profoundly related to the social.

In "Some Notes on the San Francisco Bay Area as a Culture Region: A
Memoir," Hass remembers reading Stevens' "Domination of Black" while still
at school. The poem made him "swoon"—in fact, he says, it taught him the
meaning of the word (*Twentieth* 220). "I suppose it was the acknowledgment
of … terror and beauty … that seemed to so wake me up, or hypnotize me, that
I wanted to hold it close. The sensation was physical. It was the first physical
sensation of the truthfulness of a thing that I had ever felt" (221). Hass's essay
serves to outline the two strands of influence that came to shape his project,
with one pole represented by Stevens' visceral truthfulness, another by Kenneth
Rexroth, who showed Hass that "there could be an active connection between
poetry and my own world" (223). "Art hardly ever does seem to come to us at
first as something connected to our own world," Hass suggests; "it always seems,
in fact, to announce the existence of another, different one … the next thing
that artists have to learn is that this world is the other world" (222–23). That
this world as revealed in art is the (only) other world is a lesson Stevens too
could impart. However, while Stevens shows poetry to be indispensable to Hass,
Rexroth successfully joins it with his lived experience. It is significant that Hass
describes Rexroth as the first San Francisco poet of caliber, a sign of how recently
the territory has been annexed by the United States. What is also at stake here is
the culture of the West Coast, its legitimacy and distinctiveness.

Hass speaks of an "urgent" need to be literal and "specific" in his verse,
partly as a means of rendering the terrain that is both his home and focus of his
ecological concern, as well as a way of acknowledging the workings of history
as these take shape in language ("Eight" n. pag.). In the case of California, this
includes the way language charts the course of American expansionism. In other
words, his focus on California is part of his choosing not to be abstract in ways
that demonstrate certain kinds of responsibility and ownership, as Olson and
others notice. It also highlights an alternative inheritance, placing another kind
of tradition in the center of the frame of aesthetic Modernism and its aftershocks,
and making a claim for the diversity of US culture: "I like naming Californian
places and things in my poems … I always had some feeling that the real world
was over *there* [on the East Coast]. So it seemed important to be able to put in

the names of California places, and California plants and animals—the feel of this life, and its weathers—into my poems" ("Eight" n. pag.). At the same time, "the feel of this life, and its weathers" could be a phrase of Stevens'; this is a statement that can be read on two levels. His alternative inheritance does not displace Hass's endowment from Stevens, but rather coexists with it. The lines that are sometimes taken to have bifurcated subsequent American poetry are joined in Hass.

"Wallace Stevens in the World," an essay of 1985 that treats his relationship with Stevens at more length, opens *What Light Can Do*, Hass's most recently published collection of criticism. The issue of whether or not Stevens is in the world, and if so, of how he is in it, has long preoccupied critics, as Edward Ragg, among others, has pointed out (7–8). For those responding to charges of pure aestheticism, Stevens' worldliness is presented either in relation to his engagements, even oblique ones, with the events and politics of his own times, or in terms of the more phenomenological kind of ordinariness I have alluded to—and sometimes in a way that joins both of these. In this piece, Hass defines a pressure to be in the world whereby his appreciation of Stevens' aesthetic and philosophical orientation seems to clash with the imperatives of situated experience. The negotiation of his response to Stevens, and to the issue of aesthetic value, is tied here to a 1960s context. What Hass has called his will "to get hold of the immediate world around me" increased during these years of "extraordinary public violence" (*Field* x, ix). However, the piece moves toward a more nuanced kind of conclusion than the rejection of Stevens this might seem to presage.

Characteristically, the biographical and anecdotal aspects of the essay are not casual and open out onto a larger social perspective. Hass's recollection of encountering Stevens begins with a scene of college friends "chanting" "The Emperor of Ice-Cream" while tramping through a field. "It was March in California," Hass recalls, "high spring, the hills still green, with grazing cattle in them, plum trees in blossom, the olive trees around the campus whitening whenever a breeze shook them" (*Light* 3). This pastoral idyll is in keeping with the comedic spirit in which the young Hass took the poem—somewhat inappropriately, as he notes. The scene is halcyon, the verse "delicious" (3). The second scene is another reading of Stevens among a group of friends, this time of "Sea Surface Full of Clouds," on the beach at Carmel, a poem, Hass says, by which he is still "stunned" (5). Hass describes the way that Stevens' "adjectives of experience play over the adamant nouns" in the poem (6), and the essay weaves together the importance of both the quiddities of the experiential and the adamancy of certain kinds of facts—one of the carefree student party later joins army intelligence in Vietnam, another will be seriously injured in a car crash. These early encounters with Stevens developed into a more refined kind of reading when Hass was at graduate school, though "I was never very interested in ... the wedding-cake baroque ... What I loved in him was the clarity ... I certainly didn't understand the issues implicit in the two sides of his style" (7). His admiration for Stevens' plainness was connected for him with what also attracted him in the Buddhist poetic tradition, an influence that, along with West Coast poetics, represents another kind of choice than mandarin Modernism (7).

In the same way that Stevens' attitude toward Asia feels incongruous to Hass, a representative blind spot, his discovery of politically conscious literature and the escalating turmoil of the times—the "country we were growing up into, its racism, the violence it was unleashing"—seemed at odds with an unqualified "hypnotic attraction" to Stevens (*Light* 8, 7). Political and historical consciousness and a love of Stevens seemed, then, inimical. In response to his suggestion that Stevens' subject "is epistemology," a graduate student friend of Hass's retorted that "epistemology is a bourgeois defense against actually knowing anything" (8). Hass came to feel that Yvor Winters was wrong about Stevens' "trivial hedonism," but "not entirely wrong" (8). Hass's response to Stevens in this essay could be seen as part of a search for both a usable Modernism and a usable political liberalism by a generation who came of intellectual age at a time when they felt a serious breach in the American fabric. This climate also imprinted the work of their immediate predecessors, as in the dispute between Denise Levertov and Robert Duncan over poetic responses to the Vietnam War. As Olson highlights, Hass describes his relation to Stevens in the 1960s and 1970s as "polemical": "[Stevens] felt to me like he needed to be resisted, as if he were a luxury, like ice cream, that was not to be indulged in" (10). We might note here that Stevens considered "The Emperor of Ice-Cream" to express a "gaudiness" of poetry that was "essential" to its nature (*CPP* 768). In his arguments for the importance of the imagination, Hass in his own way makes the same case, despite these anxieties.

The sense of a pressure brought to bear on a response to Stevens in the milieu of the 1960s is complicated in the essay by Hass's subsequent replaying of Stevens' lines over the course of his life, and his changing reception and interpretation of them. The resolution reached by "Wallace Stevens in the World" is that Stevens shows in lines like "and bid him whip/In kitchen cups concupiscent curds" (*CPP* 50) that "at least in language, magic can happen" (*Light* 11). The fact that this kind of "magic" can happen in language even at the most inapposite times, or in the very face of its inappositeness or unlikeliness, is something that is also registered in Hass's own verse. The essay closes with the idea that Stevens remains a presence for Hass to "brood" over and "argue with" himself about (13). Here as elsewhere, the problem of how to respond to Stevens, and how to feel about his work, seems to stand in for the problem of the Modernist legacy altogether. Stevens remains a reference point for Hass in his explorations of this question, as well as being acknowledged in this piece as a master of modulation, and thus as reflecting the imagination's ongoing relation to the world (13).

Perhaps a little contrary to the spirit of Stevens and more in that of Hass's essays, I would like to conclude by drawing on aspects of my own reactions to both poets. If hedonism, interpreted literally, is the pursuit of sweetness, what might I make of the fact that I find Hass in many respects more overtly sweet than Stevens, taken as an experience of reading? Stevens can feel tonic, and reading Hass's verse like an indulgence, despite (or, perhaps, even partly) owing to its consciously political acknowledgements. In addition to the possibilities for satisfaction afforded by Hass's evocative expressions of pleasure, our appreciation for the near and identifiable in Hass might to some degree reflect a wish for our erotic and aesthetic pleasures to resolve somehow with our political feelings, including necessary and inevitable self-questionings about the bases of our own enjoyment of poetry.

Hass's lyric pleasures are often more available than Stevens': his verse offers itself in a different kind of way to be enjoyed, identified with, or (erotically) participated in. One aspect of this difference is the way that Stevens' erotics are not as closely folded into personal sexuality as they can be in Hass. The "intensest rendezvous" in Stevens (*CPP* 444) may not be a meeting of two bodies—scenes of eros in Stevens are not exactly personal. Eros seems instead to be located more confidently in the poems themselves, pointing to the idea that they are not separate from the world, as ways of referring to or reflecting on it, but indubitably part of its materials, its fecundity and proliferation—its fruiting. Poems are sensual realities as well as forms of praise; this is the nature of Stevens' stubborn attachment to something he called "poetry." Another difference is in the confessional or autobiographical element of the verse. Certain possibilities are opened by an impersonal mode, as are others by a more personal approach. If Stevens stands at one end of this polarity, Hass moves toward its opposite.

Hass might give us more, but also sometimes less, in offering not simply bread, tea, fruit, and wine, but "On the oak table/filets of sole/stewing in the juice of tangerines,/slices of green pepper/on a bone-white dish" (*Field* 21). At one level, this is a still life such as one might find in Stevens. At another, it is a reference to the Japanese aesthetic that has inspired Hass. We also have here a located form of life, and for some critics, poems about Berkeley dinner parties, for example, can be alienating in their very cultural specificity and "bourgeois bohemianism" (see Archambeau).

Hass has explained what he sees as the need for a personal or confessional frame, since as Wes Davis describes his view, personal experience is the only lens for all experience: "the subjective lyrical poem provided us with the best model we had of the way each individual self ... experiences the sweep of history" (303). Scenes of ordinariness and domesticity are one way to render what J. M. Bernstein has called "a self-sufficient secular world" (39), but also to show the long arm of historical events as these are reflected in the particulars of the individual's life. One of the lessons Hass takes from his friend, the late poet Czesław Miłosz, is that for the most part this is the essence of how history is experienced. For Stevens, the idea of "The living man in the present place,/ Always, the particular thought/Among Plantagenet abstractions,/Always and always, the difficult inch" is an inching of specificity performed in language, rather than through the presentation of the poet (*CPP* 465). He does not aim to generate readerly intimacy with his personal life in the way practiced by Hass.

During the symposium that was organized to prepare for this volume, speakers commented on the solace to be found in the beauty of Stevens' poetry. If Stevens gives comfort, what kind of comfort is it? To find a description of this would entail a defense of the poetics of a life that is not immediately recognizably our own, and of a project that seems too austere, too playful, and too politically compromised by turns. To complicate matters further, the poetics of immanence we find in both poets need not imply a liberal political perspective of a certain kind—though it often does in the US literary context— and nor must the valence of praise they share. In Hass, these strains are often worked out together, in Stevens not quite. Hass does not think poetry can or should solve political problems, but he highlights the fact that they do not, and the feelings this generates; Stevens less so. I hope this chapter might show the relationship between Hass and Stevens to be profound, while at the same time opening a line of inquiry about the inheritances informing our contemporary critical desires. Like Hass, we are working through imperatives, insights, and an aesthetic that flowered in the cultural milieu of the 1960s in our responses to earlier phases of American Modernism. The issue of whether aesthetic value is distinctive, and what connection there can be between eros and community, remains alive. In making a case for Stevens' poetry, would we wish to make a case for a certain kind of beauty or "magic" made possible in and by language? And if so, on what ground(s)?

Works Cited

Altieri, Charles. "Stevens and the Crisis of European Philosophy." *Wallace Stevens across the Atlantic.* Ed. Bart Eeckhout and Edward Ragg. Basingstoke: Palgrave, 2008. 61–78. Print.

Archambeau, Robert. "This Nest of Gentlefolk: Robert Hass and the Bourgeois Bohemians." *Samizdat Blog.* January 8, 2006. December 28, 2015. Web.

Bernstein, J. M. *Against Voluptuous Bodies: Late Modernism and the Meaning of Painting.* Stanford: Stanford University Press, 2006. Print.

Cavalieri, Grace, and Robert Hass. "An Interview by Grace Cavalieri." *American Poetry Review* 26.2 (1997): 41–46. Print.

Davis, Wes. "Fear and Loathing at Lagunitas." *Parnassus: Poetry in Review* 31.1/2 (2009): 275–395. Print.

Filreis, Alan. *Modernism from Right to Left: Wallace Stevens, the Thirties, and Literary Radicalism.* Cambridge: Cambridge University Press, 1994. Print.

Gardner, Thomas. *Regions of Unlikeness: Explaining Contemporary Poetry.* Lincoln: University of Nebraska Press, 1999. Print.

Hass, Robert. "Common Language: Robert Hass in Conversation." *Poets.org.* May 23, 2000. *Academy of American Poets.* December 28, 2015. Web.

Hass, Robert. "Eight Years of Activism, Writing, and Reflection." *UC Berkeley News.* November 8, 2007. December 28, 2015. Web.

Hass, Robert. *Field Guide.* 1973. New Haven: Yale University Press, 1998. Print.

Hass, Robert. *Human Wishes.* New York: Ecco, 1989. Print.

Hass, Robert. "An Informal Occasion with Robert Hass." *Iowa Review* 21.3 (1991): 126–45. Print.

Hass, Robert. *Now and Then: The Poet's Choice Columns, 1997–2000.* Berkeley: Counterpoint, 2007. Print.

Hass, Robert. "Poet-Bashing Police." *New York Times.* November 19, 2011. December 28, 2015. Web.

Hass, Robert. *Praise.* 1974. New York: Ecco, 1979. Print.

Hass, Robert. "Q&A with Robert Hass." *Smartish Pace.* 2015. December 28, 2015. Web.

Hass, Robert. *Time and Materials, 1997–2005.* New York: Ecco, 2007. Print.

Hass, Robert. *Twentieth Century Pleasures: Prose on Poetry.* New York: Ecco, 1984. Print.

Hass, Robert. *What Light Can Do: Essays on Art, Imagination, and the Natural World.* New York: Ecco, 2012. Print.

Olson, Liesl. "Robert Hass's Guilt or the Weight of Wallace Stevens." *American Poetry Review* 36.5 (2007): 37–45. Print.

Ragg, Edward. *Wallace Stevens and the Aesthetics of Abstraction.* Cambridge: Cambridge University Press, 2010. Print.

Stevens, Wallace. *Wallace Stevens: Collected Poetry and Prose.* Ed. Frank Kermode and Joan Richardson. New York: Library of America, 1997. Print.

Notes on Contributors

Charles Altieri is Stageberg Professor of English at the University of California, Berkeley. An Editorial Board Member of *The Wallace Stevens Journal*, he is the author of more than ten books, including *Painterly Abstraction in Modernist American Poetry: The Contemporaneity of Modernism*; *The Particulars of Rapture: An Aesthetics of the Affects*; *The Art of Twentieth-Century American Poetry: Modernism and After*; and *Wallace Stevens and the Demands of Modernity: Toward a Phenomenology of Value*.

Angus Cleghorn is Professor of English and Liberal Studies at Seneca College in Toronto, Canada. He is the author of *Wallace Stevens' Poetics: The Neglected Rhetoric* and an Editorial Board Member of *The Wallace Stevens Journal*, for which he has also guest-edited two special issues. Since 2004, he has edited *The Elizabeth Bishop Bulletin*. He is coeditor of *Elizabeth Bishop in the 21st Century: Reading the New Editions* and of *The Cambridge Companion to Elizabeth Bishop*.

Bonnie Costello is Professor of English at the University of Boston, a former Book Review Editor of *The Wallace Stevens Journal*, and the author of many books and articles on modern poetry—most recently, *Planets on Tables: Poetry, Still Life, and the Turning World*. She has also published essays on art, travel, and memoir. The title of her forthcoming book is *The Plural of Us: Poetry and Community in Auden and Others*. With Rachel Galvin, she has recently edited a collection of scholarly essays, *Auden at Work*.

Bart Eeckhout is Professor of English and American Literature at the University of Antwerp, Belgium, and Editor of *The Wallace Stevens Journal*. He is the author of *Wallace Stevens and the Limits of Reading and Writing* and has coedited *Wallace Stevens across the Atlantic* and *Wallace Stevens, New York, and Modernism*. For the online series of *Oxford Bibliographies in American Literature*, he has recently completed an annotated survey of the primary and secondary literature on Stevens. His other areas of interest are queer studies and urban studies.

Al Filreis is Kelly Professor of English, Faculty Director of the Kelly Writers House, Director of the Center for Programs in Contemporary Writing, Co-Director of PennSound, and Publisher of *Jacket2* magazine—all at the University of Pennsylvania. Among his books are *Modernism from Right to Left: Wallace Stevens, the Thirties, and Literary Radicalism*; *Wallace Stevens and the Actual World*; and *Counter-Revolution of the Word: The Conservative Attack on Modern Poetry, 1945–60*. He is an Editorial Board Member of *The Wallace Stevens Journal*, hosts a monthly podcast/radio program, "PoemTalk," and teaches an open online course called "ModPo," which has engaged 130,000 participants in four years.

Rachel Galvin is Assistant Professor in the Department of English at the University of Chicago. She holds a PhD in Comparative Literature from Princeton. Her essays appear in *Comparative Literature Studies, ELH, Jacket2, Los Angeles Review of Books, Modernism/modernity,* and *The Wallace Stevens Journal*. With Bonnie Costello, she has edited *Auden at Work*. She is also the author of a book of poems, *Pulleys & Locomotion*, and her translation of Raymond Queneau's *Hitting the Streets* was awarded the Scott Moncrieff Prize for French Translation.

Lisa Goldfarb is Associate Professor at the Gallatin School of New York University, President of *The Wallace Stevens Society*, and Associate Editor of *The Wallace Stevens Journal*. She is the author of *The Figure Concealed: Wallace Stevens, Music, and Valéryan Echoes*, coeditor of *Wallace Stevens, New York, and Modernism* and of two special issues of *The Wallace Stevens Journal*. She teaches interdisciplinary courses focusing on poetry in English and French, music, and aesthetics.

Lee M. Jenkins is Professor of English at University College Cork, Republic of Ireland. Her main fields of research are Modernist poetry and the literature of the Americas. Major book publications to date include *Wallace Stevens: Rage for Order*; *The Language of Caribbean Poetry*; and *The American Lawrence*. With Alex Davis, she has edited three Cambridge University Press collections: *Locations of Literary Modernism*; *The Cambridge Companion to Modernist Poetry*; and *A History of Modernist Poetry*.

George S. Lensing is Mann Family Distinguished Professor of English at the University of North Carolina at Chapel Hill and a former Book Review Editor of *The Wallace Stevens Journal*. He is the author of *Wallace Stevens: A Poet's Growth* and *Wallace Stevens and the Seasons*. His essay "The Romantic and the Anti-Romantic in the Poetry of Wallace Stevens" appeared in *The Cambridge History* *of American Poetry* in 2015. He has published many essays on various American, British, and Irish poets of the twentieth century.

Rachel Malkin is Departmental lecturer in American Literature at the University of Oxford, UK. She holds a PhD from the University of Cambridge and has published articles and essays on Wallace Stevens as well as on the American philosopher Stanley Cavell. She is working on a monograph treating the dynamics of experience and the ordinary in American writing since Modernism.

Axel Nesme is Professor of American Literature at the University of Lyon, France. After graduating from the École Normale Supérieure in Paris, he obtained the *Agrégation* in English and defended his thesis on the poetry of Theodore Roethke. He is the author of a book-length study on American elegies, entitled *L'Autre sans visage*. Both in France and in the United States, he has published articles on Poe, Whitman, Roethke, Bishop, Stevens, Blau DuPlessis, and Niedecker. He has also edited or coedited two collections of essays on Elizabeth Bishop.

Justin Quinn is Associate Professor of English and American literature at the University of West Bohemia in the Czech Republic. He has published six books of poetry and is the author of *Gathered Beneath the Storm: Wallace Stevens, Nature and Community* as well as of several studies of Anglophone poetry, including *The Cambridge Introduction to Modern Irish Poetry, 1800–2000*. His most recent study is *Between Two Fires: Transnationalism and Cold War Poetry*.

Edward Ragg is Associate Professor of English at Tsinghua University in Beijing, China. He has published a collection of poems, *A Force That Takes*, and has a second forthcoming. Besides being an Editorial Board Member of *The Wallace Stevens Journal*, he is the author of *Wallace Stevens and the Aesthetics of Abstraction*, and the coeditor of a volume of essays, *Wallace Stevens across the Atlantic*, as well as of a special issue of *The Wallace Stevens Journal* on Stevens and British literature.

Joan Richardson is Distinguished Professor of English and Comparative Literature at the Graduate Center, City University of New York. She is an Editorial Board Member of *The Wallace Stevens Journal* and the author of *Wallace Stevens: The Early Years, 1879–1923*; *Wallace Stevens: The Later Years, 1923–1955*; and *A Natural History of Pragmatism: The Fact of Feeling from*

Jonathan Edwards to Gertrude Stein. With Frank Kermode, she edited the Library of America edition of Stevens' *Collected Poetry and Prose.*

Lisa M. Steinman is Kenan Professor of English and Humanities at Reed College and the author of *Made in America: Science, Technology, and American Modernist Poets*; *Masters of Repetition: Poetry, Culture, and Work*; and *Invitation to Poetry: The Pleasures of Studying Poetry and Poetics.* She has published six books of poetry and is an Editorial Board Member of *The Wallace Stevens Journal.*

Juliette Utard is Associate Professor of American Literature at the University of Paris-Sorbonne, France. She is an Editorial Board Member of *The Wallace Stevens Journal*, the author of *Poétique du fini: Le vers et l'irréversible dans l'œuvre de Wallace Stevens* and of various essays on Stevens, including in *Wallace Stevens, New York, and Modernism.* In 2015, she organized a conference on Stevens in France, which will result in a volume of scholarly essays on the topic.

Index